Absolute Fiction

SUNY series, Studies in the Long Nineteenth Century

Pamela K. Gilbert, editor

Absolute Fiction

Idealist Philosophy and British Literature

JUSTIN PRYSTASH

Cover credit: Liu Kuo-sung, *At Leisure Under the Moonlight* (月色何悠悠, 2014).

Published by State University of New York Press, Albany

© 2025 State University of New York

All rights reserved

Printed in the United States of America

No part of this book may be used or reproduced in any manner whatsoever without written permission. No part of this book may be stored in a retrieval system or transmitted in any form or by any means including electronic, electrostatic, magnetic tape, mechanical, photocopying, recording, or otherwise without the prior permission in writing of the publisher.

Links to third-party websites are provided as a convenience and for informational purposes only. They do not constitute an endorsement or an approval of any of the products, services, or opinions of the organization, companies, or individuals. SUNY Press bears no responsibility for the accuracy, legality, or content of a URL, the external website, or for that of subsequent websites.

EU GPSR Authorised Representative:
Logos Europe, 9 rue Nicolas Poussin, 17000, La Rochelle, France
contact@logoseurope.eu

For information, contact State University of New York Press, Albany, NY
www.sunypress.edu

Library of Congress Cataloging-in-Publication Data

Name: Prystash, Justin, 1980– author.
Title: Absolute fiction : idealist philosophy and British literature / Justin Prystash.
Description: Albany : State University of New York Press, [2025]. | Series: SUNY series, studies in the long nineteenth century | Includes bibliographical references and index.
Identifiers: LCCN 2024049578 | ISBN 9798855802825 (hardcover : alk. paper) | ISBN 9798855802849 (ebook)
Subjects: LCSH: English fiction—History and criticism. | Idealism in literature. | LCGFT: Literary criticism.
Classification: LCC PR830.I27 P78 2025
LC record available at https://lccn.loc.gov/2024049578

For A. M. P. and C. H.:

May joy fill all the phases of your moon

To find the real,
To be stripped of every fiction except one,
The fiction of an absolute—Angel,
Be silent in your luminous cloud and hear
The luminous melody of proper sound.

—Wallace Stevens, "Notes toward a Supreme Fiction"

Contents

Acknowledgments — ix

Introduction
Absolute Fiction — 1

Chapter 1
A Meditation on Backgrounds: Coleridge, Carlyle, Hegel — 21

Chapter 2
Absolute Realism: Constance Naden and George Eliot — 57

Chapter 3
Across Ontology and Ethics: F. H. Bradley, Samuel Butler, and Science Fiction — 93

Chapter 4
The Dark Absolute: Unveiling Divine Horror in Arthur Machen and May Sinclair — 129

Chapter 5
Amphibious Modernism: Advaita Vedānta and Aldous Huxley — 167

Conclusion
Old Idealism and New Materialism — 203

Notes — 219

Works Cited — 225

Index — 243

Acknowledgments

I would like to thank Taiwan's National Science and Technology Council for a generous five-year research grant that enabled the research and writing of this book. The grant numbers are 109-2636-H-003-008; 110-2636-H-003-008; 111-2636-H-003-012; 112-2636-H-003-003; and 113-2636-H-003-001. A brief section of the introduction was originally published in "Introduction: Idealism," *Concentric: Literary and Cultural Studies*, vol. 47, no. 1, 2021. Part of chapter 1 originally appeared in "Vexed Meditation: Romantic Idealism in Coleridge and Its Afterlife in Bataille and Irigaray," *Romantic Legacies: Transnational and Transdisciplinary Contexts*, edited by Shun-liang Chao and John Michael Corrigan, Routledge, 2019, reproduced by permission of Taylor and Francis Group, LLC, a division of Informa plc. An abbreviated version of chapter 3 appeared in "Idealist Fictions: Crossing F. H. Bradley and Samuel Butler," *Criticism: A Quarterly for Literature and the Arts*, vol. 62, no. 2, 2020.

My great thanks to Rebecca Colesworthy at SUNY Press and Pamela K. Gilbert, the series editor, for supporting this project. I appreciate the insightful suggestions of the reviewers, which improved the final version of this text. I am grateful to be surrounded by colleagues and friends who encouraged me even as I pontificated on the nature of ultimate reality, especially Hannes Bergthaller, Evan Colbert, John Michael Corrigan, Aaron Deveson, Gerardo Fernandez-Salgueiro, Justin M. Hewitson, Benjamin B. Olshin, Brena Tai, and Graeme Todd. My research assistants, Ivy Wu and Sunny Chen, were an invaluable help. It was a pleasure to invite J. Jeffrey Franklin to give a virtual keynote address in Taiwan, and many thanks also to Kevin Corrigan and Elena Glazov-Corrigan for their visit to Taiwan. I will always be indebted to Robert Aguirre, Elizabeth Grosz, and Cannon Schmitt for their instruction, inspiration, and support. And finally, thanks to my family for being there through thick and thin.

Introduction

Absolute Fiction

> The usefulness of historical knowledge in philosophy . . . is that the prejudices of our own period may lose their grip on us if we imaginatively enter into another period, when people's prejudices were different.
>
> —Peter Geach, *Mental Acts*

In *Hyperobjects: Philosophy and Ecology after the End of the World*, Timothy Morton uses a hike in Taiwan to exemplify "interobjectivity":

> In a gigantic bamboo forest on Qi Lai Mountain in central Taiwan, it is as if one is surrounded by a theater of air, leaves, and stalks. The bamboo sways, sometimes violently, sometimes delicately, to the wind that rushes through it. Each gust causes a cascade of bamboo clicks to sound in front, to the right, to the left, and behind. A ridiculously complex assemblage of high-pitched frequencies floats, resembling something between percussion and a hand stirring a bowlful of pebbles or small crystals. The wind is heard *in* the bamboo. The bamboo forest is a gigantic wind chime, modulating the wind into bambooese. The bamboo forest ruthlessly bamboo-morphizes the wind, translating its pressure into movement and sound. It is an abyss of bamboo wind. (81)

This beautifully sensuous passage is as literary as it is philosophical, employing similes, metaphors, and alliteration to assist readers in grasping

Morton's experience in the forest along with the concept of interobjectivity, the unfathomable "abyss" that "floats among objects, 'between' them." The wind, the bamboo—even the hiker who tries to find a position "in front" or "to the right" of the sounds—are not discrete but woven together into an ensemble. For Morton, this ensemble is fundamentally inter*objective* because humans are just one component of a larger, largely nonhuman whole: "intersubjectivity is just a local, anthropocentric instance of a much more widespread phenomenon, namely interobjectivity. . . . 'intersubjectivity' is really human interobjectivity with lines drawn around it to exclude nonhumans" (81–82). Objectivity, for Morton as for many of their fellow "object-oriented ontologists," must be given precedence over subjectivity because the latter is inseparable from humans' perceptual and conceptual distortion—and often practical exploitation—of the natural world. Yet one could seriously ask of this passage the most basic idealist questions. *For whom* arise the clicks in the forest? For the bamboo, seemingly, speaking its "bambooese," but also for Timothy Morton, a human. Don't clicks have to be *subjectively* registered by something or someone? Is all human perception and discourse anthropocentric, ruthlessly human-morphizing everything it experiences and separating itself from the larger nonhuman whole? Doesn't the passage itself (attempt to) refute this? Why is sensuous literary language employed here—whose senses does it address? For whom does Morton write? Does underscoring the "lines" drawn around human "intersubjectivity" have the opposite of the intended effect—namely, offsetting or privileging the human? What *is* this particular "theater," and where is the exit? Are there theaters within theaters—is there one final, absolute one? Can we listen to and describe a theater as it is "in itself," beyond the filter of the human ear, human concepts, human language?

During the writing of this book, I often walked or meditated in Daan Forest Park, a large urban park in Taipei. As I watched the birds and people laze, listened to the ambient drone and the breeze, and smelled the flowers and the haze, I often arrived at the same conclusion as Morton: this natural space (composed by humans, it is true, but also composing them) forms a theater of interconnection. I am less confident than Morton, however, that lines are drawn or can be drawn. In what way do my visits to the park "exclude" nonhumans? My subjective experience is almost entirely populated by them. If I excluded everything nonhuman, what would be left? In what way does Daan Forest Park end at the roads that encircle it? This theater must extend to include the motor traffic that still faintly reaches my ears, the air pollution that often blankets the entire island of Taiwan, the global currents of capitalism that produce the pollution, the sun that enables the capitalism, the galaxy that spins the sun, and so on, until we reach the limit of the universe. Do humans have a monopoly on subjective experience? The furtive, lurching Malayan night herons in the park, which suspiciously freeze at my approach, certainly seem to perceive me. Even the park's stands of bamboo, Morton would concede, modulate their surroundings, impart their signature. They are responsive, expressing themselves through the "other"—the wind, for instance. If one of the many late Victorian or contemporary panpsychists were sitting at my bench, she would further assert that I cannot stop at the birds and the bamboo, but must extend some kind of subjectivity, some kind of inner experience or "what it's like-ness," even to the stones and the dirt and their molecules and atoms. The theater, if we follow this line of thinking, is a vast inter*perceptual* one.

Is it possible, then, to think about Morton's description of interconnected wholes composed of local, modulating domains as inter*subjectivity* without being anthropocentric or subjectivist? In this book, I explore the modern tradition of Absolute idealism that does just this, its philosophers and literary authors (often they wore both hats) posing many of the same questions I ask above. From the late eighteenth century to today, a hybrid philosophical-literary discourse we might call "Absolute fiction" has explored the epistemological problem of how humans come to know external reality. While some Absolute idealists, like Hegel, are confident that human reason can grasp the entire extent of reality (the "Absolute"), others, like F. H. Bradley, find an abyss between our thought and this ultimate reality, an abyss that only fiction can attempt to cross.[1] These idealists also explore the ontological problem of how particular organisms and entities are interrelated across scales up to and including the Absolute—many of them arriving at an abyss here too, an alienating, dark Absolute indifferent to or even actively malevolent toward humans. Almost universally working against anthropocentrism and subjectivism, these thinkers see humans not as projectors of reality in the manner of subjective idealism, but as projections of reality, one of the latest and most complex evolutionary productions of a generative and agentic nature. They reflect upon the ethical consequences of their epistemological and metaphysical positions, articulating the need for a kind of ecological sympathy—the need to care for other humans, nonhuman organisms, and inorganic nature as you would care for yourself (because these *are* your "self"). Finally, they explore the ways in which fiction impinges on this philosophy, either in terms of epistemology, as a necessary supplement or challenge to rational argumentation, or in terms of ontology, as a constitutive element of reality. For many Absolute idealists, reality is indeed like a theater, structuring or housing fictional plots that give spectators and participants partial aesthetic experiences of the edifice itself.

Defining Idealism

Raymond Williams warns that "idealism is obviously a word which needs the closest scrutiny whenever it is used" (107). Indeed, it is a very slippery term that encompasses a range of meanings. In this section, I want to briefly survey these different senses, indicating how my own relatively narrow focus on Absolute idealism is related to each. I provide a much more detailed definition and examination of Absolute idealism in chapter 1.

The first important distinction is between idealism as a philosophical tradition and idealism as "a way of thinking in which some higher or better state is projected as a way of judging conduct or of indicating action" (Williams 106). I will be attending to idealism as a philosophical tradition, of course, but the latter meaning is often implicated in the idealist theories and narratives I examine, since almost all of them imply an ethical stance that is derived from pursuing a "higher or better state." They do not conceive of this state as higher in a spatial sense—it is not some otherworldly or ideational realm detached from this world—but because it possesses greater explanatory power or greater reality, and therefore greater value. To give a simple example, the word "hand" denotes a relatively discrete chunk of reality that I can easily identify and deploy in an action, but I better understand that hand, and can potentially use it differently or more skillfully, when I understand the skeletal and muscular systems of the body.[2] Idealist ethics is therefore often relational: I've already mentioned an idealist investment in "ecological sympathy," and one could also point to the deep influence British Idealism has had on socialist politics.[3] Moreover, this relational orientation has aesthetic implications; many of the writers I examine are driven to depict the complicated relationships between parts and wholes or individuals and societies, with George Eliot being the premier example. The novel itself, then, is a projected "higher state."

Within the philosophical tradition, I suggest that we can parse the main divisions as follows.[4] First, epistemological idealism is concerned with the ways in which the human mind is implicated in our knowledge of the external world, whereas ontological idealism articulates the ways in which mind (human or otherwise) is constitutive of reality. Kant exemplifies the former, while the German Idealists who followed him—Schelling, Hegel, etc.—exemplify the latter. The problem of epistemology is certainly a concern for the thinkers and writers I address, but all of them can be placed in the ontological category. Indeed, the genealogy I consider begins with the emergence of German Idealism (and, not coincidentally, the first European translations of Indian philosophy) in the late eighteenth century, and the characteristics of German and Indian ontological idealisms color all the later variants. A second division could be drawn between subjective and objective idealisms. Subjective idealism, often associated with Berkeley, argues that material reality does not exist—only minds and their contents exist. None of the figures I examine in this book advocates this position, although it often appears in distorted form as a fictional theme: the disconsolate, brooding character whose belief in external reality has been shattered by some terrible event, imprisoning them within a solipsistic psychological state. Objective idealism, in contrast, argues that all of reality, including material reality, is constituted or accompanied by something mental, immaterial, or ideal.

Absolute idealism, the topic of this book, is a particular type of objective idealism that revolves around the concept of the Absolute, which is synonymous with the entire extent of reality, what we usually think of as the universe. Frederick C. Beiser defines Absolute idealism as "the doctrine that everything is a part of the single universal organism, or that everything conforms to, or is an appearance of, its purpose, design, or idea" (*German Idealism* 352). I argue that the concept of the Absolute is crucial for understanding the development of British literature from the Romantic period forward. First, the Absolute is an important determinant of literary form because it provokes strategies to represent and embody unrepresentable wholes, from *Bildungsromane* to horror prose poems (it also shapes the *literary* strategies of philosophical treatises). Indeed, I suggest that idealism characterizes Victorian realism and modernism, and it also functions as an organizing premise at the emergence of the detective, science fiction, and horror genres. In this, I follow Kate Hext's contention that "literary writers in the nineteenth century expand the scope of philosophical thought through literary form" (695). Second, the Absolute affects literary theme and content because, among other things, it forces a confrontation with the ethical and political implications of interrelated wholeness. If the Absolute manifests in each particular, if each person finds their own subjectivity in the external other, if even seemingly inert matter is invested with something mindlike, then we must reimagine our responsibility and sympathy for—even identity with—other people, as in Eliot; sentient machines, as in Samuel Butler; evil creatures, as in Arthur Machen; and the impersonal, menacing Absolute that accompanies death, as in May Sinclair and Aldous Huxley. In this way, we can see the history of literature as the unfolding, in tension with Absolute idealism, of a series of generic and thematic canalizations of the totality of reality. Again, these canalizations are not an imperial enterprise but an alienating, non-subjectivist, non-anthropocentric one.

Finally, it is helpful to assert some negative definitions of idealism, especially as they pertain to Absolute idealism. Idealism is often remarked on in oppositional terms: it is not naturalist or scientific, it is not realist, and it is not materialist. These oppositions are deeply problematic and misleading, and a double negative would be closer to the mark. Idealism often draws on the latest scientific theories—for instance, Schelling on galvanism, Butler on evolution, and Samuel Alexander on relativity—and technologies to make realist arguments about the external, material world.[5] Part of the reason for these misleading characterizations, it seems, is the association of idealism with Plato and his presumed dualist ontology that separates a real world of ideas from a false world of material imitations. According to Jeremy Dunham, Iain Hamilton Grant, and Sean Watson, however, this is yet another misleading assumption: they insist that idealism is "not anti-realist," is "far from being anti-science," and is "not . . . the two-worlds idealism beloved of interpretations of Plato" (4, 6). As a resolutely monist philosophy, Absolute idealism is more closely allied in this regard to the Neoplatonist tradition, another powerful influence during the Romantic period that interprets Plato as having developed a monist metaphysical system with gradations—not a Manichean division—of reality.[6] Moreover, this graded monism entails that idealism is *not* not materialist. While it does not privilege matter as a true materialism would, it certainly does not ignore matter, denigrate it, or make it vanish in a poof. Many of the idealists I examine are keenly aware, along with Jakob von Uexküll, that consciousness is constrained (and enabled) by the specific physical configuration of the organism.[7] The fact that contemporary expressions of idealism label themselves "materialist," an observation I make in the conclusion, further belies the supposed incommensurability between idealism and materialism. One final negative definition is worth emphasizing: while Absolute idealism seeks to relate parts to wholes, it is not totalizing or homogenizing. The early-twentieth-century movement known as Personal Idealism, an offshoot of British Idealism, is just one prominent example of the desire to preserve the specificity and autonomy of the individual.

A Brief History of Absolute Idealism(s) in Philosophy: Three Flowerings

The historical period covered in this book runs from the late eighteenth century to the present, beginning with the "completely new form of idealism [that] evolved in Germany" from 1795 to 1801 (Beiser, *German Idealism* 349). This new, Absolute idealism, first formulated by the German Romantics (chiefly Friedrich Hölderlin, Novalis, and Friedrich Schlegel), did not, of course, emerge *ex nihilo* but drew upon several sources: most immediately, the critical or transcendental idealism of Kant and Fichte, which was regarded as inspiring but too subjectivist (Beiser, *German Idealism* 355–61); but also Platonist rationalism, Spinozist monism, and Leibnizian vital materialism from the Western philosophical tradition (Beiser, *German Idealism* 361–68); as well as a variety of non-European philosophies, especially those represented by recently translated texts from China, Persia, and India (Hösle 434). In *The Romantic Absolute*, Dalia Nassar examines the German Romantic conception of the Absolute, which posited that "the ideal and real are originally one, that the subjective mind is dependent on (and is a manifestation of) an archetypal idea (the absolute), and that differences in nature and mind arise on account of differences in the degrees of organization and development of the same living force" (13). Moreover, the German Romantics

> repeatedly argued that the possibility of an ethical life depended on an original unity between mind and nature. This did not simply mean that human beings should be able to transform the world with a spontaneous and free will, but also—and in some cases more significantly—that the human being should be *affected and thus transformed* by the world. Similarly, the

> work of art, the romantics contended, is neither a presentation of pure artistic freedom nor a simple mimesis or imitation of nature. Rather, it involves both a mimetic moment achieved through developing insights into the natural world and a moment of artistic creativity or freedom, such that the result is a transformation of nature. (4–5)

Thus, Nassar demonstrates that the Absolute was first conceived (in its modern form, if we bracket the historical antecedents mentioned above) as both an epistemological and an ontological idea that entailed what we might now call a specifically "ecological" ethics and aesthetics. This basic conception, while altered in various ways by other Absolute idealists in philosophy and literature over the following two hundred years, has remained remarkably resilient.

The first flowering of Absolute idealism in German Romanticism and the German Idealism of Schelling and Hegel was followed by a British, indeed, global flowering at the end of the nineteenth century and beginning of the twentieth. W. J. Mander offers 1865, the year James Hutchison Stirling published *The Secret of Hegel*, as an appropriate starting point for the British Idealist movement, which subsequently saw a "flood of writings in the 1870s and 1880s" and "continued to dominate the philosophical scene for at least thirty years, and to be a formidable force for many more" (*British* 9, 34). T. H. Green, F. H. Bradley, Bernard Bosanquet, and J. M. E. McTaggart are key figures from this movement whom I examine in the following chapters, and Mander contributes their success to a number of cultural factors. First, they and other British Idealists recognized in the earlier German idealisms "a line of reasoning whereby human knowledge might reach the metaphysical, spiritual, and moral foundations it had been seeking" (Mander, *British* 19). In responding to the mid-century crisis associated with the higher criticism and Darwin's evolutionary theory, they asserted—variously in support or not of Christianity—that "the infinite was no longer beyond the reach of human cognition but rather to be encountered, in a world transfigured, all around us." They also offered a robust political and moral philosophy that overlapped with the New Liberalism and socialism then gaining strength in British politics (35),[8] as well as the feminist and utopian movements associated with the Theosophical Society,[9] which Joy Dixon documents in *Divine Feminine*. These historical contexts help explain the phenomenal rise of the British Idealists, but we should also recall that Absolute idealism became globally dominant during the same period, helped in part by British-educated philosophy professors who traveled the imperial circuits. As Nicholas Boyle explains, "the Western world had a globalised philosophy to match its globalised economy. From St Petersburg to St Louis, and indeed to San Francisco, in Germany, France and Britain, in Australia, South Africa and Canada, the thought of Kant and Fichte, Schelling and Hegel, Schopenhauer and Lotze provided at least a reference point and often enough the substance of discussion" (36). We should also add New Zealand, India, China, Japan, and Taiwan to the list of countries where Absolute idealism was taken up, contested, and transformed (Sweet 1–42; Pong and Hung). Indian Absolute idealism is a special focus of this book, especially in chapter 5.

In her introduction to idealism in the twentieth and twenty-first centuries, Liz Disley asks how philosophy "split itself into two along analytical/Continental lines and, to some extent, put itself back together again, in only ninety years?" (42). The answer, she suggests, is that the split was never very deep. Despite a shared opposition to metaphysical system building over most of the twentieth century, analytic and especially Continental philosophers continued to adopt the methods and explore the interests of the transcendentalist and Absolute idealist projects, and by century's end, a return to metaphysics marked both sides of the divide. At the beginning of the twentieth century, British Idealism seemed to disintegrate in the face of withering critiques by the erstwhile idealists G. E. Moore and Bertrand Russell and the devastation of World War I. However, Disley points out the strong German Idealist influence on the development of phenomenology, the Frankfurt School, poststructuralism, postmodernism, and philosophies of race and gender (44–60). Even "early analytic philosophy, like so much else in the nineteenth and early twentieth centuries, can be defined as a reaction to, but not destruction of, Idealist principles and methods" (55), and this helps explain how more recent analytic philosophers like John McDowell and Robert Brandom have contributed to a third flowering of neo-Hegelianism and Absolute idealism at the end of the century. Other philosophers responsible for this recent flowering include Thomas Nagel, who associates himself with Absolute idealism (17); Timothy Sprigge, whose *The Vindication of Absolute Idealism* appeared in 1984; and Gilles Deleuze, whose philosophy—especially influential upon literary criticism—draws on both Spinoza and Henri Bergson. Sprigge and Nagel independently formed the provocative question "What is it like to be a bat?," which presaged a turn to nonhuman phenomenologies, posthuman ecologies, and panpsychism at the end of the century. This turn was assisted by Deleuze's monism, vitalism, and emphasis on geology and assemblages in his collaboration with Félix Guattari, *Anti-Oedipus*, a book that, according to Dunham et al., has been mistakenly read as materialist (284). The neo-Spinozist "materialisms" that emerged in response to these intellectual currents in the twenty-first century are in fact idealisms that often reinstate the Absolute, as I argue in the conclusion.

Finally, literature plays a critical role in maintaining this continuous interest in and centennial reflowering of Absolute idealism. Both Boyle and Disley remark on this role. Boyle mentions that George Eliot's *Daniel Deronda* (1876) "foreshadowed the [early-twentieth-century] breakdown of the attempt to marry an international Idealist perspective to an English realist tradition" (36). I examine Eliot's vexed attempt in greater detail in chapter 2. Disley contends that the use of first-person perspectives and unreliable narrators in modernist and postmodernist literature mark the continuation of idealist preoccupations: "When assessing the world [such narrators] present, the reader looks not for the thick Cartesian curtain between appearance and reality, but the situation of the narrator's perspective amongst the perspective of others, and against the possibility of a shared social truth" (43). That certain formal aspects of literature indicate an Absolute idealist orientation can also be seen in the modernist stream-of-consciousness technique and its antecedent free indirect discourse.[10] I attend to several of these formal aspects in the following chapters.

Genealogies of Literary Idealism

The genealogy of British Absolute fiction that I trace in this book begins with Samuel Taylor Coleridge and Thomas Carlyle, who first championed the new German philosophy and translated it into their quasi-literary philosophical treatise (*Biographia Literaria*) and quasi-philosophical novel (*Sartor Resartus*). These texts begin playing with the permeable boundary between self and external world that forms the basis of subsequent realist explorations, which I consider first through George Eliot. Her similar fascination with German thought found novelistic expression in what I call "Absolute realism," which seeks to represent the greater reality of the self within social wholes. After juxtaposing Eliot's fiction to the poet and philosopher Constance Naden's theory of "Hylo-Idealism," I turn to the British Idealist F. H. Bradley and the iconoclastic philosopher and novelist Samuel Butler, drawing out the ethical and ontological implications of their work, especially as they relate to science fiction. The idea here is that their inflationary account of consciousness encourages writers to explore perspectives and ethical engagements beyond the human species. This is followed by a consideration of Arthur Machen's and May Sinclair's horror stories, where I emphasize the "dark Absolute" as a structuring principle for this genre: What if the total extent of reality is not beneficent but indifferent or actively evil? My final chapter reads Aldous Huxley's fictional modification of Advaita Vedānta, an ancient Indian variety of Absolute idealism that received a modern twist as it engaged with British Idealism during the early twentieth century. Huxley uses this approach to give form to the realities that lie beyond the edges of normal states of consciousness and life itself.

This covers a lot of ground. It omits much more, however, and there are several other genealogies I regret being unable to document here. There are many philosophers in the British Idealist circle whom I can only treat glancingly or not at all in these pages. I wish I could have included chapters on Emily Brontë, Olaf Stapledon, and Iris Murdoch. Further genealogies could be derived from winners of the Nobel Prize in Literature, which was originally intended to honor "the most outstanding work of an idealistic tendency" (qtd. in Moi, "Idealism" 287). As I discuss in more detail below, most of the existing scholarship on idealism's relationship to literature focuses on poetry, so I bracket this important genre to focus on fiction, which has been comparatively overlooked. Finally, my narrow focus on British literature ignores the spread of Absolute idealism across the world during the height of the imperial period. There are plenty of histories waiting to be written. This book attempts to convey this conceptual, cultural, and historical breadth by focusing on a limited cast of exemplary figures across the nineteenth and twentieth centuries.

The modern critical study of literary idealism began with the work of M. H. Abrams and other Romanticists, and thanks to their efforts, our understanding of the relationship between idealism and British Romanticism remains the richest. The influence of German Idealism on Coleridge, Carlyle, and other Romantic writers was so direct and strong that making this link between philosophy and literature has been much easier than for later periods. Subsequent scholarship, however, has extended our sense of idealism's entanglement with poetry, including W. David Shaw's *The Lucid*

Veil: Poetic Truth in the Victorian Age (1987), Daniel Brown's *Hopkins' Idealism: Philosophy, Physics, Poetry* (1997), and Carl Rapp's *William Carlos Williams and Romantic Idealism* (1984). Naomi Schor's *George Sand and Idealism* (1993) considers the feminist and aesthetic implications of Sand's idealist fiction, and Toril Moi later takes up these insights in *Henrik Ibsen and the Birth of Modernism: Art, Theater, Philosophy* (2008), where she develops the concept of "aesthetic idealism," a "belief that the task of art (poetry, writing, literature, music) is to uplift us, to point the way to the Ideal," which remained a dominant assumption for most of the nineteenth and well into the twentieth centuries (3–4). Adela Pinch's *Thinking about Other People in Nineteenth-Century British Writing* (2010) argues that philosophical idealism informed realist depictions of thinking about, sympathizing with, and loving others during the Victorian period, and more recently, Charlotte Jones's *Realism, Form, and Representation in the Edwardian Novel: Synthetic Realism* (2021) extends Pinch's argument to the early twentieth century, revealing how British Idealist metaphysics affected literary realism during this period. This sketch of the existing literature suggests that, while we now have a better understanding of the imbrication of idealism and literature beyond the Romantic period, for which we have the fullest account, most scholarship on this topic is period-based and focuses on poetry or realism. My own argument, while indebted to all these sources, seeks to examine idealism and fiction across periods, across genres, and across cultures.[11]

In his essay "Idealism in Nineteenth-Century British and American Literature," Richard Eldridge offers a model of how to conduct such a broader survey of idealism and literature. First, he argues that when idealism permeates the culture—as it does from the nineteenth century forward—one need not restrict one's analysis to cases where it is easy to document a direct line of influence. We should therefore keep in mind that there are "two different kinds of influence of German Idealism on English-language writers: immediate engagement by way of direct reading, including traceable borrowings of images, phrases, themes, and so on; and indirect engagement, as English-language writers take up, develop, revise and criticise some of the thinking about human life that is both evident within some major German Idealist texts, but also more broadly circulating within the culture" (121). Eldridge then constructs his own idealist genealogy—William Wordsworth, Jane Austen, George Eliot, Charles Dickens, Thomas Carlyle, Ralph Waldo Emerson, Henry David Thoreau, Walt Whitman, Herman Melville, and Virginia Woolf—that reveals a series of narrative attempts to counterbalance a predominantly skeptical cultural attitude in the face of social unrest, to tell stories *"exemplary for the possibilities of humanity as such within social life*, of the overcoming of alienation and anxiety, and of the achievement of stable orientation and felt confidence in relationships and activities," or at the very least to represent the lamentable foundering of such narratives (139). *Absolute Fiction* allows us to add two observations to Eldridge's helpful account. First, there are at least three more kinds of influence between idealism and literature over the course of the long nineteenth century: the influence of idealist movements other than German Idealism, such as British Idealism and Advaita Vedānta; the bidirectional influence of philosophy on literature *and* literature on philosophy; and the recursive influence philosopher-authors (and there are many of them) have on the development of their own work. Second, by examining a slightly different genealogy, I suggest that the overcoming of alienation and anxiety and achievement of stability and confidence comes about—when it does—only through an intensification of alienation and anxiety to the absolute limit, for it is extremely unsettling to unsettle the self.

Polemics and Literary Criticism

The writer of a book on idealism today labors under a double difficulty. Like everyone else, he or she must present a convincing, detailed argument. But it is also necessary to neutralize the pervasive skeptical or dismissive attitude toward the topic itself, something most scholars needn't confront. Thus, in the preface of Jones's 2021 book, even after decades of literary scholarship on idealism, she feels the need to push against "the enduring philosophical unfashionability of a metaphysics of abstractions, universals, and absolute forms," suggesting that "our 'postmetaphysical' outlook, or those who aspire to its disenchanted condition, may feel inclined to dismiss [the metaphysical character of a broader philosophical history] as nonsense, yet it is an important kind of nonsense which has shaped intellectual life for millennia" (xviii–xxiv). Unfortunately, such well-intentioned statements can easily become or be taken as polemical, thereby estranging the very readers one most wants to attract. While it is true that literary criticism in general tends to dismiss idealism in the service of a stated commitment to materialism, those critics intrigued by idealism should resist the reverse temptation to reject materialism and lionize idealism. I am not implying that Jones does this; rather, in this passage she helpfully redirects the problem of polemics by calling for a shift in perspective from the personal to the historical. In other words, writing or reading a book on idealism is not *necessarily* a question of one's personal *belief* in the doctrines under consideration. We might personally consider these doctrines to be "nonsense," and I confess that some of those I examine in this book strike me as such (while others I find quite convincing). Putting aside the question of belief, however, it should be clear that even the most nonsensical or fictional philosophy can be extraordinarily provocative and productive *for fiction*. If, on top of this, we find idealism attractive for personal or political reasons, as I do, so much the better.

In addition to presenting and digesting idealism as objectively but also as charitably as possible, we should remind ourselves that idealism as a category is plural in actual expression. We are dealing here not with a totalizing dogma but with a multiplicity of conflicting and contested positions that we, personally, can find more or less persuasive and useful in our specific historical context. Despite its insistence on the Absolute—perhaps because of it—Absolute idealism has no absolute form or purpose; it is non-exclusionary. Indeed, we can conceive of the history of philosophy itself as the unfolding of Absolute idealism in the sense that each new philosophical position, idealist or materialist, must reckon with its predecessors by rising to a higher (i.e., more absolute) perspective than they could have achieved within *their* historical horizon. On this point, Leon Chai is worth quoting at length:

> [I]f interest in German idealism is on the rise in different quarters, it's almost uniformly characterized by a trait we don't find in idealism itself: the impulse to evade any kind of absolute. Here the instinctive worry would seem to be that any absolute is equivalent to conceptual determinacy. In other words, we don't want to get boxed in. On this view, absolute idealism is problematic because it tries to determine the end point of philosophy. And even if the end point it envisioned somehow managed to subsume all its predecessors into itself, it still wasn't good enough. While it displayed a kind of metalevel awareness, it nonetheless fixed the form theoretical awareness could take. That meant we couldn't employ the perspective any other way. With the history of philosophy since Hegel, however, it has

become increasingly clear that metalevel awareness of some kind is the only game in town. In other words, every new system or perspective has to have a way to critique its predecessors such that it can't itself be subjected to the same kind of critique. But to do that, it has to have a "higher" viewpoint by which it can summarize or describe its predecessors, one to which they themselves don't have access. . . . Without the capacity to take metalevel awareness in a different direction, then, you couldn't hope to offer a new version of the history of philosophy. And without your own version, sooner or later you'd have to accept the version German idealism had to tell. (96–97)

We can therefore conceive of Absolute idealism as what Tilottama Rajan calls "an idealism without absolutes": "Idealism is not only reconfigured by materiality but also itself reconstitutes the material: both 'materiality' as a concept, and the material with which philosophy deals" (2). The polemic between idealism and materialism seems like badly misspent energy, since idealism in its modern, Absolute form has always embraced materiality, while materialism must somehow add in the ideal. The engine of philosophy is dual chamber.

I draw on self-described "materialist" literary critics throughout this book because I usually find their approaches and goals entirely compatible with idealism. This may be because the history of literary criticism, like the history of philosophy, is less a struggle between idealist and materialist camps and more the accumulated demarcation of *present* perspectives as more all-encompassing than *past* ones. Whether or not we agree with Philippe Lacoue-Labarthe and Jean-Luc Nancy's claim in *The Literary Absolute* that literature and/as literary criticism was formed in the crucible of German Romanticism and Absolute idealism, it is hard to deny that the tension between idealism and materialism has structured and continues to structure literary criticism. The various "turns" throughout its history seem to mark the demise of one or the other approach, but because even the most ardent idealist refuses to completely disavow the material (and vice versa), the turns are hairpin. Consider New Criticism. On the one hand, as Joshua Gang argues in *Behaviorism, Consciousness, and the Literary Mind*, the quintessential New Critical method of close reading, which is still ubiquitous among literary critics today, has its roots in the behaviorist-materialist emphasis on the "body" (of the text), which also accounts for the New Critical dismissal of biographical-psychological readings as enshrined in the intentional fallacy (32–65). On the other hand, because of their emphasis on holistic form and seeming disregard for social and material context, the New Critics appear incorrigibly "idealist." Indeed, the turn against New Criticism—which stressed the analysis of all the material contexts left out by its formalism, including racial, gendered, sexual, economic, geographical, and other realities—(re)asserted a materialist approach to the interpretation of literature that opened up productive new strains of analysis. And yet this turn, too, bleeds into the idealist: the Foucauldian emphasis on intangible power, the Derridean emphasis on language and texts, the Butlerian emphasis on the social construction of gender, and, more generally, the arealist emphasis of postmodernism, have all been accused by adherents of the subsequent turn of being too disembodied and "idealist." For example, with "new materialism," which tosses aside the "idealist assumptions" that have led to an "eclipse of materialism" since the 1970s (Coole and Frost 2, 3), we seem to have arrived at a proper materialism. But as I argue in the conclusion, the assumptions and conclusions of new materialism are much the same as those of Bradley, Butler, and the "old idealism" of the Victorian era. Meanwhile, a recently resurgent "new formalism," which swings us back toward New Criticism, is careful to attend, in Platonic fashion, to the reality and materiality of forms. Despite the various names on the road signs, we seem to be turning in a circle, revolving around the same problematic. This is not to say that we are going nowhere—one can ascend in a spiral—but perhaps it would be more correct and helpful to chart our critical journey in genealogical or dialectical rather than oppositional or polemical terms. Thus, throughout this book I try to stress not only the strong relationship between Absolute idealism and contemporary literary criticism but also the interpretative benefits to be gained by working across the idealism/materialism binary.

Chapter Outline

In chapter 1, "A Meditation on Backgrounds: Coleridge, Carlyle, Hegel," I survey Absolute idealism in Germany and Britain as it emerged in response to newly translated Indian texts like the *Bhagavad Gita* and practices like meditation. Coleridge, Carlyle, Hegel, and their later reinterpretations embody the three contextual and three conceptual characteristics of idealism in the long nineteenth century: idealism is interdisciplinary (uniting philosophy, literature, and literary criticism); continuous (despite a mid-nineteenth-century lull, its development was sustained across this time period); Indian-inspired (making it a transnational and transcultural phenomenon); realist (material objects, like ideal ones, exist); objectivist (the ideal emerges and is grasped *through* and not *against* materiality); and mereological (the microcosmic or metonymic logic of the Absolute preserves and values difference). I end with a section that considers Wilkie Collins's *The Moonstone*, which played an important role in generating the modern detective story because its use of idealism gives it an incredibly powerful conceptual framework for pursuing the formal strategies of the genre. By foregrounding the importance of the protagonist Franklin Blake's personality quirk—his frequent lapse into German Idealist meditations—my reading of Collins sets up the subsequent pursuit of Absolute idealism through the rest of the book.

In chapter 2, "Absolute Realism: Constance Naden and George Eliot," I contend that literary realism—especially as exemplified in George Eliot—*is* Absolute idealism, stressing with Naomi Schor that "[r]ealism in the nineteenth century signified *only* in relation to idealism, so much so that to consider one term in isolation from the other is to deplete, even distort its significance" (59–60). I begin with a consideration of the poet Constance Naden's philosophy of Hylo-Idealism (literally, "matter-idealism"). A highly paradoxical variant of Absolute idealism that insists on both radical subjective idealism (the universe is the creation of the mind) and radical materialism (all phenomena, including mental states, are reducible to a material basis), Hylo-Idealism starkly delineates the extremes within which realism operates. I see realism emerging as a fraught conceptual and aesthetic site within which idealism and empiricism battle for dominance, with Absolute idealism serving to both sustain and resolve this tension. My analysis of Eliot traces her version of this "Absolute realism" across three novels: *Romola*, *Middlemarch*, and *Daniel Deronda*. I argue that these novels radically perforate and extend the self by exteriorizing the mind and interiorizing the environment, marking out a spectrum of selves that runs from solipsistic absorption to Absolute diffusion. Taken together, Eliot and Naden embody the creative interplay between realism and Absolute idealism in the mid- to late Victorian period and suggest how the anti-subjectivist logic of realism encourages the proliferation of seemingly quite distinct genres like science fiction and horror.

Chapter 3, "Across Ontology and Ethics: F. H. Bradley, Samuel Butler, and Science Fiction," explores the late-nineteenth-century flowering of panpsychism—a term coined in 1879 by Eliot's partner, George Henry

Lewes, to describe the idea that all matter, down to the smallest atom, is imbued with some type of consciousness, mind, or volition. Panpsychism invites literary writers to artistically render the consciousness, agency, and perspectives of nonhuman subjects, from aliens to robots. Thus, I argue that there is a natural affinity between panpsychism and science fiction: Butler's sentient machines in *Erewhon* form the conceptual basis for an array of science fiction, and Bradley's science-fictional excursions in his most well-known and influential philosophical work, *Appearance and Reality*, are surprisingly innovative and prescient. After considering how panpsychism is aligned with the inhuman science fiction of Eliot and Edward Douglas Fawcett, I gesture toward its continued presence in the genre. I take as my main example the Cellarius Universe, a franchise launched in 2018 that takes Butler as an explicit inspiration. The franchise was originally intended to build a massive "universe" of content through a multiplicity of perspectives, encouraging artists and fans to produce fiction, film, animation, music, playing cards, and other aesthetic objects related to its conceptual premise. I argue that this collaborative, transmedia project embodies the visionary panpsychism of the late Victorian period.

May Sinclair begins *A Defence of Idealism* by framing her philosophical treatise as the resurrection of a horror story: "As long ago as the early 'nineties Idealism was supposed to be dead and haunting Oxford" (v). Idealism never seems to die, perhaps because it is the expression of a horrific, shambling universe. In chapter 4, "The Dark Absolute: Unveiling Divine Horror in Arthur Machen and May Sinclair," I pose the question, "What if the Absolute is not benign but evil?" The answer is nowhere more evident than in the weird horror fiction of the late nineteenth and early twentieth centuries, which often explores human interactions with what I call the "dark Absolute," a menacing, inhuman(e) totality that elicits ecstasy as often as fear. I begin by examining Machen's novels, short stories, and prose poems for their depictions of sexual relationships between individual characters and the dark Absolute. Being literally fucked by the universe often leaves characters "fucked" in various ways, but ecological penetration also brings ecstasy in the sense of being taken out of the self, redistributed. I then turn to a consideration of Sinclair's idealist philosophy and her weird short story "The Flaw in the Crystal," which together suggest the horrific sexual ecstasy associated with the integration of experiences beyond the "veil" that normally isolates the individual subject from other people and the Absolute. Other weird stories by Sinclair articulate the structure of the Absolute experienced after death. In some, the Absolute is a hellish labyrinth or claustrophobic simulacrum; in others, it is no less dizzyingly but less darkly characterized as an infinite cycle of imaginative acts of creation, a concept she also explores in her explicitly Indian stories. In this chapter, we see how the formal brevity of stories and prose poems enable a distinct approach to the Absolute. Unlike the phenomenological experience of reading a novel, one can perceive again and again the totality of the weird text in a single sitting—yet this totality is horrifying and incomprehensible. Such dark Absolutes—like their real-world political counterparts, from the imperial concentration camp to the totalitarian state—are created and sustained through the dynamics of fear and desire.

The modernist suspicion that spiritual or even Absolute meaning can be discovered in thoroughly earthbound experiences—from liminal states of consciousness to confrontations with death—reveals the affinity not just between modernist novels and the weird fiction of Machen and Sinclair, but also between them and southeast Asian philosophies as interpreted by Aldous Huxley in his novel *Time Must Have a Stop*, the subject of chapter 5, "Amphibious Modernism: Advaita Vedānta and Aldous Huxley." Amphibiously bringing together Victorian and modernist formal structures, Western and Eastern philosophy, individual spiritual quest and collective politics, Huxley's work requires an amphibious, comparative approach to unravel. Thus, I first examine Advaita Vedānta, an ancient Indian Absolute idealism that gained a modern inflection through the spiritual eclecticism of Bengali saint Ramakrishna, his disciple, Swami Vivekananda, and Indian philosophers who drew equally on British Idealism and Advaita Vedānta, such as A. C. Mukerji. Advaita Vedānta's insistence on the identity between individual consciousness (*Ātman*) and the timeless Absolute (*Brahman*), as well as how one comes to realize this identity through what Eliot Deutsch calls the process of "subration," or retrospective falsification, are key Advaita concepts that help unlock Huxley's novel. Like Advaita Vedānta and *The Tibetan Book of the Dead*, Huxley's novel seeks to demonstrate—through both content and form—how individuals grasp the Absolute through rites of self-estrangement or, to put it another way, in demystifying the fictions that distract them from perceiving their real identity with the Absolute. I conclude by suggesting that Huxley's descriptions of bad psychedelic trips, which mirror the after-death experience of a character from *Time Must Have a Stop*, presage the turn to postmodernism, in which there is no Absolute "stop" to retrospective falsification, leading to a paranoid style of subjective idealism in culture and criticism.

The conclusion, "Old Idealism and New Materialism," begins by noting the recent resurgence of interest in idealism evidenced by the philosophical movement known as speculative realism—from Iain Hamilton Grant's resuscitation of Schelling to Steven Shaviro's defense of panpsychism, an unmistakable idealism characterizes this loose association of thinkers who have proven so influential on literary criticism. Even Quentin Meillassoux, who takes an uncompromisingly materialist approach to reinstating the importance of the Absolute, argues in *After Finitude* that postmodern attempts to "end" absolutes and metaphysics have ironically accelerated a covert return to spirituality, religion, and idealism, granting "unprecedented license" to the idea of the Absolute (45). This paradoxical attack on that which is being implicitly promoted is nowhere more evident than in another, related philosophical movement known as new materialism. In the edited volume *New Materialisms*, Diana Coole and Samantha Frost argue against the (subjective) idealism they say characterizes postmodern philosophy, positing instead a materialism that finds, for example, "generative powers (or agentic capacities) even within inorganic matter" (9). The similarity between such "new materialism" and the "old idealism" I examine throughout *Absolute Fiction* is striking. I end by using new materialism to read Huxley's final novel, *Island*, drawing out the literary-critical and political benefits to be gained from an open (re)turn to the Absolute and a commitment to generating new idealisms.

Chapter 1

A Meditation on Backgrounds

Coleridge, Carlyle, Hegel

> What fine chisel / Could ever yet cut breath?
>
> —William Shakespeare, *The Winter's Tale*

In a pair of essays, "Bentham" (1838) and "Coleridge" (1840), John Stuart Mill respectively considers the merits of the two forms of philosophy that came to dominate the long nineteenth century in Britain: materialism and idealism. Although Mill himself, as an empiricist and utilitarian, was a staunch advocate of materialism, he offers a reading of Samuel Taylor Coleridge that acknowledges the misunderstandings that arise from becoming entrenched in only one of the two perspectives. "Were we to search among men's recorded thoughts for the choicest manifestations of human imbecility and prejudice," he writes in "Coleridge," "our specimens would be mostly taken from their opinions of the opinions of one another" (Mill and Bentham 187). Mill attempts to move beyond division and polemics, arguing that "these two sorts of men, who seem to be, and believe themselves to be, enemies, are in reality allies" (206). In this book, I follow Mill's generous rhetorical approach: although I explore literature and philosophy from an idealistic perspective, I assume that idealism must be allied to materialism in order to create a compelling account of aesthetics and reality. Idealists of the long nineteenth century shared this assumption from the time idealism first reemerged as a powerful and widespread philosophy at the end of the eighteenth century, in the wake of Kant's transcendental idealism.

The fact that British idealism reached its insights *through* and not *against* materialism has been obscured by the philosophical prejudices of Western academia since the mid-twentieth century, prejudices that tend to cloud and oversimplify our understanding of this period's philosophy. As Anthony Quinton acknowledges in the third issue of *Victorian Studies* (1958), "no oblivion is so profound as that which envelops the British philosophers of the nineteenth century" (248). Unfortunately, little has changed to lift them—especially the idealists—from such obscurity in the sixty-plus years since *Victorian Studies* began publication.[1] In this chapter, in order to shed light on a vast idealist movement that emerged across decades, nations, and continents, that was embraced by men and women, philosophers and literary writers, and that employed the concepts of both Western and Eastern philosophical traditions, I explore its early backgrounds through the figures of Coleridge, Thomas Carlyle, and Hegel: the three philosophers who had the biggest impact on the subsequent development of British idealism. In the following paragraphs, I provide a brief overview of three contextual and three conceptual characteristics of idealism in the long nineteenth century. These characteristics, which certainly don't apply *in toto* to every idealist, nevertheless help capture the spirit of the three thinkers I focus on in this chapter, the other philosophers and writers I examine in the rest of the book, and, I believe, the idealist spirit of the modern age as a whole.

1. *Interdisciplinary.* German Idealism "raised the whole issue of the relation of philosophy to aesthetic writing" (Ameriks 7), while the closely allied German Romantics explored the fictionality of philosophy and the philosophical nature of fiction in their experiments with aesthetic form and the purposeful confusion of genre (Lacoue-Labarthe and Nancy 91). The German Idealists also transcended the distinctions between several other disciplines, including religious studies, politics, and art (Ameriks 1). It is notoriously difficult to identify the genre to which Coleridge's *Biographia Literaria* (1817), Carlyle's *Sartor Resartus* (1833–34), and Hegel's *Phenomenology of Spirit* (1807) belong: Are they a blend of philosophical treatise, novel, and autobiography? Idealism in the long nineteenth century is discursively promiscuous and eclectic. Thus, to understand it properly, we must employ an interdisciplinary methodology.

2. *Continuous.* We should emphasize historical continuity and geographical contiguity as much as breaks. There is a direct genealogical line from the (German and British) Romanticism and German Idealism that suffused the beginning of the Victorian period to the British Idealism

that suffused the end. After the great flowering of idealist philosophy in Romanticism, there was indeed a relative dearth of British idealist works in the middle of the nineteenth century until the publication of James Hutchison Stirling's *The Secret of Hegel* (1865) led to another flowering at Oxford University in the 1870s. By 1890, almost all English-speaking philosophers were idealists (Hedley 291), and they remained the largest group in the philosophical professoriate until 1945 (Mander, introduction 3). But the apparent lull at mid-century can only describe philosophy proper (if we can speak of a "proper" anymore). When we take into account idealism's characteristic of interdisciplinarity, it becomes clear that Absolute fictions flourished during the mid-Victorian period in, for example, the novels of Charles Dickens, Emily Brontë, and George Eliot. Of course, the idea of a lull at mid-century also fails to consider American Transcendentalism, the St. Louis Hegelians, and other movements that this book, unfortunately but necessarily, leaves unexamined.

3. *Indian-Inspired.* In this chapter and in chapter 5, I place special emphasis on the extent to which Indian philosophy influenced the emergence and development of Absolute fiction. In the late eighteenth and early nineteenth centuries, newly translated Sanskrit texts by scholars like Charles Wilkins, Henry Thomas Colebrook, and Friedrich Schlegel brought Vedantic thought into widespread intellectual currency.[2] Opponents of idealism, like Mill, were quick to make negative (Orientalist) associations between Indian and idealist philosophy, while its supporters, like Walt Whitman, made positive associations. But these two traditions are certainly associated, and I will draw attention to the Vedantic references, imagery, and concepts that play a crucial role for Coleridge and Hegel, who were directly acquainted with Vedantic texts, and to a lesser extent in Carlyle, who was more indirectly influenced. Idealism's Indian flavor in the long nineteenth century further underscores the way that idealism emerges at the confluence of transnational and transcultural currents.

4. *Realist.* The word "idealism" often conjures up the notion that everything is merely a construct of the human mind and therefore unreal, but such "subjective idealism" is a minority position in the history of philosophy, and it is almost entirely absent from the nineteenth century forward. As Greg Ellermann remarks in an essay on the union of idealism and realism in Coleridge, "Once held to be indifferent, or even hostile, to the external world, idealism is now seen to be at its most daring, and most startlingly prescient, when theorizing nature as a network of nonhuman

forces" ("Late" 33). Rather than opposing realism, nature, science, or materiality, the idealism of this period did have two genuine enemies: dualism, the idea that there is a sharp distinction between mind and matter; and mechanism, the idea that the world operates like a machine, with atomistic parts affecting one another in a predictable fashion. Karl Ameriks notes that for Plato, among others, the "ideal" means precisely *the most real*, and it is only recently that the term has taken on the opposite meaning; moreover, the ideal is not projected into "another" world in a dualistic manner but adds ontological depth and significance to this one (8). In other words, not only are material objects real, but so are *immaterial forms*, both subjective forms like one's concept of "blue" and objective forms like the sequential nature of time or the hierarchical structure of a corporation. Caroline Levine recasts this essentially Platonic argument in her influential book *Forms: Whole, Rhythm, Hierarchy, Network* (2015), which demonstrates that matter and form are piled together inseparably.

5. *Objectivist.* This characteristic elaborates on the previous one. Counterintuitively, modern idealism approaches reality from the objective rather than subjective standpoint: the ideal emerges and is grasped *through* and not *against* materiality. In *German Idealism: The Struggle Against Subjectivism, 1781–1801*, Beiser documents how philosophers writing in the aftermath of Kant's great revolution, including the German Idealists and Romantics, became increasingly distanced from Kant's tepid endorsement of objective reality, which he relegates to the inaccessible "in-itself." For example, Schelling's *Identitätssystem* of 1799–1804 makes subject and object identical at the level of the Absolute (the entire natural order), and this originary indifference explains how the human mind can arise from *within* nature and gain knowledge of it. Because humans are always already nested within an ecological system, one significant effect of objective idealism is to displace the centrality of the human. Such anti-anthropocentrism is manifest, for instance, in Coleridge's and Hegel's opposition to the instrumentalization of nature (Ellermann, "Hegel" 12n41).

6. *Mereological.* There is another negative definition of idealism worth emphasizing: it does not subsume everything within an all-encompassing, static whole. The organic, dynamic universe or Absolute would not be what it is without all the parts that compose it, and each part, no matter how seemingly small or insignificant, can be treated as the end for which all other parts and the whole exist. This microcosmic or metonymic logic stresses the importance for the idealists of maintaining

the integrity of *difference* within their metaphysical system-building. It also makes the novel and other literary forms particularly suited for grasping reality because, no less real and impactful than any other part of the Absolute, these fictions are also in many ways homologous to it. For example, novels are also "wholes" that only unfold and have meaning through their particular contents. Like the Absolute, then, literature has an internally metonymic (mereological) and metaphorical (relational) logic; unlike the Absolute, which has no outside, a novel also points beyond itself to a wider ecological whole composed of other texts, social contexts, readers, etc.

This sixth characteristic could also be identified as *organicist*, although to better encompass variants, I prefer the more neutral term *mereological*. In *Romantic Organicism: From Idealist Origins to Ambivalent Afterlife*, Charles I. Armstrong demonstrates the ubiquity of organicist thinking among the German and British Romantics as well as Kant and the German Idealists, who used the organism as a model to explain "the functioning of philosophical, literary, and also political wholes" (5). This desire to think meaningfully about wholes drives, for example, Coleridge's pursuit of the "absolute literary-philosophical work" and Wordsworth's "architectonics of the absolute" (107). Karen Ng claims that "describing the activity of reason and thought in terms of the dynamic activity and development of organic life" is "a central, recurring rhetorical device" for Hegel—but it is more than a rhetorical device, for "he means to suggest not that reason is *like* life but that reason *is* a dynamic, living activity in constant development" (3). Moreover, much like idealist philosophy, organicism continued to exert an influence well into the Victorian period and beyond; indeed, it can be understood as anticipating the very twentieth- and twenty-first-century tendencies in philosophy and literary criticism that denounce it (2). I will return to this irony in my conclusion by pursuing the legacy of idealism and organicism and their value for articulating political wholes that are "far from precluding heterogeneity and difference" (C. Armstrong 27). Organicism is implicit in many of my readings throughout this book.

Perhaps it is conceptually appropriate, in this idealist context, to think of the above six characteristics as various expressions of one final, encompassing term: "backgrounds." First, to understand how idealism unfolds after the beginning of the nineteenth century, it is helpful to keep in mind the historical backgrounds that made its emergence possible in the first place: the myriad contextual filaments that together serve, to borrow the words of Dylan Thomas, as the "force that through the green fuse drives the flower" (12). These backgrounds include, most distantly, Cambridge Platonism, which Coleridge invokes with his opening reference to Thomas Burnet in "The Rime of the Ancient Mariner."[3] We find an echo of this earlier Platonism in the Neoplatonism exemplified by Thomas Taylor during the Romantic period; this (Neo)Platonic heritage provided sophisticated arguments for the objective reality of ideas, which structure a divine and monistic universe. A background that closely shades into this is the late-eighteenth-century revival of Spinoza, which strengthened the turn toward monism and pantheism among many of the German Idealists and Romantics. Indian philosophy, as we have seen, added further depth and richness to the picture. Then, of course, powerful streaks of idealist thought during this period are to be found in Kant and Fichte, the post-subjective German Idealism and German Romanticism that emerged in response to them, and the British Romanticism that adopted and adapted many of these ideas.

The second reason the word "backgrounds" captures the spirit of idealism is that it resonates with the three conceptual characteristics I discuss above. For idealism to be realist, it must bring into focus that which is merely the background in an anthropocentric world: material objects, nonhuman species, nature. For the post-Kantian idealists especially, we cannot conceive of the human subject without its natural background because the human subject emerges from it as its expression. Separating the human from its natural surrounds—indeed, isolating any subjective or objective entity from its contextual backgrounds—is an arbitrary cut in the total canvas of reality. Just as the foreground of a traditional painting depends on its negative relation to the background, or the abstract surfaces of a modern painting depend on the minimal fringe of a frame or the spaces of a museum, all finite things depend on other finite things and ultimately the Absolute—which likewise depends on each one of its constitutive filaments.

In the remainder of this chapter, I trace just a few of these backgrounds by reading the works of Coleridge, Carlyle, and Hegel as Absolute fictions that exemplify the characteristics of idealism enumerated above. I conclude by considering how the late Victorians interpreted these backgrounds and what they portend for the subsequent development of literature over the course of the nineteenth century and after, using Wilkie Collins's *The Moonstone* as an example.

Coleridge: Interior Atmospheres

Throughout Coleridge's poetry and philosophy, we find the desire for self-transcendence: a desire to smudge the lines dividing the subject from myriad encircling objects; a mystical desire, ultimately, to dissolve subjectivity into the animate universe, variously identified with Spirit, Mind, or God. Coleridge offers at least two methods for achieving this desire, methods grounded in his philosophical system and exemplified in his poetic practice: meditation and poetry itself.[4] For Coleridge, these practices are mutually reinforcing, because meditation facilitates the composition of poetry, which in turn causes its readers to meditate. His poetic meditations are deeply vexed, reflecting the often incomplete and contradictory nature of his work, but many of these inconsistencies can be navigated by attaching Coleridge to a larger genealogy. Through a consideration of the immediate influence of Indian philosophy, it becomes clear that Hindu imagery and concepts suffuse his writings, and this incorporation was done not (only) in an Orientalizing manner, but out of genuine respect.

Pantheism, hylozoism, and Spinozism are the early Coleridge's preferred terms for what is essentially the same concept: objects are alive, and therefore the distinction between subject and object does not hold. These terms may assume a different basis for the vital element itself—God, spirit, soul, or mind—but, following Coleridge's relatively interchangeable usage and in order to simplify a dizzying cascade, we can identify them as part of the same general philosophical approach that effloresced around 1800 and influenced many of the German Idealists. Coleridge also participated in this approach,[5] which clearly aligns with his philosophy and praxis of self-transcendence. Thomas McFarland describes Coleridge's ambivalent relationship with pantheism as "the central truth of Coleridge's philosophical activity" (107). Moreover, he notes the affinity between pantheism and poetry, both of which "tend to obliterate the boundaries between the realm of thing and the realm of mind" (275). Coleridge sometimes expresses this affinity in the content of his poetry, as in "Frost at Midnight," when, after engaging in "vexe[d] meditation," the speaker's mind finds a "companionable form" in a fluttering cinder. This leads to the further insight that God is "in all, and all things in himself" (*Complete Poems* 231–32). The poems of Wordsworth, Shelley, and other Romantics contain many similar expressions of vibrant things.[6]

Another current of thought that converges with pantheism during this period is Indian philosophy, which was introduced through the work of Orientalists and Sanskrit scholars like William Jones, whose work Coleridge read.[7] Indeed, Coleridge absorbed Eastern ideas more intensely than any of his peers: "Coleridge engages more profoundly with oriental ideas and cultures—and in ways more extensively informed by contemporary and earlier scholarship—than any other British Romantic" (Vallins, introduction 2). Coleridge locates the origin of all Western philosophy in the pre-Socratic Pythagoras because he was traditionally believed to be the first to receive influence from the East. As Andrew Warren explains, "The origin and subsequent history of philosophy consists of, first, a rupture between subject and object, and then various attempts to reconcile that division. This is how Coleridge thinks about philosophy, and the history of philosophy. Pythagoras takes up Thales' search for first principles, tears asunder self and world, and then attempts to reconcile that divide by drawing upon Eastern wisdom about the pantheistic unity of the world" (109). Coleridge admires (and emulates) Pythagoras for attempting to create an ontological system grounded in first principles. The catalyst for such an attempt emerges, for both men, in the productive commingling of Western and Eastern traditions. They find in Eastern philosophy conceptual tools for negotiating the central problem they identify within their own tradition: the subject/object split. Coleridge's idealism is therefore, like Western philosophy itself, fundamentally intercultural.

Eastern praxis, particularly meditation, also informed Coleridge's poetry. For instance, Natalie Tal Harries documents several of Coleridge's "poetic expressions of meditative contemplation" (133), as in "The Eolian Harp," when the speaker ponders whether "all of animated nature / Be but organic harps diversely framed, / That tremble into thought, as o'er them sweeps / Plastic and vast, one intellectual breeze, / At once the Soul of each, and God of All?" (*Complete Poems* 88). Just before this realization, he beholds "through [his] half-closed eye-lids . . . / The sunbeams dance, like diamonds, on the main, / And tranquil muse[s] upon tranquility" (85–86). What is remarkable here, in addition to the pantheistic language, is his use of meditative, half-closed eyes to symbolize a kind of valve that streams energetic external objects into and across the "passive brain" (88). In other words, the speaker does not gaze with what Mary Louise Pratt calls "imperial eyes" (7), the characteristically Western vision that objectifies the Other and Nature in order to control them. Quite the opposite: natural objects—and in the contextual background, Eastern discourses—play his passive brain like a lute. Thus, we can think of Coleridge's idealism as the articulation of a "contact zone" (7) where traditional binaries are powerfully blurred.

In *Biographia Literaria*, Coleridge identifies Shakespeare and Milton as quintessential poets because they mark the polarity of poetic self-transcendence: Shakespeare centrifugally "becomes all things," shifting the subject into objects; Milton "attracts all forms and things to himself," gravitating objects into the subject (2: 27–28). Poetry creates an ontological relation, an opportunity to expand and contract, to breathe. It exceeds language, forming a "chain of flowers" that link poet and pen, reader and words, breath and body, mind and imagination.[8] It distills an entire ambient atmosphere that exists beyond the conscious mind or, rather, allures consciousness beyond itself: poetry as meditation, incantation, dilation. To support this conception, Coleridge pays particular attention to poetic form. Meter is like a subtle drug that acts through "the continued excitement of surprize, and by the quick reciprocations of curiosity still gratified and still re-excited, which are too slight indeed to be at any one moment objects of distinct consciousness, yet become considerable in their aggregate influence. As a medicated atmosphere, or as wine during animated conversation; they act powerfully, though themselves unnoticed" (2:66). This extends poetic structure outside the reader's consciousness. Meter creates an "atmosphere" of "objects" too subtle to discern, like the alcohol in wine or the medicated particles in a puff of smoke that, once imbibed or inhaled past a certain threshold, elicit conscious feelings of curiosity, gratification, and excitement. Poetry is not just a mental exercise, but a series of intellectual and affective states that arise when imperceptible objects permeate the body. Poetry is therefore an essentially *relational* phenomenon.[9]

In his notebooks, Coleridge stresses the importance of breathing for developing this relational cohesion between mind and body, subject and object. Punctuation marks, he writes in 1809, are not "logical Symbols" but "dramatic *directions* representing the process of Thinking & Speaking conjointly—either therefore the regulation of the breath simply . . . or as the movements in the Speaker's Thoughts makes him regulate his Breath" (3: 3504). In other words, punctuation, like meter, functions outside of rational consciousness. It plays a somatic role, regulating the breath so that speech can be dramatically enacted and meaning imparted. One could say that all these objects—meter, punctuation, all the particles in the "medicated atmosphere"—expand consciousness after being inhaled.[10]

Coleridge says as much in another entry from 1806, where the Greek letter *theta* symbolizes breath and existence:

> The ⊙ [is] a Circle, with the Kentron, or central Point, creating the circumference & both together the infinite Radii /—the Central point is primary Consciousness = living Action; the circumference = secondary Consciousness <or Consc[iousness]: in the common sense of the word> and the passing to and fro from the one to the other Thought, Things, necessary Possibilities, contingent Realities. . . . The • is I which is the articulated Breath drawn inward, the O is the same sent outward, the ⊙ or Theta expresses the synthesis and coinstantaneous reciprocation of the two Acts. (2: 2784)

This passage contains a rich condensation of Coleridge's philosophical views. Taken as a description of subjectivity, it divides the subject into two layers of consciousness. The first is primary consciousness, where "living Action," or dramatic interaction with external objects, occurs. Secondary consciousness is our "common sense" understanding of mental activity as rational awareness. These layers are connected (forming a "contingent" constitution of the subject) when "Thought" and "Things" circulate between them during the act of breathing. Moreover, just as primary imagination is "a repetition in the finite mind of the eternal act of creation in the infinite I AM" (*Biographia* 1: 304), Coleridge's *theta* can also be read as a symbolic rendering of the entire universe, with primary consciousness—the dot at the center of the circle—representing God. The radii then trace the thoughts and objects that connect God to the secondary consciousness of human subjects, which form the circumference. According to this metaphysical structure, humans can approach God by "inhaling" objects, just as they were generated by an exhalation.

Coleridge's *theta* embodies a dense amalgamation of Neoplatonic and Hindu concepts, a synthesis characterizing many of his early writings (Vallins, "Immanence" 122–24). The Hindu strain in his account of meditation becomes clearer when we consider Charles Wilkins's translation of *The Bhagvat-Geeta* (1785), which Coleridge read in the 1790s (Harries 132–33). In a letter appended to the beginning of the text, Warren Hastings, Governor-General of India, suggests that its "highly metaphysical" nature is best understood through a consideration of Hindu "spiritual discipline," in which the attention must "be abstracted from every external object, and absorbed, with every sense, in the prescribed subject of their meditation" (8). In the act of approaching Krishna through meditation, the devotee begins to experientially grasp that the division between subject and object is merely an illusion to be transcended. Krishna says that "all things rest in me, as the mighty air, which passeth every where, resteth for ever in the aetherial space" (78). Employing one of Coleridge's favorite pantheistic metaphors, he says that as "a single sun illuminateth the whole world, even so doth the spirit enlighten every body. They who, with the eye of wisdom, perceive the body and the spirit to be thus distinct, and that there is a final release from the animal nature, go to the Supreme" (106). In these passages, Krishna sometimes appears to advocate a metaphysical dualism, where body and spirit are completely divorced or objects are merely illusory. But in fact, Krishna is overturning dualism: objects are real, but one animating principle—Krishna's spirit—suffuses all these objects. "There is not any thing greater than I," Krishna says, "and all things hang on me, even as precious gems upon a string. I am moisture in the water, light in the sun and moon" (70).

Through meditation, one recognizes that all objects, like subjects, are vitalized by the universal spirit. Acquiring this vision of the universe is difficult, requiring a rigorous program of meditation to intensify one's relation to objects. Krishna advises his follower to sit "with his mind fixed on one object alone . . . keeping his head, his neck, and body, steady without motion, his eyes fixed on the point of his nose, looking at no other place around" (63). By lowering the eyelids and repetitively allowing one object to pierce the mind, the meditator grasps the animating principle of spirit and, through an expansion of consciousness, approaches a fuller union with God. Krishna insists that through this spiritual practice, "thou shalt behold all nature in the spirit; that is, in me" (55). One's mind becomes intensively focused on the body and then extends until, ultimately, it comes into full contact with the universe. This supreme object of wisdom is "all hands and feet; it is all faces, heads, and eyes; and, all ear, it sitteth in the midst of the world possessing the vast whole. Itself exempt from every organ, it is the reflected light of every faculty of the organs. . . . It is the inside and the outside, and it is the moveable and immoveable of all nature" (103). This experience is self-transcendence taken to the limit, but it nevertheless occurs "in the midst of the world," within "all nature," emanating in the glow of organs.[11] It is the infinite extension of body *as* spirit.

With its frequent use of simile, metaphor, and lush visual imagery, Wilkins's *Bhagvat-Geeta* offers a poetic description of how to overcome the split between subject and object. Meditation resolves the problem from an object-oriented perspective because it starts by literally focusing on objects: physical objects, one realizes, are infused with mind or spirit, and therefore form a continuity with the mind and body of the meditating subject (and with God). As we have seen, Coleridge incorporates this idea into his poetics and poetry. It also forms the basis of his philosophy, despite frequent hesitations and disavowals. For example, consider his dismissal of hylozoism, a term taken from the Greek words *hyle* (matter) and *zoē* (life):

> The hypothesis of Hylozoism . . . answers no purpose; unless indeed a difficulty can be solved by multiplying it, or that we can acquire a clearer notion of our soul, by being told that we have a million souls, and that every atom of our bodies has a soul of its own. Far more prudent is it to admit the difficulty once for all, and then let it lie at rest. There is a sediment indeed at the bottom of the vessel, but all the water above it is clear and transparent. The Hylozoist only shakes it up, and renders the whole turbid. (*Biographia* 1: 131–32)

After admitting that the relation between body and soul[12] is a recalcitrant problem, Coleridge considers the solution offered by hylozoism, the idea that all matter is alive (with soul). Hylozoism appears to overcome the binary that troubles Coleridge because it argues that soul is everywhere; in other words, there is no fundamental difference between living subjects and (apparently lifeless) objects. Yet, he reflects, doesn't this just multiply the problem? He begins with the question of how soul relates to his body, and now he must explain how soul relates to each atom in his body! Thus, at this point in the *Biographia*, he argues that hylozoism may further obscure, rather than resolve, the subject/object problem. He does not reject hylozoism outright but contends that it would be more "prudent" to allow subject and object to settle into the familiar opposition.

In later chapters of the *Biographia*, however, Coleridge explains how soul relates to body in a way that is consonant with hylozoism. Certainly, he flirted with hylozoism in 1801, some fourteen years before *Biographia* was composed. In that year, he wrote "The Night-Scene: A Dramatic Fragment," in which the character Earl Henry describes life with his lover in identical terms to the passage on hylozoism: "Life was in us: / We were all life, each atom of our frames / A living soul." Such love, he states, "is joy above the name of pleasure, / Deep self-possession, an intense repose." His interlocutor, Sandoval, replies, "No other than as eastern sages paint, / The God, who floats upon a lotos [sic] leaf, / Dreams for a thousand ages; then awaking, / Creates a world, and smiling at the bubble, / Relapses into bliss." As it does with the speaker of "The Eolian Harp," love provokes a meditative state of "intense repose" in which Earl Henry paradoxically finds both "deep self-possession" and realizes that this self is atomized into a million souls. Yet, although Sandoval makes his rejoinder "with a sarcastic smile" (*Complete Poems* 291), Coleridge had imagined becoming this same god in a 1797 letter to John Thelwall: "I should much wish, like the Indian Vishna [sic], to float along an infinite ocean cradled in the flower of the Lotus, and wake once in a million years for a few minutes just to know that I was going to sleep a million years or more" (*Collected Letters* 1: 350). For Coleridge, meditation can make one like a god: it brings tranquility, bliss, and the potential for an endless cycle of creativity. As we have seen, these earlier, positive depictions of hylozoism or Hindu pantheism become more ambivalent by the time of the writing of the *Biographia*, but there is more continuity in his thought than is often acknowledged.[13]

In the *Biographia*, Coleridge proposes a unification of subject and object through the faculty of the imagination, an essential part of the poetic—and therefore meditative—process. Like Krishna's meditation, Coleridge's imagination vitalizes objects (including the subject *as* object) and enfolds them within a provisional, more expansive relation. This attempt to bring aesthetics, epistemology, and ontology into one unified theory is indebted to contemporaneous German philosophers[14] as well as the "pantheistic" or "hylozoistic" Hinduism I explored above. Before highlighting certain passages of the *Biographia*, it may be worthwhile to review the main content of chapters 12 through 15. These chapters are famously convoluted and full of digressions, but essentially, chapter 12 gives a philosophical account of the subject/object problem and suggests that it can be resolved, chapter 13 provides a mechanism for its resolution in the faculty of the imagination, and chapters 14 and 15 discuss poetry. This arrangement suggests that Coleridge sees poetry as a crucial practice, one that exemplifies and embodies his philosophical system.

Coleridge begins this section of the *Biographia* by setting forth a system of "idealism," which is "at the same time, and on that very account, the truest and most binding realism" (1: 261). In other words, his is not the type of idealism where nothing exists outside the mind of the perceiving subject; rather, he defends objective idealism, where objects are real and, like the subject, composed of something mind- or spirit-like. He argues that "things without us" are "unconsciously involved" within us (1: 260), just like the "chain of flowers" that entangles the writer and reader of poetry. Indeed, objects are "identical, and one and the same thing with our own immediate self-consciousness" (1: 260). This is because spirit is the foundation of all subjects and objects, and the totality of this spirit is God, in which, as in Krishna, "all things rest." Coleridge then turns to a definition of the primary and secondary imagination. The former is "a repetition in the finite mind of the eternal act of creation in the infinite I AM" (1: 304), which resonates, as I suggested earlier, with the use of *theta* as symbol of meditation. The secondary imagination "dissolves, diffuses, dissipates, in order to re-create; or where this process is rendered impossible, yet still at all events it struggles to idealize and to unify. It is essentially *vital*, even as all objects (*as* objects) are essentially fixed and dead" (1: 304). This is the practice through which the subject, by creating new assemblages with objects, idealizes and vitalizes them—or more precisely, *realizes* that objects are never just "objects (*as* objects)," but inherently ideal and vital in themselves. Finally, Coleridge argues that we see the imagination vividly at work in poetry: Shakespeare, he says, "gives a dignity and a passion to the objects which he presents. Unaided by any previous excitement, they burst upon us at once in life and in power" (2: 23–24). Shakespeare's excellence marks an ontological becoming: through poetry, he "becomes all things, yet for ever remaining himself" (2: 28), and anyone who breathes while reading the lines of Shakespeare or Milton also becomes entangled in things. Ultimately, Coleridge's writings suggest that both meditation and poetry are carefully orchestrated practices for experiencing and expressing self-transcendence. Such spiritual becoming is not diaphanous, dreamy, or detached from reality, but always grounded in bodies and materiality.

Carlyle: Transcendent Descendentalism

Carlyle is not commonly thought of as a philosopher. Charles Frederick Harrold refers to him as merely a "gifted amateur," stressing that Carlyle never considered himself a philosopher (3–4). Nevertheless, it's worth remembering that Carlyle applied, unsuccessfully, for a chair of philosophy at both St Andrews and London University. It's also remarkable that he "took much of his own 'German philosophy' pre-digested from

Coleridge" (Ashton 72), another literary figure whose philosophical stature is often diluted by his indirect, seemingly subordinate relationship to greater philosophical sources. In this sense, Carlyle's relationship to "real" philosophy is at a further remove and doubly diluted. I will argue, however, that the streamlet of Carlyle's philosophy—fed, indeed, by other upstream currents—became a torrent in its own right, integrating various aspects of Absolute idealism into a singular discourse that powerfully affected the next generation of authors and philosophers. For instance, in his careful analysis of twenty-eight philosophers located in Britain, Canada, Australia, South Africa, and the United States, Alexander Jordan argues that "the British Idealists were enormously influenced by Carlyle in almost every aspect of their thought, including their theology, their moral and ethical philosophy and their social and political thought" (444). In one of the greatest and most influential Absolute fictions of the century, *Sartor Resartus* (1833–34), readers can find the following idealist positions expressed in densely layered, self-referential (that is to say, idealist) literary form: (1) the explanatory and ethical poverty of radical materialism forces us to see that (2) all finite things are vestures or appearances of the Absolute and that (3) the Absolute, in turn, appears in its entirety in each of these finite things; another way to think such interpenetration is through (4) the paradox of selfhood, in which the self both dissolves into a general whole and gains specific integrity and value through that dissolution; finally, (5) literature plays a crucial role in this realignment of our ontological and ethical perspectives through techniques such as anthropomorphism, science-fictional thought experiments, and the rhizomatic yet teleological unfolding of narrative itself. These paradoxes are contained in and expressed by the figure of Diogenes Teufelsdröckh, a German idealist philosopher who combines in his own name the divine and the defecatory.

The young Carlyle clearly looked up to Coleridge as an important thinker, visiting him several times in 1824 and 1825. Despite Carlyle's later dismissal of Coleridge as intelligent but addled, the older sage was a crucial inspiration for *Sartor Resartus*. As James Treadwell puts it, "Coleridge signifies for Carlyle the possibility of a doubly productive Idealism. He stands for the refinement of materialism into a vitalist universe saturated with divinity; and he also stands for the prophetic man of letters whose task it is to communicate this new scripture to his contemporaries, as Teufelsdröckh does" (69). Treadwell is right to stress that their idealism is a refinement, rather than an outright rejection, of materialism. Indeed, both Coleridge and Carlyle—who read the first 150 pages of the first *Critique* (Ashton 92)—misread Kant in Absolute idealist fashion. That they misread him is not surprising, given that many other readers, from Mill to Lord Macaulay (who complained that it might as well have been written in "Sanscrit"), found Kant baffling (Dibble 22). But Teufelsdröckh's philosophy is "essentially a simplified version of the leading themes of German Idealist philosophy" rather than Kantian philosophy, since for Teufelsdröckh the rational faculty of the Understanding requires supplementation from the imaginative faculty of Reason, which gives access to "things-in-themselves or about noumenal (as opposed to phenomenal) objects of thought" (McSweeney and Sabor xxv). Of course, this is precisely Coleridge's post-Kantian philosophical approach. It also reflects Carlyle's familiarity with Novalis, Friedrich Schlegel, and Schelling (Harrold 10–11), all important Absolute idealists. As Carlyle grew older, however, he became more and more detached from his early enthusiasm for idealism, as evidenced by his increasingly strident defense of Great Men and racial hierarchies, ideas of division that are antithetical to the harmonizing, mereological spirit of Absolute idealism.

Indeed, not only the content but also the formal structure of *Sartor Resartus* works to harmonize disparate cultures and perspectives. Jerry A. Dibble argues that the novel employs many of the same rhetorical techniques as the German Idealist philosophers, who tried to create a new style of writing philosophy in the face of skeptical and uncomprehending readers. Carlyle similarly required "a special kind of rhetorical strategy, one which would work toward communication and persuasion and yet, paradoxically, would also manage to delay full comprehension until the whole of the writer's message could be set fairly before his audience" (4). This explains the function of the commonsensical British editor of Teufelsdröckh's texts—he embodies not Carlyle's doubts about idealism but his British readers', and as the editor's skepticism erodes, so (ideally) does theirs (5). In this way, Carlyle attempts to bring together British and German, empiricist and idealist perspectives. Moreover, as Dibble suggests, Carlyle employs a strategy of delay where the ultimate doctrine finally becomes clear at the end of the narrative. Dibble mentions the *Bildungsroman* structure of *The Phenomenology of Spirit* in this regard, but as we will see in the next section, Hegel's *The Science of Logic* (1812–16) has the same teleological arrangement in which everything that comes before the end is retrospectively grasped and recast by that end. But it is not just philosophical perspectives, narrative expectations, and genres that

Carlyle harmonizes in this Absolute fiction: an often-overlooked aspect of the text is the extent to which Teufelsdröckh is associated with Indian philosophy and the frequency with which he and the editor engage in "meditations." In several ways, then, *Sartor Resartus* underscores the fact that modern idealism is a fundamentally mosaicking activity.

In the second chapter of *Sartor Resartus*, the editor advises his audience to adopt a particular attitude toward the text: "Let the British reader study and enjoy, in simplicity of heart, what is here presented him, and with whatever metaphysical acumen, and talent for Meditation he is possessed of" (10). This suggests that the reader will explore philosophical issues with the help of a particular skill—meditation—which, as in Coleridge, has the double valence of deep consideration and focused attentiveness on a "presented" object, in this case "the Book itself" (10). The reader's meditation is meant to retrace Teufelsdröckh's, who has likewise "unfolded" his doctrine through "infinitely complected tissues . . . of Meditation" (41). The enfolded, layered form of the novel therefore embodies, and encourages, a process of meditation. The reader must wander, as Teufelsdröckh has, through a series of ideas in order to arrive at the final truth, which is that the process itself—the struggle to know and love particular things—is the truth. In this sense Teufelsdröckh is a spiritual leader, a guru who guides the reader along the proper path of meditation. This explains the insistence with which Teufelsdröckh is associated with the East. He is "Dalai-Lama," meditating in solitude (21); his history has "something of an almost Hindoo character" (78); like "Hindoo Worshippers," he attends equally to spiritual content and form (182). Perhaps Carlyle is merely using the editor to represent the widespread British association of idealism with India (see Lord Macaulay's comment above), but the last comparison is Teufelsdröckh's own. Nor is the editor ultimately repelled by Teufelsdröckh's language and ideas, for by the end of the novel, he admits that "This stupendous Section ["Natural Supernaturalism"] we, after long, painful meditation, have found not to be unintelligible; but on the contrary to grow clear, nay radiant, and all-illuminating" (193).

Thus, the editor's distanced skepticism is replaced, in the end, by an embrace of alterity, and this precisely matches the spiritual conversion Teufelsdröckh undergoes in his passage from the Everlasting No to the Everlasting Yea. This famous transformation seems like a straightforward shift from materialism to idealism and, in general, it is that, but it is important to consider how Teufelsdröckh reinvests the material world with life and meaning instead of rejecting it. In other words, his conversion rests on a successful balancing of emphasis between matter and spirit, and he makes this apparent dualism concordant by learning to release the hard distinction between himself and the "other" outside himself. In "The Everlasting No," we see that both extremes—radical materialism and radical idealism—are isolating and intolerable. The materialist vision of the universe as "one huge, dead, immeasurable Steam-engine, rolling on, in its dead indifference, to grind me limb from limb" is directly preceded by an equally terrifying vision of other humans as pure forms with no content: "The men and women round me, even speaking with me, were but Figures; I had, practically, forgotten that they were alive, that they were not merely automatic" (127). In both cases, the self is encircled by, but utterly detached from, the "rolling" "round" of indifferent machines, whether engines or figures.

Far from annihilating the self, however, being the lone sensible nucleus in a dead world of whirling automata augments it. Teufelsdröckh's solitude and anguish are keened to a heightened pitch, and "The Everlasting No" ends with his "whole ME" delineating itself through defiant protest, echoing the mechanistic universe's NO with a negation of his own (129). Within this "Centre of Indifference," Teufelsdröckh must struggle to release his subjectivist perspective by "clutch[ing] round him outwardly, on the NOT-ME for wholesomer food" (130). Clutching and devouring what is outside the self may sound like a deeply problematic *increase* in subjectivism, but it is actually a necessary stage in the process of realizing that the self is dependent upon the other, as Hegel demonstrates in the famous "The Truth of Self-Certainty" and "Lordship and Bondage" chapters of the *Phenomenology*.[15] Just as Hegel's philosopher and consciousness respectively find in those chapters, Teufelsdröckh learns that the desire to consume is a bad infinity (endless regress) that provides no lasting satisfaction: Alexander the Great, he remarks, would not be content with the conquering of one planet but would require another, and then a solar system, and then a universe (139). In contrast, although he still has no positive philosophy of his own at this point and remains a "dissevered limb" (139), Teufelsdröckh has become acquainted with the wider world through a "Meditation" (134) on nature, cities, politics, war, cultures, and books. He has humbly "grown familiar with many things" (138), and this begins to knit him to the wider world.

Finally, we reach "The Everlasting Yea," which completes Teufelsdröckh's turn from materialism through subjective idealism to Absolute idealism. The "Annihilation of Self" is now complete (142), for he finds that his "self" is actually a part of a larger ecological reality: namely, God, which inhabits and enlivens all of nature, including himself (143). Thus, the realization of true infinity (an organic whole, the Absolute) is achieved not through the expansion of a consuming self ("increasing your Numerator") but through the elimination of the difference between subject and object ("lessening your Denominator . . . [to] Zero") (145). By doing so, Teufelsdröckh transcends the partial reality of time to directly grasp the Absolute: "On the roaring billows of Time, thou art not engulphed, but borne aloft into the azure of Eternity. Love not Pleasure; love God. This is the EVERLASTING YEA, wherein all contradiction is solved" (146). In an earlier essay, I cited this passage as evidence that Carlyle advances a dualist conception of temporality, but this now seems incorrect to me.[16] Dualism implies an absolute distinction, usually with an accompanying hierarchical ordering, between two things. Carlyle's eternity and time are not distinct, however, but integrated realities, and while it is true that eternity encompasses time, it is in the same non-dualistic, nonhierarchical sense that a lung encompasses alveoli. Later in the century, Bradley makes a similar argument about temporality in relationship to the Absolute, as we will see in chapter 3, and he draws from it the same science-fictional conclusions that Carlyle does, as we will see below.

In line with the objectivist and mereological characteristics of Absolute idealism, Teufelsdröckh's ascent into the empyrean of the Everlasting Yea is balanced by his reverence for the gravity of particular objects. He is, after all, "Professor of Things in General" (14), an obviously oxymoronic title that conjoins content and category, material and ideal. The editor remarks that the "grand unparalleled peculiarity of Teufelsdröckh" is his combination of "Descendentalism" with "Transcendentalism" (51)—and there are many instances where he arrives at the Absolute by descending into the contemplation of a specific thing. For instance, he remarks that even the "drop which thou shakest from thy wet hand" is imbued with "Force" and therefore is not "utterly dead;" moreover, each droplet is part of the circulations of climate, riding "the wings of the Northwind," just as the Sun kindled this fire "where the sooty smith bends over his anvil" (55). The specific thus participates in the general to such an extent that the two ontological scales collapse: "Rightly viewed no meanest object is insignificant; all objects are as windows, through which the philosophic eye looks into Infinitude itself" (56). Looks into—and modifies. Each event, however mundane, is full of meaning because it shifts the universal: "It is a mathematical fact that the casting of this pebble from my hand alters the centre of gravity of the Universe" (186). This idea of ontological entanglement across scales is also made by Hegel. "As regards the reciprocal determinations that hold the whole together," he writes in *The Science of Logic*, "metaphysics could make the basically tautological claim that if one speck of dust were destroyed the whole universe would collapse" (62).[17]

Humans (and nonhumans) enact such ontological entanglement most visibly by using tools. A tool is a material prosthesis that connects a specific organism to its specific ecology, providing a means to act and affect across scales of magnitude. Humans, whom Teufelsdröckh defines as "a Tool-using Animal," are incredibly adept at augmenting their reach through tools: "he can use Tools, can devise Tools: with these the granite mountain melts into light dust before him; he kneads glowing iron, as if it were soft paste; seas are his smooth highway, winds and fire his unwearying steeds" (32). Humans speak to matter and compel it to life: "He digs up certain black stones from the bosom of the Earth, and says to them, *Transport me, and this luggage, at the rate of five-and-thirty miles an hour;* and they do it" (33). But Teufelsdröckh's definition ultimately breaks down because all animals—or living things, however we define that—use tools in much the same industrial mode: "there is not a Man, or a Thing, now alive but has tools. The basest of created animalcules, the Spider itself, has a spinning-jenny, and warping-mill, and power-loom, within its head; the stupidest of Oysters has a Papin's-Digester, with stone-and-lime house to hold it in: every being that can live can do something; this let him *do*" (150). The relentless emphasis on industrial machinery further confuses the distinctions between human, nonhuman, and thing: just where does one body end and another begin, and who is using whom? These are precisely the questions Samuel Butler asks at the end of the century. In his panpsychist tract *Unconscious Memory* (1880), Butler points out the "remarkable analogy between the development of living organs or tools and that of those organs or tools external to the body" (146). Not only do all organisms have external organs or tools, but also, as Butler proposes in *Erewhon* (1872), machines have their own consciousness, and they may well be using humans as tools. Carlyle was certainly aware that the "black stones" humans seem to command in fact radically alter human life and relations in unanticipated ways, while coal becomes increasingly ontologically involved, extending its power and influence. This is an entangled web, indeed.

The ontological reticulations explored in *Sartor Resartus* are reflected in the novel's idiosyncratic formal structure, which suggests that the expression of Absolute idealism requires aesthetic experimentation, as the German Romantics insisted. The editor complains about the "almost total want of arrangement" in Teufelsdröckh's texts, which form a "Chaos" "wherein all courses had been confounded, and fish and flesh, soup and solid, oyster-sauce, lettuces, Rhine-wine and French mustard, were hurled into one huge tureen or trough, and the hungry Public invited to help itself" (26-27). As daunting as the editor's gustatory hyperbole appears, however, Teufelsdröckh's narrative is not utterly indigestible: that is reserved for "Fashionable Novels," which for Teufelsdröckh are tougher than his own "tough faculty of reading" (210). The implication is that novels—like the universe itself—must continuously produce new forms as part of their organic and autopoietic logic. In other words, they must defamiliarize themselves. This explains *Sartor Resartus*'s unconventional ordering principles, which follow the form of the Absolute because they are mereological or metonymic, emphasizing the ways in which part and whole open onto and mutually shape one another. As I suggest throughout the rest of this book, such Absolute logic also shapes the formal and thematic characteristics of fiction in the long nineteenth century writ large, from realism to detective fiction, science fiction, weird horror, and modernism—even postmodernism.[18] To put it another way, Absolute idealism compels the differentiation of genre from its basis in *realism*.

In addition to its mereological content, which I have discussed above, *Sartor Resartus* is formally mereological because it integrates parts and wholes across scales of magnitude, and such scalar shifts open up a range of generic and interpretive possibilities for literature. Despite its seemingly incoherent organization, the "Sheets," "Shreds," and "Snips" of Teufelsdröckh's narrative are swathed in six paper bags marked by zodiac signs, thus connecting the mundane events of his life to cosmic trajectories. His continual digressions, then—what the editor calls his "play[ing] truant for long pages" (23) and a tendency toward "almost wearying minuteness" (70)—are not irrelevant detours but integral paths toward an Absolute view of reality. This is, coincidentally, precisely the same formal device we find in nineteenth-century realist narratives, which are riddled, as Amy M. King points out, with long, seemingly banal descriptive passages that nevertheless index the cosmic, "an ontology of particulars that fed a vague sense of the divine" ("Natural History" 461). King suggests that this formal relation borrows the following structural and ethical assumptions from natural history and natural theology, but we could equally claim that these aptly describe Absolute idealism: "a delimited focus of attention on small objects or minute areas; the requirement to dilate at length upon such detail, finding much in the small and the quotidian; and the absolute value of close attention upon the detail, which yields truths inaccessible to wider gazes" (461). Of course, modern literary criticism seizes on these same assumptions in its fundamental reliance on close reading, a technique in which general truths emerge from intense meditation on particular textual objects.

Taking the same mereological relation but focusing on the cosmic rather than the particular side of reality invites science-fictional, rather than strictly realist, narratives. In "Natural Supernaturalism," Teufelsdröckh turns his attention to the "two grand fundamental world-enveloping Appearances, SPACE and TIME" (197), introducing the thought experiment of time- and space-annihilating hats. "Had we but the Time-annihilating Hat," he writes, "we should see ourselves in a World of Miracles, wherein all fabled or authentic Thaumaturgy, and feats of Magic, were outdone. But unhappily we have not such a Hat; and man, poor fool that he is, can seldom and scantily help himself without one" (199). But we do have such a hat—literature, especially historical and science fiction—and Carlyle dons it for a moment in his brief but startling sketch of a time traveler who walks streets filled with ghosts and visits the "Beginnings" and "Endings" of the universe (200). The cosmic scope of this excursus does not provide a totalizing perspective that dissolves all particularity, as one might expect, but instead impresses upon us, to borrow King's words again, "the absolute value of close attention upon the detail." When one wears a time-annihilating hat, which is to say when one reads *Sartor Resartus*, "[t]hen sawest thou that this fair Universe, were it in the meanest province thereof, is in very deed the star-domed City of God; that through every star, through every grass-blade, and most through every Living Soul, the glory of a present God still beams" (200).

This last reference to the City of God puts us in mind of Augustine, perhaps especially Emerson's apocryphal invocation of him in "Circles": "St. Augustine described the nature of God as a circle whose centre was everywhere and its circumference nowhere" (*Complete Essays* 279). If the center of the Absolute is everywhere, giving everything absolute value, then no single part is privileged, not even Beginnings or Endings. Despite the teleological structure of the novel, which traces the *Bildungen* of Teufelsdröckh, the editor, and the reader, we are left, in the end, in the middle of nowhere: according to the editor, the novel "leads to nothing, and there is no use in it" (Carlyle 204). Yet, it is meant to lead us back to a renewed appreciation of every thing and everything that "is passing under our very eyes" (4), positioning us to see that nowhere and everywhere "thy daily life is girt with Wonder, and based on Wonder, and thy very blankets and breeches are Miracles" (205). Carlyle's belief that literature and philosophy defamiliarize reality in a way that fosters a greater awareness of the miraculous that inheres in the banal, a sense of wonder at the everyday, frequently appears as an ethical stance in Absolute fiction. It also, however, marks a difference between Carlyle, on the one hand, and Coleridge and Hegel on the other. The latter believe that the Absolute can be adequately conceptualized through philosophy. The more mystical Carlyle preserves it, through the gap of wonder, from being comprehensively grasped by any human discourse. According to Teufelsdröckh, the man without a sense of wonder, though he carries the whole of Hegel's philosophy in his head, is blind (54). Hegel would no doubt disagree.

Hegel: Proleptic Memories

Coleridge, who had a slight familiarity and felt a strong frustration with Hegel's philosophy, may well be considered "the first of the nineteenth century British Idealists" (Hedley 2). For the cluster of British Idealists at the end of the Victorian period, the familiarity was stronger and the frustration slighter. Hegel was a powerful influence on these later idealists, so much so that they are sometimes referred to as the British Hegelians or Oxford Hegelians, although such labels unfortunately imply that their work is merely derivative. The Hegel treatise that most influenced them (Mander, *British* 19) was the one Hegel himself considered "the fundamental keystone of his system" (Pinkard 161): *The Science of Logic*, which will be the focus of this section. Because I am primarily concerned with the Absolute fictions of the long nineteenth century, I will approach the *Logic* through the interpretive lens of nineteenth-century Anglophone writers in order to suggest how Absolute idealism was absorbed into their philosophical and literary texts. In other words, I am less interested in identifying Hegel's actual project than in reading him through the lens of later interpretations; following Katrin Pahl, I believe that one "remain[s] true to the Hegelian text by transforming it" (14). These later interpretations understand his philosophy as consonant with Coleridge's and Carlyle's: Hegel provides a realist, objectivist, mereological ontology that explains the logic, or formal characteristics, of the entire cosmos (which is therefore the same logic that governs human thought). For instance, in an essay comparing Carlyle and Hegel, Walt Whitman suggests that the movement from Kant to Schelling and Hegel is a movement away from subjectivism toward an objectivism and naturalism that unifies the subject and object (175). He commends Hegel for his "scientific" (175) demonstration that "the contrarieties of material with spiritual, and of natural with artificial, are all, to the eye of the *ensemblist,* but necessary sides and unfoldings, different steps or links, in the endless process of Creative thought, which, amid numberless apparent failures and contradictions, is held together by central and never-broken unity" (176). Whitman leaves the subject of "Creative thought" ambiguous, thereby suggesting that the mind of an individual self is formally analogous, even ontologically identical, to "the thought of the universe" (175). The similarity here to Vedantic philosophy was not lost on Whitman, who notes that Hegel elaborates on "an old nucleus-thought, as in the Vedas" (175). In this section I will follow Whitman in reading Hegel as an ontological monist who was deeply indebted to Indian thought.

The single work most responsible for igniting late-Victorian interest in Hegel was James Hutchison Stirling's *The Secret of Hegel: Being the Hegelian System in Origin, Principle, Form and Matter* (1865). Although "its writing style, full of exclamation and mock-quotation, is so much influenced by Carlyle as to be in places almost unreadable" (Mander, *British* 18), it nevertheless revived interest in Hegel after a mid-century lull in which he was marginalized by being associated with David Strauss and the higher criticism, an association underscored by George Eliot's praise of Hegel in her translation of *Das Leben Jesu* (Willis 92, 94). Kirk Willis describes how the British perception of Hegel shifted dramatically (and ironically) from the middle to late Victorian period. In the middle of the century, Hegel was considered an anti-Christian thinker; Mill "dismissed all forms of Absolute Idealism as pantheism, and [made] a bald conclusion that Hegelian and Straussian philosophies of religion therefore had as little applicability to the study of Christianity as did the doctrines of the Vedantists" (Willis 94). But for Stirling and many of the British Idealists at the end of the century, Hegel was a bulwark *against* the crisis of faith, albeit in a loosely Christian mode inflected by the pantheism Mill deplored: "[British Idealism] largely abandons the traditional conception of God as ontologically distinct from the world, replacing it with a God that is immanent in nature, and most especially immanent in the finite self; a position whose reverse expression, of course, is to say that the finite self is implicitly infinite or divine" (Mander and Panagakou 5).

In *The Secret of Hegel*, Stirling takes on the role of Teufelsdröckh's editor, attempting to "mitigate" the "uncouth unintelligibleness" of German philosophy for dubious British readers (xvii). He frames the trajectory of classical German philosophy in identical terms to Whitman: the movement from Kant to Hegel is one from (anthropocentric) subjectivism to objectivism, for "Hegel was enabled to get beyond the limited subjective form of Kant's mere system of human knowledge, and convert that system into something universal and objective" (89). The "secret," then, is that humans need to turn their usual perspective on reality inside out. To borrow the catchphrase of speculative realism, we can no longer adopt a "correlationist" or anthropocentric view of reality, which is an abstract projection; instead, we must move from the outside in, from object to subject, to grasp the actual concrete: "it is the background that contains the true, the immediate outside and surface is untrue" (41). Thus, *pace* Karl Marx, Hegel is not standing on his head, lost in mystical clouds of thought, but "wholly down on the solid floor of substantial fact" (xlix). Moreover, another common misconception or "fear" that Hegel advocates an "absorption into the universal"—thereby sinking all particulars into a totalizing soup—is baseless (720). Instead, each particular maintains its integrity as a crucial part of the Absolute: "the Whole would perish were a single link to fail, for each is as a centre of the relations of the all" (718). Despite his repeated avowals of Christianity, Stirling admits the "pantheistic" implications of such mereology (86). Reverting to French, he proclaims that Hegel's God is "le Dieu Absolu, that which is, but that is Thought, Spirit: moi, je suis l'Absolu; toi, tu es l'Absolu; lui, il est l'Absolu" (74).

Stirling also underscores the literary significance of Hegel's writing style, which is described in much the same terms as Teufelsdröckh's: "never were such words written—selcouth, uncouth, bizarre, baroque—pertinent and valuable only to a Hegel. Style and terminology how clumsy, inelegant, obscure! Then the figures, like 'life in excrement,' an endless sprawl—an endless twist and twine—endless vermiculation, like an anthill" (41). Like Teufelsdröckh's language, Hegel's is difficult but startling; his sentences are rhizomatic, densely layered, and filled with metaphorical "figures." His style (or at least this description of it) also infects Stirling's own, which oscillates between dry philosophical discourse and flights of purple prose, the latter of which is apparent in one of his definitions of the Absolute: "the vibration of a mathematical point, the tinted tremble of a single eye, infinitesimally infinite, punctually one, whose own tremble is its own object, and its own life, and its own self" (678). Such blending of philosophy and literature in Absolute fiction could be contrasted with the "Photographic" novels of the Victorian period—Stirling has in mind the sensation novel—which he excoriates as purely subjectivist and superficial, "a succession of optical presentments followed easily by the eye" (xlii, 716). Stirling derides such literature because it has no temporal or ontological depth; in other words, it concerns itself with, and produces in its readers, subjective, physical sensations lodged in the "present" rather than systematic thought that unfolds objectively and diachronically. We need not agree with Stirling's diagnosis to observe that, for the late Victorians, Absolute idealism was as much a literary as a philosophical provocation.

Stirling's attention to both the ontological and literary/linguistic aspects of Hegel's work marks the two main interpretative approaches that continue to inform Hegelian scholarship up to the present time (di Giovanni lv–lvi). In his introduction to the *Logic*, George di Giovanni suggests that the British Idealist J. M. E. McTaggart represents the former, ontological or metaphysical, approach, since for McTaggart the *Logic* provides a "cosmogony" or account of the origins and development of the universe (lvii).[19] This metaphysical approach held sway from the late nineteenth to the late twentieth century. The discursive or non-metaphysical (or "post-Kantian") approach, which emerged in the final decades of the twentieth century, examines the historical development of normative claims. In the words of Christopher J. Insole, it contends that "the truth is worked out by telling a story. It is not just that the story attempts to tell the truth that is already there. Rather, in telling the story, we partly create the truth we are attempting to articulate" (qtd. in di Giovanni lix). These two approaches are not incommensurable: one could point out that discourses and stories are obviously "part" of the universe and "partly create," however modestly or significantly, that ontological reality. For example, Slavoj Žižek maintains, in books such as *Less Than Nothing: Hegel and the Shadow of Dialectical Materialism*, that Hegel makes an "epistemologico-ontological" argument about the nature of reality: our inability to grasp the ultimate truth of reality, that relentless epistemological gap or lack, is itself "a crack in the thing itself" (17). In other words, for (Žižek's) Hegel, reality is lack all the way down, "less than nothing." This overlapping of epistemology (language, discourse, etc.) and ontology allows Žižek to claim that "although we can clearly distinguish between reality and fiction, we cannot simply drop fiction and retain only reality; if we drop fiction, reality itself disintegrates, loses its ontological consistency" (370). Drawing the two approaches to Hegel together, one could say that reality simply *is* Absolute fiction, the creative unfolding of a universal narrative that self-reflexively apprehends and alters itself through logic, language, and art.

This is far from saying that the universe is fictional in the sense of illusory or unreal. The notion that idealism in general or Hegel in particular advances such a claim is itself an intractable fiction that many commentators attempt to dispel. Understanding Hegel seemingly requires a series of apophatic definitions of what is *not* being argued. Hegel is not an antirealist (Dunham et al. 145; Beiser, *Hegel* 68–69; Houlgate 429), nor is he anthropocentric (Dunham et al. 152; Ellermann, "Hegel"). Hegel's system is not an all-devouring subjectivism that liquidates difference and otherness: "the Hegel of the absolute Subject swallowing up all objective content is a retroactive fantasy of his critics" (Žižek 261). Perhaps the basic misunderstanding about Hegel stems from the assumption that "ideas" and "matter" can only be thought dualistically. Instead, for Hegel as for Plato, ideas are (also) objective: they do not exist only in the minds of human beings, nor are they "the hidden reality beneath appearances"—instead, ideas are "the very form of appearance, this form as such" (Žižek 31). In other words, a thing must have an idea, form, or organization to appear or exist; its idea is inseparable from its existence, just as its matter is inseparable. Indeed, it seems rather uncontroversial to claim that everything in nature has a particular organization and is positioned within a larger organization, which is why "much of contemporary science is . . . implicitly idealist. Any domain of science that asserts the existence of systems, and/or uses the language of 'functionality' and 'organization,' in order to explain the existence of components of those systems, is idealist in character" (Dunham et al. 153). Another negative definition, therefore, is that Hegel is not "anti-rationalist or anti-science" (152).

A final negative definition that we can apply to Hegel, one that will again bring together the literary and the cosmic, is that he is not Orientalist—at least not entirely. Although we cannot ignore the many negative, dismissive statements he makes about Indian thought (and other non-Western cultures), we should also emphasize his prodigious, genuine interest in India. In *Hegel's India*, Aakash Singh Rathore and Rimina Mohapatra note that

> what remains passed over in silence in the vitriolic attacks on Hegel's obnoxious prejudice is, precisely, that he spent an enormous amount of time in close and constructive study of diverse writings on Indian art, religion, and philosophy, and drafted hundreds of pages of reflective copy about them. . . . [I]t is arguable that given the changed global environment and proliferation of accurate source material, Hegel showed *less* prejudice and arbitrary cultural preference than contemporary philosophers and philosophy departments continue to do today. (18–19)

Rathore and Mohapatra point out that Hegel wrote more on the "oriental" world than on the ancient Greeks (14), and he was uncomfortably aware of the similarity between Indian philosophy and his own thought, such as the conception of *Brahman* and the Absolute (4). A comparative study of Hegelian and Indian philosophy is beyond the scope of this chapter; I simply want to draw attention to the deep influence Indian ideas and practices had on Hegel. This is especially evident in his consideration of the relationship between literary form, reality, and meditation. In "On the Episode of the Mahabharata Known by the Name *Bhagavad-Gita* by Wilhelm von Humboldt" (1827), Hegel underscores the way in which reading literature can induce a state of meditation meant to provide insight into the nature of reality. He writes, "the preserved meter of the original [poem], which might have caused a lot of difficulties, appears here in a specially suitable way, since its slow pace forces the reader to meditate on the contents, which deals with meditation" (qtd. in Rathore and Mohapatra 107). Later, he gives the story of the poet Valmiki, who was told to compose the *Ramayana* in a particular metric rhythm by *Brahman*/the Absolute, a divine being who nevertheless "stays characterized as deep meditation" (127).[20] Although Hegel ultimately dismisses meditation as a source of true insight, he takes seriously the idea that the composition of language and the composition of the universe are folded together and can be accessed at the pleat through meditation.

Hegel acknowledges that meditation offers a *beginning* because it allows one to grasp "being," the idea with which he begins the *Logic*. At this initial stage, being is completely abstract, indeterminate, and empty: "It is altogether the same as what an Indian calls Brahma, when for years on end, looking only at the tip of his nose, externally motionless and equally unmoved in sensation, representation, phantasy, desire, and so on, he inwardly says only *Om, Om, Om*, or else says nothing at all. This dull, empty consciousness, taken as consciousness, is just this—*being*" (*Science of Logic* 73). He thus grants meditation a rather etiolated role in divining metaphysical truth, since it is only by carefully following the immanent logic of being through to the end, to the "absolute idea," that one retrospectively understands all of the determinations that being generates. The opening of the *Logic* shows how the idea of "being" as absolute truth (an idea first advocated by Parmenides) necessarily leads to the idea of "nothing" (Buddhism) and then "becoming" (Heraclitus) (60) and on through a series of further determinations, and we must follow this entire dialectical exposition because it makes the beginning "*ever richer and more concrete*" (750). The dialectic reaches its end—also its completely articulated beginning—with the absolute idea, which brings together form and matter, universal and particular, and all of the determinations of the dialectic into one system, organization, or concept: it "alone is *being,* imperishable *life, self-knowing truth*, and is *all truth*" (735). Catherine Malabou reminds us that Hegel's conception of the dialectic and the Absolute (or "absolute idea") does not entail the consumption of the Other (*Future* 4) nor a totalizing stasis, but rather provides a plastic and open-ended "process where the universal and particular mutually inform one another" (*Future* 11).

Such a process, which follows the development of an indeterminate beginning to an "end" in which that beginning and everything that follows is retrospectively grasped and thereby *recomposed*, invites an analogy: Does it describe the unfolding of the cosmos from its simple beginning to its articulation by human thought? Or does it describe the development of an individual subject? Or is it remarkably akin to a novel and the experience of reading a novel? As we have seen, all of these interpretations have been explored by readers of Hegel, but I want to dwell on this last question: Is a novel—or a philosophical treatise, for that matter—an Absolute fiction in the sense that, like the Absolute or *as* the Absolute, it does not transcend but *is* (an expression of) the contexts and contents, the selves and experiences, that compose it? Is the novel, like the reader of a novel, like the Absolute, a certain in-betweenness or "crack in the thing itself" (Žižek 17) that, in its particularity, actively mediates form and content, universal and particular, beginning and end? "Reading Hegel," Malabou argues, "amounts to finding oneself in two times at once: the process that unfolds is both retrospective and prospective. In the present time in which reading takes place, the reader is drawn to a double expectation: waiting for what is to come (according to a linear and representational thinking), while presupposing that the outcome has already arrived (by virtue of the teleological ruse)" (*Future* 17). She subsequently suggests that "the situation of 'in-between' [is] *par excellence* the situation of reading" (184). Hegel's implicit philosophy of reading therefore depends upon a certain experience of temporality—glancing forward and backward from a liminal, always-shifting position—that helps us better understand his literary significance as a writer of Absolute fiction.

In both the form and content of the *Logic*, Hegel employs temporal "in-betweenness" in a way that appeals to literary form and content. In the introduction, he draws attention to the distinction between form and content, which for him is the distinction between the perspective of the philosopher and the subject matter, respectively. He reminds his reader that "the divisions and the headings of the books, the sections and chapters given in this work, as well as the explanations associated with them," are given from the philosopher's vantage point, who "has already gone through the whole of the exposition [and] therefore knows the sequence of its moments in advance and anticipates them before they are brought on by the matter at issue itself" (34). The author and the reader have access to this perspective because Hegel has obviously "gone through the whole of the exposition" and the reader (in a more limited sense, at least at first) because she can peruse the table of contents, skip ahead, reread, etc. This creates both a prospective/anticipatory and retrospective/historical experience for these extratextual agents (34). The author and reader are also able to perceive the formal depth of the exposition: for example, Hegel's division of the text into abstract arguments and down-to-earth "remarks" layers the text into less and more concrete planes, just like the distinction between translation and editorial comment in *Sartor Resartus* or poem and gloss in "The Rime of the Ancient Mariner." From the immanent perspective of the subject matter, however, the exposition proceeds according to its own inner logic, without foreknowledge of future events: being does not "know" that it will become nothing in the next section or the Absolute at the end of the *Logic*. This is akin to the limited perspective of a character, who is likewise ignorant of future plot developments or the overall structure of the novel she exists in. These formal restrictions suggest a nested ontological series where the character's storyworld unfolds within, and in the same manner as, the reader's world. These different worlds are therefore not "unreal" and "real" but lie on a gradient: depending on "where," "when," and "who" one is, one has a more comprehensive or restricted view of the various sequences and textures of the aesthetic-ontological whole.

Thus, a Hegelian literary approach assumes that reader and text are entangled and recomposed through a reading process that continuously synthesizes past, present, and future in myriad unpredictable and unrepeatable ways. Wolfgang Iser is helpful in elucidating this idea. He proposes that a reader's knowledge of past events in a literary text are often "set against a different background" in the present, thereby bringing "hitherto unforeseeable connections" into view and engendering "complex anticipations" of future events, but also altering past events through a "retrospective effect on what has already been read" (283). The reading process is therefore a "kaleidoscope of perspectives, preintentions, recollections" (284) that blurs the distinction between subject and object: "Text and reader no longer confront each other as object and subject, but instead the 'division' takes place within the reader himself" (298). This division or gap within the reader is precisely what opens him (and the text, and the Absolute) to alterity and alteration. In other words, the self-consistency of the reader and the text are destroyed through their entanglement. As Žižek puts it, "If there is a "semantic choice" that underlies Hegel's thought, it is not the desperate wager that, retroactively, one will be able to tell a consistent, all-encompassing and meaningful story in which every detail will be allotted its proper place, but, on the contrary, the weird certainty . . . that, with every figure of consciousness or form of life, things will always somehow 'go wrong,' that each position will generate an excess which will augur its self-destruction" (207). Žižek offers two literary examples that demonstrate how the end retroactively shifts the beginning: T. S. Eliot's argument in "Tradition and the Individual Talent" (1919) that the new literary work readjusts the entire literary tradition (208–09); and *Great Expectations* (1861), a "Hegelian novel" in which the ending (or endings, since Dickens wrote alternatives) recomposes Pip's original expectations for the future along with his entire character and "the very ethical standard by which we measure his character" (518–19). Similarly, at the end of Hegel's *Logic*, being is made fully determinate and concrete in the "absolute idea," yet we are left with the sense that we must meditate once more upon the beginning.

Collins: Detecting Idealist Influences

In *The Literary Absolute*, Lacoue-Labarthe and Nancy argue that German Romanticism, in conjunction with German Idealism, marks the beginning of an entirely new understanding of literature as "production" and "auto-production" that continues to define the way we conceptualize literature and criticism:[21]

> Romantic poetry sets out to penetrate the essence of poiesy, in which the literary thing produces the truth of production in itself, and thus . . . the truth of the production *of itself*, of autopoiesy. And if it is true (as Hegel will soon demonstrate, *entirely against* romanticism) that auto-production constitutes the ultimate instance and closure of the speculative absolute, then romantic thought involves not only the absolute of literature, but literature as the absolute. Romanticism is the inauguration of the *literary absolute*. (12)

Like the Absolute, literature produces (itself). It produces new poetry, fiction, drama, and self-reflective criticism within and across ever-shifting formal parameters like meter, plot, and genre. We must think of "literature as the absolute": not just as a simile for the Absolute but as a metonymic instance of it, a generative organ(ism) that coincides with the unfolding of various planes and phases of reality. As Frank Kermode suggests, drawing on Hans Vaihinger's Kantian philosophy of fictionalism, we should push our sense of what constitutes fiction to the absolute limit. In addition to fictions like *Great Expectations*, there are fictions of science, mathematics, law, reality, causality, and what Vaihinger calls "the last and greatest fiction," fiction of the Absolute (qtd. in Kermode 41). Such an expansive definition of literature is appealing because it explains the imbrication of philosophy and literature and the frequency with which idealist concepts appear in cultural productions of the long nineteenth century, but it also obliges us to attend even more rigorously to textual differences in order to preserve the integrity of individual texts and evaluate them comparatively.

In other words, how does one select paradigmatic examples of Absolute fiction when everything is Absolute fiction? It certainly seems difficult to conceive of a text that would be completely external to the concerns of idealism as I've discussed it in this chapter, but some texts do seem more amenable to an idealist reading. Žižek's description of *Great Expectations* as a Hegelian novel, along with Dickens's known affinity for Carlyle, suggests that Dickens would be an appropriate place to begin. Before turning to George Eliot's work, however, which I find even more amenable, I want to conclude by quickly inspecting Wilkie Collins's *The Moonstone* (1868)—a novel that, on the surface, appears hostile to idealism—to suggest that idealism turns up in many unexpected places (my selections in this book are therefore merely the beginning of an investigation). In the case of Collins, idealist assumptions underpin the content and form of a text that played an important role in generating the modern detective novel. Its use of idealism, especially objectivism and mereology, gives it an incredibly powerful conceptual framework for pursuing the formal strategies of the genre.

I will pass by some of the more obvious ways in which *The Moonstone* and the detective genre speak to the themes I have been discussing in this chapter: the way in which particular, seemingly meaningless "trifles" are crucial for understanding the whole truth; the retrospective shift that occurs as the reader realizes "whodunit" at the end of the novel.[22] Instead, I want to foreground the importance of Franklin Blake's personality quirk—his penchant for lapsing into German Idealist meditations—that would otherwise appear as a touch of comedy, a superfluous trifle. Throughout the novel, Blake struggles to articulate the difference between "subjective," "objective," and "subjective-objective" approaches to grasping the truth. I want to suggest that these approaches correspond, respectively, to "subjective idealist," "materialist," and "Absolute idealist" perspectives. The first two are shown to be inadequate and misleading, whereas the last, finally achieved through Ezra Jennings's experiment, resolves (through an imperfect recapitulation of the past) the central mystery of how and why Blake took the Moonstone.

In the novel's first discussion of idealism, Blake asks Gabriel Betteredge whether they should consider the question of why John Herncastle bequeathed the Moonstone to his niece, Rachel, from the "Objective side" or the "Subjective side" (42). Although Betteredge is confused by such "foreign gibberish" (43), he offers a subjective explanation: Herncastle knew that a young woman would desire such a diamond, and he also knew that it would vex his sister, Julia. Blake counters with a "Subjective-Objective" explanation, suggesting that Herncastle did it "to prove to his sister that he had died forgiving her" (43). This presumably combines the subjective and objective because it emerges from Herncastle's subjective desire to "prove" something, but also from the objective, selfless relinquishment of both resentment and an extremely valuable object. This may be granting Blake's idea more explanatory consistency than it deserves, because he often seems as flummoxed by idealism as Betteredge. For instance, later in Betteredge's account, Blake again falls "down in the bottomless deep of his own meditations, past all pulling up," and indeed his logic is cast as nonsensical for it leads him to the "Objective-Subjective" epiphany that "Rachel, properly speaking, is *not* Rachel, but Somebody Else" (175). Blake also lapses from subjective-objective claims to pure subjective idealism at the dinner party, where he absurdly proposes that "the proper way to breed bulls was to look deep into your own mind, evolve out of it the idea of a perfect bull, and produce him" (70). At the other end of the spectrum, however, Sergeant Cuff's purely empirical and objective methodology—"an abominable justice that favoured nobody" (166)—also fails to grasp the reality of what occurred. The novel seems to satirize all three positions—subjective, objective, and subjective-objective—despite Blake's protest that Betteredge's depictions of his idealism are themselves a form of subjective idealist projection, "never [having] any real existence, except in our good Betteredge's own brain" (294).

Near the end of the novel, however, Blake struggles once again to figure out how to bring the conceptual architecture of idealism to bear on an "experiment" (361) that will unravel the mystery. He spends all night "building up theories, one more profoundly improbable than another," and awakens "with Objective-Subjective and Subjective-Objective inextricably entangled together in my mind . . . doubting whether I had any sort of right (on purely philosophical grounds) to consider any sort of thing (the Diamond included) as existing at all" (362). Blake, "lost in the mist of my own metaphysics" (362), finds that his idealism inevitably bends toward the subjective pole, thereby bringing the reality of the external world into doubt. Enter Ezra Jennings, associated with "the ancient people of the East" (325), who combines the empirical, scientific expertise of a Cuff with his own "metaphysical" (391) insight that mind exists "connectedly" beyond any particular fragmentation of language or deterioration of the brain (376–77). Jennings's proposed experiment, which seeks to "replace" Blake "as nearly as possible, in the same position, physically and morally, in which the opium found [him] last year" (392), is based on the hypothesis that one's physical and mental states are not just "in" the body and brain but emerge relationally in concert with all the objects in one's environment. Blake is therefore not just the "subject" of the experiment but an "object" among others (399). Jennings's hypothesis anticipates Jonathan Kramnick's, in *Paper Minds*, that "physical action brings objects into view through attention and movement and so smears or spreads the locus of experience from interior states of the brain to entire bodies located in specific ecologies" (5). Kramnick supports this claim with reference to Tom McCarthy's *Remainder* (2005), whose protagonist, like Blake, attempts to recover lost memories by precisely recreating past situations. It is remarkable that these novels, so dissimilar in historical context and other respects, strike upon the same subjective-objective method for articulating the joint between mind and matter: the Absolute idealist method.

Finally, it is worth considering how critical interpretations of *The Moonstone* offer their own idiosyncratic shades of idealism. My first example traffics in many of the problematic ideas associated with stereotypical "idealism": D. A. Miller's essay "From *roman policier* to *roman-police*: Wilkie Collins's *The Moonstone*" (1980), later incorporated into his influential book *The Novel and the Police* (1989). Miller correctly regards Jeremy Bentham's panopticon, as famously read by Michel Foucault in *Discipline and Punish*, as an "ideal" model of modern state power because it exerts power intangibly and invisibly, "by enlisting the consciousness of its inmates as a primary means of supervision" (166). For Miller, this "policing power" (162) is diffused in such a totalizing manner throughout *The Moonstone* that the solute cannot be extricated from the solvent or even be discerned: "it is already everywhere. It cannot be resisted for long since it exerts the permanent pressure of 'reality' itself. Finally, it cannot even be seen, for it is a power that never passes as such: therein lies its power" (164). Miller's numinous concept of power does not stop, of course, at the confines of Collins's text but saturates "the Novel" in general, which is "the form that results when the detective story is exploded and diffused" (164)—he cites *Great Expectations* and *Middlemarch*, among many other nineteenth-century works, as exemplifying the fact that there is no outside to this ideality in literature; it even infects the world beyond the text through the ideological interpellation of the reader (167). Ultimately, *The Moonstone*, like all other "traditional novels" (170), is "thoroughly *monological*—always speaking a master-voice that corrects, overrides, subordinates, or sublates all other voices it allows to speak" (168). This implies that nontraditional novels may be subversive, but for Miller those of the long nineteenth century are "ideal" because they establish a hierarchy of power in which the ideal completely dominates material conditions and dissolves particularities into "blandly mute positivity" (153).

Against Miller's paranoid reading, Christiane Gannon's "Hinduism, Spiritual Community, and Narrative Form in *The Moonstone*" (2015) bluntly insists that "the novel lacks a monological narrator" (299). Instead, "the desire for monological expression is revealed to be merely a symptom of radical subjectivity, each narrator wishing to become the source of the novel's truth, each individual hoping to become omniscient" (307). In other words, the novel's formal fragmentation underscores the futile desire—common to individualistic Western cultures—to recast the world in subjectivist terms, to arrogate to oneself all explanatory power (one could argue that Miller's essay, obsessed as it is with mastery, has the same "desire for monological expression"). Gannon suggests that *The Moonstone* offers an alternative to this subjectivism in the "intersubjective collaboration" pursued by Blake and Jennings, which "prefigures the concluding scene of the novel in which we are left with a triumphant image of Eastern spirituality and the collective unconscious" (315). This scene, described by the adventurer Mr. Murthwaite as "the grandest spectacle of Nature and Man, in combination, that I have ever seen" (Collins 472), blends the hills, plains, rivers, forests, humans, and gods of Kathiawar into one variegated ecology: we could invoke Jennings by saying that the novel's denouement in India retrospectively reveals that a certain spirit persists "connectedly" behind the novel's linguistic fragmentation.

Gannon's reading, like Miller's, finds expressions of idealism in both the content and form of the novel, although hers is less extreme, more balanced, more Absolute idealist. It is not surprising that a novel so concerned with idealism elicits idealist interpretations. Nor is it surprising that these interpretations fundamentally disagree, because each critic reveals a different facet of *The Moonstone* depending on the balance they discern between, or emphasis they place on, subjectivism and objectivism. Idealism is not monological or monolithic but marks an approach that encompasses myriad conceptions of the relationship between subject and object, mind and matter. Moreover, it is expressed variously in myriad genres, from literature to philosophy to literary criticism. The careful critic must acknowledge these distinctions even as she perceives them connectedly and values them discrepantly.

Chapter 2

Absolute Realism

Constance Naden and George Eliot

> Art aims always at the representation of Reality, i.e., of Truth; and no departure from Truth is permissible, except such as inevitably lies in the nature of the medium itself. Realism is thus the basis of all Art, and its antithesis is not Idealism, but Falsism.
>
> —George Henry Lewes, "Realism in Art: Recent German Fiction"

> [T]he true meaning of Idealism is precisely this vision of realities in their highest and most affecting forms, not in the vision of something removed from or opposed to realities.
>
> —George Henry Lewes, *The Principles of Success in Literature*

Far from being opposed to realism, most idealism—especially Absolute idealism—*is* realism. We could also say, conversely, that most literary realism—especially as exemplified in its greatest and most philosophical exponent, George Eliot—*is* Absolute idealism. This, the central argument of this chapter, runs counter to commonplace assumptions about realism. These assumptions might be written out as follows: the aim of realism is to capture reality as it actually exists; realism therefore empirically attends to the specificity of material objects and their dynamic participation with and within human social and economic networks; idealism—associated with romance and romanticism, the subjective distortion of reality, and immateriality—is thus opposed to realism. Such an anti-idealist perspective easily aligns itself with the governing assumptions of Victorian studies as a field. In the 1950s, Victorian studies emerged in opposition to New Critical formalism because it had to account for the aesthetic value of realist novels rather than poetry. Given the tentacular nature of these novels, Victorianists were forced to venture beyond the confines of the texts themselves, and they found in various nineteenth-century (pseudo-) scientific discourses, and the philosophical tradition of empiricism that subtends them, extraordinarily fruitful resources to explain their form and content. Thus, Victorian studies has been oriented toward materiality and materialist philosophies from its beginnings up to the present day.[1] And yet, idealism has always been (in) the (back)ground of realism. As the epigraphs above indicate, even George Henry Lewes, who held a deeply ambivalent view of idealism, recognized that idealism and realism are not opposed but constitutive.

This constitutive nature appears in the history of the term "realism" itself. As Raymond Williams notes in *Keywords*, "[t]he old doctrine of Realism was an assertion of the absolute and objective existence of universals, in the Platonic sense. These universal Forms or Ideas were held either to exist independently of the objects in which they were perceived, or to exist in such objects as their constituting properties" (198). In the early nineteenth century, there was an ironic shift from this medieval conception of "realism" to its modern sense as "a term to describe new doctrines of the physical world as independent of mind or spirit" (199). But the emergent (and now dominant) meaning retains traces of the residual one. The new meaning "can be said to have overlain and suppressed [the older one]. But this is not wholly true. Our common distinction between *appearance* and reality goes back, fundamentally, to the early use—'the reality underlying appearances'" (198). Again, this suggests that idealism is not opposed to realism—rather, realism emerges in the nineteenth century as a fraught conceptual and aesthetic site *within which* idealism and empiricism battle for dominance. The respective formal and thematic weight that realist novels give to idealism (including subjective idealism) and empiricism varies across historical period, subgenre (e.g., psychological realism vs. naturalism), and even the oeuvre of a single author. This is why I believe that literary realism is a manifestation of Absolute idealism: Absolute idealism best accounts for the divergent tendencies of realism. Absolute idealism—like Constance Naden's (1858–1889) philosophical tracts and Eliot's novels—paradoxically asserts, *pace* empiricism, the reality of ideas as the "constituting properties of objects" *and* insists, *pace* subjective idealism, on the reality of the physical world as "independent of mind or spirit." As Marshall Brown puts it, "the nineteenth-century debate [over realism] articulates (voices) Hegel's dialectic of reality [as expressed in the *Logic*] while Hegel in turn articulates (structures) the debate" (225).

I will frame my reading of literary realism and Eliot's fiction not with Hegel, however, but with a consideration of Naden's philosophy of Hylo-Idealism (literally, "matter-idealism"). A highly paradoxical philosophy that insists on both radical subjective idealism or solipsism (the universe is the creation of the mind) and radical materialism (all phenomena, including mental states, are reducible to a material basis), Hylo-Idealism is one of the nineteenth century's most marvelously bizarre examples of Absolute idealism. Juxtaposing Naden and Eliot helps us view them both from a fresh perspective—despite their obvious differences (for example, Naden, unlike Eliot, exclusively wrote poetry), they share some surprising similarities. Obviously, they were both extraordinarily intelligent; Herbert Spencer said that Naden reminded him of Eliot (Stainthorp 65n120) and (somewhat patronizingly) remarked that both women possessed a "union of high philosophical capacity with extensive acquisition" (qtd. in Stainthorp 65). Naden and Eliot both grew up in the Midlands, rejected their early Nonconformist faith, became thoroughly acquainted with contemporary science and philosophy, and created their own versions of Absolute idealism to find meaning, purpose, beauty, and wonder in a world devoid of the transcendent God of Christianity. We gain a sharper sense of the philosophical structure of Eliot's novels through comparison with Naden's more traditionally philosophical essays; in turn, we hear echoes of Eliotic themes in Naden, who cherished Eliot as one of her favorite writers (*Further Reliques* 222). Taken together, Naden and Eliot suggest the creative interplay between Absolute idealism and realism in the philosophical treatises and novels of the mid- to late Victorian period. More specifically, Naden's emphasis on the extremes of absolute solipsism and absolute material determination mark out the aesthetic and ethical boundaries of realism, boundaries that can encompass everything from personal hallucinations, dreams/nightmares, thoughts, and emotions to the social, economic, ecological, and cosmic forces that shape subjectivity: a very broad tent that houses subgenres from science fiction to weird horror.

Naden is remarkable in her own right as a principal figure in the development of nineteenth-century idealism. One of the first women to become a member of the Aristotelian Society, she, like Eliot, "devoted much of her scholarly life to translating German philosophical and literary ideas" (LaPorte 428). Marion Thain notes the "striking" similarity between Naden and the German Idealists (163–64) and also compares her to Bradley (157); Charles LaPorte suggests that she may have influenced another British Idealist, J. M. E. McTaggart (440n7). It is also worth noting that late in her short life she traveled to India, conceivably to extend her acquaintance with Eastern philosophies, themes of which appear in her poetry and philosophy (Stainthorp 252–53). The nature of her philosophical intervention remains contested, with scholars offering various, sometimes contradictory, interpretations of Hylo-Idealism, which was first developed in collaboration with Robert Lewins (1817–1895) and defined Naden's theoretical orientation from 1876 to 1886 (Stainthorp 12). Despite Lewins and Naden's attempts to disassociate Hylo-Idealism from Absolute idealism, I will suggest that it offers the only coherent way to articulate the seeming contradiction between Hylo-Idealism's simultaneous embrace of both solipsism and radical materialism. The argument that Hylo-Idealism is a variety of Absolute idealism was already made by Naden's contemporaries: according to Robert William Dale, the physicist John Tyndall called Hylo-Idealism "an old friend, though in a new dress," while Dale himself remarked that it is only intelligible insofar as it corresponds to Absolute idealism (*Further Reliques* 234–35). Finally, I will end this introductory section by suggesting that Naden's epistemological and ontological arguments entail an ethics that closely approximates Eliotic sympathy as well as the ethics advanced by Bradley, which I analyze in the next chapter.

Although most research on Naden attends to her poetry, scholars that do examine Hylo-Idealism are confronted by the conundrum of a philosophy that attempts to unite the extreme poles of idealism and materialism: solipsism and radical materialism. Interpretations vary, but they tend to privilege the materialist side of the equation and/or fail to explain how Naden integrates the *entirely* idealist mental construction of reality with the *entirely* materialist insistence that reality is matter, all the way down (admittedly, her explanation on this point is unsatisfyingly brief). Clare Stainthorp, who has written the most exhaustive examination of Naden's life and works, acknowledges that the German Idealist "absolute . . . is a significant starting point for Naden's philosophy" (61), but she accepts Naden's description of her own position as a rejection of Absolute idealism in favor of "relative idealism" (76, 82, 117). The reference here is to Naden's essay "The Brain Theory of Mind & Matter; or Hylo-Idealism," where she writes, "Although rejecting that Absolute

Idealism which will deny the existence of aught that is corporeal, even of the sensifacient hemispheres and the sensiferous nerves, we are forced to accept that Relative Idealism which declares that the only Cosmos known to man, or in any way concerning him, is manufactured in his own brain-cells" (*Induction and Deduction* 160). In this passage, Naden (incorrectly) conflates Absolute idealism with subjective idealism (nothing corporeal exists) and describes her own position in terms of epistemological idealism (we can only know reality through our own mental constructions, although matter—"sensiferous nerves," "brain-cells"—must exist to feed these mental constructions). Naden's problem, which was Kant's problem, is to explain *how* we can know that matter exists *if* we only know reality through mental constructions. Stainthorp and other scholars tend to sidestep these definitional and conceptual problems, which leads, I think, to some confusion. For instance, Thain calls Hylo-Idealism a "materialist creed," although she also concedes that it attempts to reconcile matter and spirit (152, 153). In contrast, Nour Alarabi categorically states that the "objective world, i.e., the world existing beyond our perception, is of no interest to Naden and Lewins" (848), which seems difficult to square with a "materialist creed." Like Alarabi, Patricia Murphy argues that "[i]n Hylo-Idealism . . . objective meaning cannot exist" (162). She also contends, however, that Naden "elevate[s] matter . . . as a kind of embodied spirituality" and connects Hylo-Idealism to Darwinian evolutionary theory (161, 163). But how can Naden accept Darwinian evolutionary theory if objective meaning cannot exist? More broadly, how are such contradictory assessments of Naden's philosophy possible?

They are possible because her philosophy is fundamentally contradictory, which is not at all meant as a criticism—indeed, this is what makes Hylo-Idealism so unusual and exciting. We can only grasp it, however, by acknowledging its basis in contradiction. First, we must recognize Naden's absolute insistence on solipsism. In several places, she and Lewins make Protagorus's famous statement that "man is the measure of all things" a kind of motto for Hylo-Idealism. In "The Brain Theory of Mind & Matter" as elsewhere, Naden unequivocally supports the idea that each individual creates one's own, utterly unique universe: "man is the maker of his own Cosmos . . . all his perceptions—even those which seem to represent solid, extended, and external objects—have a merely subjective existence" (157). Second, we must recognize Naden's absolute insistence on radical materialism. In the same essay, she writes, "Matter, so far from being a nonentity, is the *fons et origo* of all entities" (161). How is it possible to reconcile such baldly contradictory first principles? Naden explains by quoting Lewins: Hylo-Idealism "in no sense denies the objective, but only contends for *identity* of object and subject, proved as it is by natural Realism itself, from the doctrine of *molecular metamorphosis*, which shows the Ego continually undergoing transubstantiation with the 'Non-Ego,' and *vice versâ*, so as to form *one* indivisible organism" (161). Lewins gives the metaphor of "a porous vessel of ice, filled with water, immersed in an infinite ocean" to capture the distinction and circulation between subject and object—but also their fundamental identity as variations in form, "like the mystic Athanasian trinity" (161–62). The religious imagery here—which is invoked in an attempt to resolve Hylo-Idealism's fundamental contradiction by emphasizing difference in unity, what Hegel calls "the identity of subject-object identity and subject-object non-identity" (Beiser, *Hegel* 61)—reminds us that despite being an atheist, Naden, like Eliot, often infuses her work with religious significance, and not always in the Christian mode Lewins adopts here.

Indeed, the epigraph to "The Brain Theory of Mind & Matter" is taken from the Orientalist Max Müller's *India: What Can It Teach Us?* (1883): "The Vedic poets dimly recognized their Gods as only symbols of the ultimate power that manifests itself in the world,—the Atman or Self—the Self of all things—the Self in which each individual must find rest" (qtd. in *Induction and Deduction* 156). A linked footnote explains that Müller "quite identifies Hylo-Idealism . . . with Vedantism." Hinduism thus becomes another touchpoint to explain how solipsism and radical materialism are linked: for Naden, the self *is* God, the universe, ultimate reality. This position requires an immanent God, a pantheism that Naden connects, in "What is Religion? A Vindication of Neo-Materialism," to the "ancient scriptures of India" (*Further Reliques* 118). In this essay, which anticipates our own "new materialism," Naden describes a "sense of identity with the material universe" wherein "the visible heaven and earth, and the human body itself, seem transient forms or incarnations of an eternal mind, which includes all finite and mortal beings, as drops of water are included in the ocean" (117). Such straightforward idealism is simultaneously a proper materialism, a materialism that sees matter not as dead and inert but instinct with agency and force: the "indwelling energy [of matter], impelling and restraining the suns and satellites of heaven, belongs not less to every ultimate particle of their mass. Our solid earth is no mere dead weight, but an active body" (124). The proper philosophical attitude, Naden seems to suggest through such juxtapositions, is to deflate all dualisms—self and universe, body and mind, temporality and eternity, idealism and materialism, etc.—through an identification that nevertheless preserves the distinction. One must embrace both poles: "If we are Pantheists in moments of exaltation and ecstacy, we shall be Materialists in hours of introspection and stern self-analysis" (122).

We have still not completely resolved the dilemma at the heart of Hylo-Idealism. To say that a solipsistic self knows that the material universe exists because that self is identical with the universe begs the question. How can we *know* that a material universe exists, and that the self is identical with it? How can we be certain that anything exists outside of our own mind? Naden most explicitly confronts this problem in "Hylo-Idealism: The Creed of the Coming Day." This essay begins with an epigraph by Lewes, who suggests that each "man" perceives "a different world" but believes he perceives "the same one," which is not a "delusive" belief because all men share similar "states of consciousness" (qtd. in *Induction and Deduction* 167). Naden seeks to explain how we can know that other humans who share similar states of consciousness exist. This is "the most critical point of the inquiry . . . . how are we to know that there is any such thing as matter?" (172). Her answer, which occupies two paragraphs, unfolds as follows: 1) mental states must be active, producing an effect on subsequent mental states, because otherwise it would be impossible to explain how new mental states arise; 2) we must therefore assume "some active basis of thought, that is, of something which thinks"; 3) by analogy, we can assume that other men are also "something which thinks"; 4) seeing that the thoughts of other men are affected by stimulating or destroying the brain, we can assume that the brain is that which thinks; 5) thus, the material world exists outside the human mind (173). Leaving aside the question of whether this is a convincing epistemological argument, it is clear that Naden intends it as part of the overall effort to strengthen her ontological one, which interests and engages her much more. In "Philosophical Tracts," for example, she continues to explore the ontological argument made in "The Brain Theory of Mind & Matter" and "What is Religion?" The self is the entire universe, she argues, because the self implies "certain conditions," and these imply other conditions, until we reach the limit of the universe (152). In other words, without the air and sun, I would not be a self; therefore, the air and sun—my conditions—*are* my self. Although I have a particular and "distinctive content" as a self, I am also identical with the universe or Absolute as a whole (152). Ultimately, the only way we can understand Hylo-Idealism's two contradictory principles as a coherent system is to suppose that each self (we need not restrict "self" to human selves) perceives/creates its own unique Absolute, while the Absolute expresses itself uniquely, but fully, in each self. Self and Absolute are "one thing regarded from different points of view" (153). Self is fully material, and matter is fully conscious.

This ontology entails an ethics. To say with Protagorus that "man is the measure of all things" is not self-centered, or even anthropocentric, because of "the solidarity between Man and the Universe, animate and inanimate, sentient and senseless" (*Induction and Deduction* 158). If we acknowledge the self as continuous with objective reality, with the persons, animals, plants, and things around it, we will find, paradoxically, a selfishly social desire to help (others as) ourselves. Indeed, such a desire would be society thinking and enacting itself: "society . . . *constitutes* [each person's] very mind and character" (*Further Reliques* 134). Yet the "distinctive content" of self persists, and it is by no means given that any single self will *recognize* its translucence. Like Gwendolyn Harleth in *Daniel Deronda*, "we may be constantly mentalising our fellow-creatures, without being in any way impressed with the solidarity of mankind" (*Induction and Deduction* 175). The real distinction of selves means that "no man can cross the frontier of his neighbour's personality. But in another sense it is equally true that such immigration is continually taking place" (174). Every interaction with someone or something outside me is an "immigration," a colonization of the self by the environment that acts as an invitation to expand my ethical horizon. Even an ordinary conversation can open onto the Absolute. Naden likens two speakers to "opposite mirrors" that imperfectly contain the mental and physical content of the other, each mirror "reflect[ing] its own reflexion" (174). Such self-contained infinity also reflects an epigraph from *Middlemarch*: "Full souls are double mirrors, making still / An endless vista of fair things before, / Repeating things behind" (*Middlemarch* 733). We are reminded of all the ways in which Eliot's characters see—or do not see—themselves and others in looking-glasses, burnished steel, and the eyes of the beloved.

Together, Naden and Eliot offer idealist realisms that insist on the primacy of the individual self. Like ice in water, however, each self is translucent, refracting its surrounds according to its surfaces and liquefying as the flows that sustain it lap for as long as it lasts. If the self I normally conceive of as my own, delimited, perhaps, by the extent of my body or my thoughts, is but a partial self, I can only fulfill myself through what

Eliot calls sympathy. Her meditations on ontology and ethics are mostly confined to human selves. She does glance, occasionally, at the perceptions of a cat, dog, or squirrel, and these animal fringes subtly remind readers of that "tempting range of relevancies called the universe" (*Middlemarch* 141)—relevant for many reasons including ethical ones, although in Eliot's case the temptation is largely resisted. As we will see in the next chapter, other writers more fully indulge this temptation, considering the astonishing range of possible physical entities, perceptual compositions, and ethical demands that Absolute idealism logically forces us to confront. This is why elements of romance, science fiction, horror, and fantasy persist in the margins of literary realism: whatever limned parcel of reality the novel represents, there are always other perceptions, other realities, clamoring in the background. One of Naden's science-fictional thought-experiments is illustrative of this temptation to imaginatively range far beyond the human. In "Scientific Idealism," she asks us to suppose that our sensory ganglia have all atrophied, with the exception of the olfactory ganglia. She then asks us to imagine that all the nerves in our body are grafted onto the olfactory ganglia. "What would be the result?" she asks. "The world would seem one great odour. We should smell with eyes, ears, fingers, and tongue. A beautiful picture or song would be perceived as a succession of harmonious perfumes" (*Further Reliques* 215–16). Absolute realism can be extraordinarily bizarre, displacing what we assume to be most "real." By grafting the self into larger and larger ecological circuits of reality—into "[c]limate, the structure of the earth's crust and the conformation of its surface, the flora and fauna of the inhabited region" (*Induction and Deduction* 186)—realism necessarily compels new perceptions, new forms, new genres, into existence.

What Is Literary Realism?

Before considering Eliot's Absolute realism and then venturing into its more bizarre, nonhuman fringes in the following chapters, we must first examine how realism has been traditionally understood: as the straightforward representation of the material conditions of a particular human society. Such representations assume a certain *philosophy*: but which one? Scholarship on the rise and development of the novel has emphasized the close relationship between philosophy and literature, although Absolute idealism is not usually invoked. Ian Watt's classic *The Rise of the*

Novel closely ties realism to the empirical tradition of Descartes, Locke, and Thomas Reid: "Modern realism, of course, begins from the position that truth can be discovered by the individual through his senses" (12). Michael McKeon complicates this picture in *The Origins of the English Novel, 1600–1740*, suggesting that the novel developed dialectically across this period, from "romance idealism" to "naive empiricism" to "extreme skepticism," positions overlaid with the political stances of "aristocratic ideology," "progressive ideology," and "conservative ideology," respectively (21). In contrast to Watt, McKeon asserts the constitutive, rather than vestigial, nature of the "traditional categories" of idealism and romance: "the traditional categories do not really 'persist' into the realm of the modern as an alien intrusion from without. Now truly abstracted and constituted *as* categories, they are incorporated within the very process of the emergent genre and are vitally functional in the finely articulated mechanism by which it establishes its own domain" (21). In other words, while the novel and modern realism are indebted to empiricism's attempted rejection of universals and shift of focus to the inductive, sensory epistemology of discrete individuals, they remain within the frame of idealism's larger tectonics.[2] It is no surprise that Victorian empiricism and literary realism disavow idealism—even as they embrace it.

Indeed, this contradictory attitude is precisely what we find when we examine the trajectories of Lewes and Eliot, who can conveniently act as important representatives of empiricism and realism. Lewes, one of the last great Victorian amateur scientists and Eliot's romantic partner from 1854 until his death in 1878, believed in the empirical scientific method as the only reliable way to discover truths about reality. Although he was an early enthusiast of Carlyle and Hegel, publishing the first article on Hegel to appear in a major British review (the *British and Foreign Review*) in 1842, he quickly soured on idealist metaphysics, writing a scathing indictment of Hegel and Absolute idealism in the first edition of his *Biographical History of Philosophy* (1845–46). By 1871, in response to the rising influence of British Idealism, he revised his entry for the *Biographical History*'s fourth edition, tripling the number of pages devoted to Hegel but retaining, even intensifying, his repudiation of Hegelian thought (I. Armstrong, "George Eliot, Hegel, and *Middlemarch*" 1–10). Nevertheless, his own empiricism ironically began to incorporate what can only be called Absolute idealism. George Levine demonstrates how Lewes's *Problems of Life and Mind*, "like George Eliot's last novels, verges, at times, on the mystical" (*Realistic Imagination* 264). For example, the first two volumes of *Problems of Life and Mind*, written concurrently with Eliot's *Middlemarch*, are full of idealist claims such as the following: "[Every Real] is the complex of so many relations, a conjuncture of so many events, a synthesis of so many sensations, that to know one Real thoroughly would only be possible through an intuition embracing the universe" (qtd. in Levine, *Realistic Imagination* 265). Levine concludes that Victorian empirical science was "a movement that was turning the world upside down, making matter ideal and the ideal material, and implying a secular world as mysterious as the religious" (263).[3] Eliot's relationship to idealism follows a similar arc. In an article on John Ruskin published in 1856, just before launching her novelistic career as George Eliot, Marian Evans defines realism as "the doctrine that all truth and beauty are to be attained by a humble and faithful study of nature, and not by substituting vague forms, bred by imagination on the mists of feeling, in place of definite, substantial reality" (Eliot, *Selected Essays* 368). However, the "complex but confident empiricism" of her early fiction becomes supplemented with a non-misty idealism in *Romola* (1862–63), when the "'ideal' had become for her an essential component of reality" (George Levine, "George" 3). By the end of her career, idealism saturates the form and content of both *Middlemarch* (1871–72) and *Daniel Deronda* (1876).

Despite the default allergy to idealism built, as it were, into the field, some scholars of the long nineteenth century have variously traced the parallel developments of realism and idealism across the period. Levine argues that, following the shift of realism from Platonic realism to "hard-nosed" empiricism in the early nineteenth century, literary realism then "edges back" toward Platonic realism in the later nineteenth century and eventually collapses into subjective idealism with the advent of modernism (*Realistic Imagination* 8–9). Charlotte Jones contends, contrarily, that Absolute idealism characterizes several turn-of-the-century authors, perhaps most especially May Sinclair, herself an idealist philosopher. The "synthetic realism" evinced by these authors is an exploration of the "tension between surface impressions and a reality behind appearances and beyond material surfaces. . . . [R]ealist writers aim at what is at once both a more abstract and a more concrete notion of truth, one whose material manifestations carry with it the mark of its relation to a whole range of universal truths of which it is part" (xvii). Drawing attention to the biases of the field, Jones argues that the "enduring philosophical unfashionability of a metaphysics of abstractions, universals, and absolute forms should not obscure the extent to which realist writers often had recourse to its terminology, aspirations, and quandaries" (xxiii–xxiv). Finally, although Pamela K. Gilbert argues that realism is a fundamentally materialist mode that "intersect[s] with and even absorb[s]" idealism, she acknowledges that these two traditions formed a "spectrum" with most thinkers in the "slippery middle," and she is "very surprised to see the continued and powerful influence of the German idealists throughout the [nineteenth century]" (22, 28, 4). Following Levine and Jones and reversing the order of Gilbert's absorptive thesis, I believe that literary realism is the sustained aesthetic exploration of idealist philosophy, although I would express that relationship as marking the gradual ascendancy of Absolute realism across the Victorian period to World War II (when the need to move beyond subjective idealism and engage with scientific empiricism is foregrounded), followed by a turn toward subjective idealism and arealism in the postwar period, when British Idealism disappears from philosophical preeminence. This increasing tendency toward arealism appears both in literature and literary criticism, especially the postmodernism of the latter half of the twentieth century (Beaumont 2–3; G. Levine, "Literary Realism" 13).

In the twenty-first century, as evidenced by Jones's work, we are witnessing a robust pushback against the arealism of postmodernism. Not too surprisingly, a lot of this pushback has come from Victorianists, who tend to be both interested in realism and suspicious of idealism, and who have had, as the V21 Collective puts it, a "historically pervasive resistance to 'theory'" ("Manifesto"). However, this pushback against postmodernist *subjective* idealism—almost always shorn of its adjectival modifier—has unfortunately deepened the disrepute of idealism in general, preventing us from grasping the relationship between *Absolute* idealism and realism and blinding us to the idealist antecedents and allies of contemporary theoretical approaches, even those that most vigorously oppose "idealism." Consider Anna Kornbluh's *The Order of Forms: Realism, Formalism, and Social Space*. She offers a powerful and compelling reimagining of literary realism that, in my view, implicitly argues for its inherent Absolute idealism while explicitly attacking "idealism." Kornbluh seeks to affirm "the order made by forms and the forms made by order," arguing that "the novel theorizes what infrastructures of relation support a world, abstracting from concrete content to produce and limn wholes," especially "the collectively lived experience of social relations" (4, 13, 19). She opposes this argument to what she sees as the ubiquitous tendency in literary studies to work "against abstraction: ending metaphysics, impugning grand narratives, spurning institutions" (1), and she takes as the central representatives of this tendency Agamben and Foucault. In place of their postmodern idealism, Kornbluh offers her neoformalism of abstractions with its admitted "Platonic overtones" (27). Yet, far from delineating how her own idealism differs from that of Agamben's and Foucault's, as one might expect, Kornbluh repeatedly attacks idealism and insists that her approach is materialist: "the field of relations precedes individuals. . . . 'Organization' is the elementary, primary fact, the ratification of which distinguishes a materialist from an idealist" (18). As refreshing as I find her approach and goals—they are entirely compatible with Absolute idealism—the distinction she makes here between materialism and idealism is inexact. Her argument may well be materialist, but it is also idealist.

"[T]he Idea," write Dunham, Grant, and Watson, "is, in fact, another word for 'organization'" (153). The British Idealist Bernard Bosanquet (1848-1923) describes mind and society as "organizations" in a way that nicely captures Eliot's ethics of sympathy and anticipates Dunham, Grant, and Watson's synonymy as well as Kornbluh's argument about the primacy of social form. According to Mander, Bosanquet argues that mind and society are analogous "organizations . . . he suggests that society has the same type of unity as a mind, that of an interconnected structure of ideas" (*British* 502). Indeed, for Bosanquet, as for Eliot and Kornbluh, the structure of mind and society are not just analogous but ontologically continuous, with the individual mind arising from within the larger social organization. In *Psychology of the Moral Self* (1897), Bosanquet writes, "the operative content, the actual being of the soul, comes from the environment. How else, indeed, should we have a real communion with other souls?" (10). An individual soul or mind, like a society, develops not through an empirical "process of compounding units distinctly given," but through "a process of discrimination within a mass which cannot and does not change its character all at once" (16). That is to say, the abstract form of the whole (mind or society)—the "environment"—conditions the expression of the individual (perception or person). For Bosanquet, morality consists in perceiving this "wide self . . . a recognition of unity between ourselves and others, or even between ourselves and nature" (67). His identification of "the private self with the universal self" (113), which he terms "sympathy," accords with sympathy in Eliot and nineteenth-century realism more broadly. As Rae Greiner explains, sympathy in these novels is "formal," a "cognitive exercise," "a form of thinking geared toward others, including the other that is myself as others see me" (1). It turns out that sympathy is not so much thinking outside the self as thinking the self within the outside.

In the following two sections, I use Eliot to explore Absolute realism, by which I mean literary realism that engages the ontological, epistemological, and ethical assumptions of Absolute idealism through the idiosyncratic constraints and advantages of novelistic form. Absolute realism assumes that characters are individual organisms who also function as organs of multiple larger, variously overlapping organizations, including family, political party, class, society, nation, sex, species, nature, and God.[4] This organicism is also a monism because the transcendent God is made immanent to the universe; the divine is purely secular, and all natural things participate, with various degrees of awareness, in the divine. One of the main formal challenges for Absolute realism, then, is to provide a mereological or metonymic account of how each person or thing attaches to larger wholes and, ultimately, to God or the Absolute as the total extent of reality. This challenge is compounded by the problem of consciousness because each mind has a limited perspective on reality, and what little scope of knowledge each person has is often distorted by their own desires and fears, as well as the enlarging or enervating influence of their physical and social environment, the people, things, and ideas that surround and constitute them. The problem of self is therefore tied to the problem of ethics: a self narrowly limited to a small sphere of reality (perhaps merely the capricious currents of one's own mind) is an inefficacious and even dangerously diseased social organ (e.g., Tito Melema, Rosamond Vincy, and Henleigh Mallinger Grandcourt); an expansive self, one that is capable, through sympathy, of perceiving larger and larger spheres of reality *without neglecting the particular*, approaches the Absolute self (e.g., Romola de' Bardi, Dorothea Brooke, and Daniel Deronda). Characters who realize themselves in the Absolute are able to renovate others (including the reader) and reenchant the world. Absolute realism is thus not a mimesis but a poiesis.

Several realist authors of the long nineteenth century, such as Emily Brontë, Dickens, and Sinclair, can be considered Absolute realists in the sense given above, although I am taking Eliot as perhaps its best exemplar. It is worth emphasizing that none of these authors merely regurgitates the philosophy of Coleridge, Carlyle, Hegel, or any other Absolute idealist; they all give idiosyncratic accounts of ontology, epistemology, religion, ethics, the mind-body problem, and other issues that are irreducible to a formula but nevertheless affiliate under a broad category. My analysis of Eliot traces her version of Absolute realism across three novels: *Romola*, *Middlemarch*, and *Daniel Deronda*. I argue that these novels radically (and increasingly) perforate and extend the self by exteriorizing the mind and interiorizing the environment, creating a kind of spectrum of selves that runs from solipsism to the Absolute. Although many of her characters remain selfish from beginning to end, Eliot often charts the progress of the solipsist who gradually expands his or her perspective to embrace more and more of the Absolute. This difficult shift in perspective, which demonstrates the ethical attainment of sympathy, also depicts the difficult shift in assumptions that readers must make in order to move from subjective idealism (which seems quite natural, if rather unfortunate) to Absolute idealism (which, in its complete reversal of the consensus view of reality, seems—depending on one's perspective—either absurd or breathtaking). The apparently romantic or supernatural elements in Eliot that have met with the most hostility from readers and critics—the "Jewish plot" of *Daniel Deronda* is the best example—often mark the irruption of the Absolute, not as an alien intrusion into the realist novel but as an acknowledgment of its constitutive principle.

George Eliot as Absolute Realist

Not everyone would agree that it is possible to read Eliot as an Absolute realist. For instance, Avrom Fleishman flatly states that "idealist metaphysics are foreign to her thinking" (87). Others prefer to call some of the hallmarks of her Absolute idealism—the externalization of the individual mind and self; the objective reality and efficacy of forms, ideas, and abstractions; the rejection of material and spiritual dualism—"materialism." Nevertheless, in this section I will attend to what I see as the idealist inflections of Eliot's ontology, epistemology, ethics, and aesthetics. The intimidating range and extent of her reading makes it impossible to assign any single overriding influence on her work, but before turning to her novels, I would like to underscore three important genealogical strands that help position her within the context of Absolute idealism: science, philosophy, and aesthetics.

First, as I discussed in the previous section, Victorian science increasingly became the site of a contest between empiricist and idealist approaches to reality. As Rick Rylance demonstrates, from 1850 to 1880, the nascent field of psychology began to imagine "the mind's comprehensive embodiment for the first time in history" (80). While this new orientation could certainly lead to a materialist understanding of mind as the passive, epiphenomenal result of stimulated nerve tissue (T. H. Huxley's well-known metaphor of the mind as a steam-whistle on a locomotive engine), it was not necessarily so. As we have seen, Lewes was much more syncretic. He developed what Suzy Anger describes as "a dual-aspect theory that maintained that the description of neural processes and the description of mental states are two ways of explaining the same underlying reality" (227). This, along with his mystical passages, explains why he has typically been understood as an idealist and was even accused by the British Idealist T. H. Green of being a kind of closet idealist who didn't have the courage to admit it (Rylance 328, 315).[5] Eliot went even further than her partner in this direction. Isobel Armstrong suggests that Eliot "was far more relaxed about the conflict of ideational and empirical that was so important to Lewes," and she was also "less prone than Lewes to adopt dualistic positions" ("George Eliot, Hegel, and *Middlemarch*" 12). Her *Daniel Deronda* notebooks reveal a fascination with thinking about nature along non-dualistic lines, noting the continuums within, or identity between, seeming opposites. In the section "Physical science," for example, she transcribes the following from her reading materials: metals that grow like vegetables; ring vortices, an ideal configuration of matter that can generate perpetual motion; skies formed from a single handful of matter; curved lines that appear straight and varied motions that appear uniform; and substances that blur the lines between physical and spiritual, like phlogiston and "air & gas (geist)" (16–23).

As for Eliot's philosophical contexts, Anger argues that she was deeply influenced by the empiricist tradition but also, "to some degree," by the idealism of Coleridge, Carlyle, and Spinoza (222). Again, such melding of empiricist and idealist positions was widespread in the Victorian period. Pinch reveals how "the grafting of German idealist ideas about the priority of mind onto British empiricism resulted in some strangely literal accounts of the mind's power in and on the world around it" (*Thinking* 6). This "weirdly muscular" idealism (21) intrigued many philosophers and authors, including Eliot—indeed, there were "a great number of Victorian writers and thinkers who were untroubled by, or saw themselves as transcending, any opposition between materialism and idealism" (47). Eliot was attracted to this nexus through her longstanding interest in Spinoza's monist ontology and ethics,[6] which had also acted as "[o]ne of the strongest influences on absolute idealism" in the late eighteenth century (Beiser, *German Idealism* 361). Perhaps most importantly, Eliot was drawn to idealism through her involvement in the Hegelian tradition. Both David Strauss and Ludwig Feuerbach, whom Eliot translated in the 1840s and '50s (she translated Spinoza's *Ethics* in 1856), were and are considered Hegelians. We can similarly read Eliot herself as responding to Hegel's legacy of critiquing the dualism of Kantian thought (Nazar 414). Some scholars have emphasized the Hegelian logic that structures elements of Eliot's fiction,[7] while others argue that Eliot's late work anticipates British Idealist ethics.[8] Finally, we should make note of the "Platonic revival that far outshone that of the Renaissance" from the 1850s onward (Turner 372). These various strands suggest that idealism was "in the air" during the Victorian period, and Eliot was certainly breathing it in.

Victorian aesthetics, broadly conceived, was also engaged in what Pinch calls "weirdly muscular" idealism: not only through the theme of "thinking about other people" that both she and Greiner see at work in realist novels, but also though the ascription of spiritual and/or mental characteristics, such as agency, to seemingly inert objects. Benjamin Morgan calls this an aesthetics of "outward mind": "If many worried that scientific and aesthetic materialisms would render mind and soul mere epiphenomena of nerves or atoms, it was also the case that a nineteenth-century fascination with matter occasioned new speculation about the agencies of physical things that had previously seemed still and inert: in aesthetic objects, matter became spiritualized, animated, and enminded" (6). Morgan chooses, like the new materialists, to think of the spiritualization of matter as a form of "materialism," but whatever we call this hybrid of idealism and materialism, the "outward mind" is a strong theme in Eliot's novels. Thinking about other people and spiritualizing objects largely appear as questions of thematic content, but it is also worth remarking the extent to which novelistic form was an important site for inscribing connections between mind and matter. Melissa Anne Raines argues that at the small-scale level of syntactical form, Eliot carefully composed her sentences in order to induce vibrational "shocks to the system *beneath* the contextual level of story and character" (vii). Readers of her novels are therefore subtly but physically induced to "develop a level of observation that is almost extrasensory" (xi). At the large-scale level of unqualified "form," we see a similar aesthetic ontology whereby the author's creation and the reader's perception are guided by a dialectical engagement with form that leads them to grasp more and more of the Absolute. In "Notes on Form in Art," written in 1868 but not published, Eliot examines the crucial importance of form in creating literary art. Knowledge of wholes, generalities, and abstractions is no longer reached exclusively through induction, as it was in "The Future of German Philosophy" (1855), but through a dialectical process of induction and deduction:

> [A]s knowledge continues to grow by its alternating processes of distinction & combination, seeing smaller & smaller unlikenesses & grouping or associating these under a common likeness, it arrives at the conception of wholes composed of parts more & more multiplied & highly differenced, yet more & more absolutely bound together by various conditions of common likeness or mutual dependence. And the fullest example of such a whole is the highest example of Form: in other words, the relation of multiplex interdependent parts to a whole which is itself in the most varied & therefore the fullest relation to other wholes. (*Essays* 433)

This nicely describes the process of arriving at knowledge of the Absolute; it could just as well describe the process of reading *Middlemarch* or *Daniel Deronda*. And the process is physical as much as mental: it arises through the "rhythmic persistence" of emotion "in adjustment with certain given conditions of sound, language, action, or environment" (435).

The scientific, philosophical, and aesthetic developments sketched above provide the broader context for situating Eliot as an Absolute realist, but I would like to conclude by pointing to a specific shift in her thought—from the rejection to the embrace of idealism—that occurs between the mid-1850s and the mid-1860s. We can first consider this shift from the perspective of her published essays. In "The Future of German Philosophy" (1855), Eliot argues in support of inductive empiricism: "the expressions *all, universal, necessary* . . . have their origin purely in the observations of the senses" (*Essays* 151). Thus, the abstract is derived from the particular on the "*à posteriori* path," whereas Absolute idealism is associated with the ultimately misleading "high *priori* road" (153): "the very ideas which have been enthroned as the *absolute*" are the result of "unprecise expressions and mere devices of language" (152). Her attack on idealism continues in "Silly Novels by Lady Novelists" (1856). There she ridicules "mind-and-millinery" novels for their "philosophic reflections" of Absolute idealism: "Lady novelists, it appears, can see something else besides matter; they are not limited to phenomena, but can relieve their eyesight by occasional glimpses of the *noumenon*" (*Essays* 310). (Kant, we recall, strictly bars epistemological access to the *noumenon* or thing-in-itself, apart from its qualified appearance through the human senses as *phenomenon*; in contrast, the Absolute idealists incorporate the *noumenon* directly into their metaphysical systems.) In "A Word for the Germans" (1865), however, Eliot defends German philosophers against the stereotype of the "cloudy metaphysician" (*Essays* 387) by invoking Samuel Johnson's famous "refutation" of idealism: "The sound British thinker kicks a stone to prove that matter exists, and so confound the metaphysicians; concluding that their arguments are necessaily [sic] shallow because he can't see far into them" (388). In other words, Eliot is suggesting that the kneejerk British dismissal of idealism as shallow is itself shallow, for it is easy to dismiss what you don't understand. What is valuable about the "German mind," for Eliot, is its tendency to harmonize "largeness of theoretic conception" (abstractions, idealism) with "thoroughness in the investigation of facts" (particulars, empiricism) (389). This defense of German philosophy is markedly different from the clear preeminence given to empiricism in her essay from ten years earlier, and it marks the beginning of a shift, an openness, to idealist philosophy that only increases over the remaining decade and a half of her life.

"Your German," Eliot writes in "A Word for the Germans," "sees that everything is related to everything else" (*Essays* 389). In an 1876 letter to Barbara Bodichon, Eliot writes of *Daniel Deronda*, "I meant everything in the book to be related to everything else there" (*Letters* 290). I believe that her novels—especially *Romola, Middlemarch,* and *Daniel Deronda*—provide a full expression of Eliot's Absolute realism as it moves from tentative experimentation in *Romola* (written from January 1862 to June 1863) to complete embrace in her final novel, *Daniel Deronda*. It is no coincidence that she became increasingly preoccupied with the question of consciousness—the ontology, epistemology, and ethics of conscious beings—over the course of her career. In quantitative terms alone, as Jill L. Matus documents, the word "consciousness" grows in centrality, appearing 23 and 25 times in *Scenes of Clerical Life* (1857) and *Adam Bede* (1859), respectively, compared to 60, 90, and 110 in *Romola, Middlemarch,* and *Daniel Deronda*, respectively (462). These novels are endlessly fascinated with the various permutations of the individual mind: how it can lose itself in solipsism, how it can enlarge itself through others, through nature, and through abstractions until it grasps Absolute reality and the absolute value of each particularity therein—even the state of solipsism from which the quest for knowledge and love begins.

Subjectivism, Form, and the Absolute in George Eliot's Fiction

Romola depicts the social and political fragmentation that characterized republican Florence from the death of Lorenzo de' Medici in 1492 to the public execution of Christian visionary and reformer Girolamo Savonarola in 1498. Eliot's central plotline follows Romola, daughter of Casaubon-like Aristotelian philosopher Bardo de' Bardi, as her marriage to the scholar and Machiavellian political schemer Tito Melema collapses and she finds spiritual purpose through the influence of Savonarola. Like *Daniel Deronda*, which is similarly framed within the context of an ideal national unity, *Romola* has an unusual formal structure that shifts from historical realism to the description of what Dorothea Barrett calls "an ahistorical ideal realm" shot through with "transcendental symbolism" (xv, xvi). This shift in formal mode is not accidental, however—we see it again, more mutedly, in *Middlemarch* and even more strikingly in *Daniel Deronda*—nor is it contradictory. Instead, in all three novels we see Eliot exploring the ethical bearing of various types of idealism, with a general plot trajectory from solipsism (Tito and Gwendolyn) and naïve subjective idealism (young Romola and Dorothea) to Absolute idealism (mature Romola and Dorothea, Daniel). I will trace this trajectory in *Romola* by focusing first on Tito—along with Rosamond and Grandcourt, one of Eliot's rare unsympathetic characters—whose solipsism works to literally dismember other people, social bonds, and political order. Next, I will consider Savonarola, whose idealism is depicted as a noble but vexed form of Christian Neoplatonism. Savonarola's desire to unify a dismembered society through spiritual purpose is repeatedly defended by Romola and the narrator, but his too-dualistic idealism is ultimately flawed by a denigration of the material world and his willingness to destroy people as a means to the Absolute. It is Romola who best achieves what Savonarola fails to do, uniting self-sacrifice and a broad sympathy for humanity with a passionate love for the people who immediately surround her. Selfless and self-centered, she learns to integrate abstract duty and the material particularity of love. Through her suffering and perseverance, she gains the most *real* perspective in the novel: more real than the self-constructed fantasies of Tito and the self-deceptive visions of Savonarola. Hers is the attainment of Absolute realism.

Before examining these three characters in more detail, a few words on Platonism and Neoplatonism will help us better articulate the various idealisms at play in the novel. First, it is worth mentioning that Plato's famous distinction between immaterial forms and their shadows, the material world, does not necessarily entail dualism, as is often assumed (Dunham et al. 6; Milbank and Riches v). Indeed, the centuries-long Neoplatonic tradition is a monist interpretation of Plato: the philosopher Plotinus (205-270), who is largely responsible for the conceptual architecture of Neoplatonism, divides reality into three "hypostases" (the One, Intellect, and Soul), but these hypostases all emanate from the highest Form, the Absolute "One": in other words, they are ontologically continuous, like water flowing from a fountain. Moreover, the hypostases exist within external nature and the mind (Wallis 2), which makes it possible for humans to unify with the One *through* material particularity. Plotinus, like Savonarola, does approach a kind of *evaluative* dualism, denigrating the material world in favor of the immaterial (Adamson, *Philosophy in the Hellenistic* 207–08). But other Neoplatonists, such as Iamblichus (c. 245–320), much more tightly integrate materiality and immateriality. In his investigation of Iamblichus's theurgy—the communal, ritualistic use of numinous objects to interact with the divine—Gregory Shaw argues that Iamblichus provides "a radically non-dual vision that sees the physical world as radiantly transformed, not rejected or denied in favor of a 'spiritual' reality" (xxi). These Neoplatonic themes are very much alive in *Romola*: there are textual references to Marsilio Ficino, who "attempted to revive Iamblichean Platonism in fifteenth-century Florence" (Shaw 7); Tito disparagingly associates Ficino and Savonarola (via his disciple Fra Luca) with Neoplatonism (*Romola* 177); up to his death, Bardo de' Bardi labors to compose a refutation of Neoplatonism (242);[9] meanwhile, Romola's admiration for Savonarola and Cassandra Fedele (54)—friend of Angelo Poliziano and Giovanni Pico della Mirandola (Fedele 90–95)—align her with the Neoplatonists; finally, numinous objects, such as rings, gems, and crucifixes, are scattered throughout the novel, blending the distinction between divine and mundane. Thus, the negative characters of the novel are opposed to Neoplatonism while the positive characters are associated with it (we will see this again in the association between Neoplatonism and Kabbalah in *Daniel Deronda*).

Tito is a premier example of the solipsist, a person on the extreme subjective end of subjective idealism who makes no distinction between himself and the entire structure of reality. From the outside (despite the solipsist's assumption, there *is* an outside), we perceive that the solipsist selfishly seeks to impose his desires on or extract his desires from the world without any regard for, or even concept of, alterity. Using free indirect discourse (a technique that itself resists solipsism), Eliot takes readers into Tito's mind to watch him ask himself, "What, looked at closely, was the end of all life, but to extract the utmost sum of pleasure?" (115). In the midst of his rationalizing away of any external standards of conduct, he convinces himself that "maxims that required a man to fling away the good that was needed to make existence sweet" are themselves selfish, "made by men who wanted others to sacrifice for their sake" (116). Although it would be misleading to say that Tito never believes in the existence of any person or thing outside himself (his descent into self-absorption is gradual and cumulative), his general attitude toward life is one of pervasive subjectivism—his own. And this attitude is repeatedly condemned by the narrator, who remarks that the "problem of arranging life to his mind had been the source of all his misdoing" (276).

Although he fails in the end, Tito poses a serious threat to the rest of the characters in the novel because he is so skillfully effective at arranging life to fit his mind. Indeed, the division and duplicity everywhere on display in Florence reflects his dissembling and desultory mind. This is shown most vividly in the remarkable chapter "The Peasant's Fair," in which Tito wanders aimlessly through a fair in the piazza, serendipitously finds Tessa in the church of the Nunziata after thinking about finding her, and then marries her in a mock ceremony conducted by Vaiano, a street charlatan. This dreamlike chapter—full of symbolic repetitions, surreal imagery, improbable coincidences, wish-fulfillment, and the theme of appearance versus reality—could just as easily take place in Tito's head as on the streets of Florence. Three rings surface in the chapter: the peddler Bratti sells false Roman rings with supposedly hidden potency (139); Tito asks Bratti to sell his father's ring after rejecting "superstitious scruples about inanimate objects" (140); and Tito forbids Tessa to wear a betrothal ring after their "marriage" (150). The bond symbolized by rings—the bond between present and past, father and son, husband and wife—are here rendered false, broken, or absent. Moreover, the duplicitous street spirituality embodied by Vaiano, who makes a living out of manipulating his audience's superstitious scruples about inanimate objects, and whose pet monkey causes a violent scene by jumping onto a woman's head (143), spills into the official religious space of the church of the Nunziata. Waxen images cover the walls and ceiling of the church, "exact doubles of the living. And wedged in with all these were detached arms, legs, and other members . . . . It was a perfect resurrection-swarm of remote mortals and fragments of mortals, reflecting, in their varying degrees of freshness, the sombre dinginess and sprinkled brightness of the crowd below" (144). The vertiginous lack of coordinates, the doublings, deceptions, and dismemberment, the contempt for numinous objects: this is Tito's Florence as projected from his mind, and his dream has very real effects, including the beheading of Bernardo del Nero and the ascension to power of "the rapacious Italian States that wanted to dismember their Tuscan neighbor" (570).

Savonarola asserts a very different path for Florence, one that attempts to eliminate falsity and unite people under a shared vision of Absolute truth. This ideal seems preferable to Tito's nihilism, but Savonarola's tactics for achieving it will incense those aware of the history of the twentieth century even more than they incense Romola and the narrator, who venture occasional defenses of Savonarola's most egregious actions. A deeply uncomfortable chapter shows Savonarola's youth patrols assaulting Monna Brigida, stripping her of her jewelry and false hair, and intimidating her into "conversion" to the Piagnone cause (434–38). Savonarola's infamous Bonfire of the Vanities destroys "impure" artwork, books, games, musical instruments, clothing, and "all the implements of feminine vanity" in a pyramidal conflagration (419). These violent, misogynist scenes attest to Savonarola's rigid separation of body and spirit: his idealism remains trapped in a dualism that seeks not to integrate material and immaterial but to expunge the former. The ascetic friar Fra Luca—Romola's estranged brother and Savonarola's disciple—most vividly embodies this anxiety about flesh. Fra Luca abandoned his father because he was afraid Bardo's scholarship led to "worldly ambitions and fleshly lusts," and to the end he refuses to acknowledge ties of kinship: "I must have no affection, no hope, wedding me to that which passeth away; I must live with my fellow-beings only as human souls related to the eternal unseen life" (154, 155). This rejection of earthly love is precisely what Romola cannot countenance. Nor can the narrator, who observes that Fra Luca seeks "wisdom apart from the human sympathies which are the very life and substance of our wisdom" (160). Without regard for the human and substantial, wisdom can be dangerously detached and unbalanced. Unfortunately, Savonarola uses the same conceptual language as Fra Luca: "the pride of the body is a barrier against the gifts that purify the soul," he tells Romola (157).

Despite this crucial flaw, however, Savonarola is lauded throughout the novel because, unlike almost any other character, he perceives a spiritual ideal beyond narrow self-, party, and material interests. Indeed, to a certain extent his actions belie his dualistic beliefs, for he doesn't merely see a transcendent ideal in his visions, he channels it into the actual world, invigorating those who listen to his orations with a tangible, vibrational force. Romola is literally struck by his speeches, having "the sense of being possessed by actual vibrating harmonies" that "penetrated [her] with a new sensation—a strange sympathy with something apart from all the definable interests of her life" (247). Savonarola's vibrational influence enlarges Romola's sense of sympathy and responsibility toward others even as it shrinks her self-concern: he "had created in her a new consciousness of the great drama of human existence in which her life was a part; and through her daily helpful contact with the less fortunate of her fellow-citizens this new consciousness became . . . [a] definite motive of self-denying practice" (388). Despite this salutary effect on others, Savonarola himself is split. On the one hand, in his "moments of ecstatic contemplation, doubtless, the sense of self melted in the sense of the Unspeakable"; on the other hand, "in the presence of his fellow-men for whom he was to act, pre-eminence seemed a necessary condition of his life" (573). In other words, he loses himself in the Absolute while paradoxically asserting himself as the Absolute. For Romola, such a paradox is a sign that Savonarola's concept of the Absolute isn't capacious or objective enough. When Savonarola arrogantly claims that "[t]he cause of my party *is* the cause of God's kingdom," Romola, "her whole frame shaken with passionate repugnance," retorts, "God's kingdom is something wider—else, let me stand outside it with the beings that I love" (492).

Savonarola's fault, then, lies in his blindness to the particular and concrete. In his passion for the Absolute, he is willing to sacrifice individuals to his universal aims, and he even subjectively identifies himself with the Absolute instead of acknowledging his own partiality and finitude. Romola seeks to integrate such passion for the Absolute with equal passion for those closest to her. In comparing Fra Luca's spiritual love for God with her own mundane love for Tito, she asks, "What thought could reconcile that worn anguish in her brother's face—that straining after something invisible—with [Tito's] satisfied strength and beauty, and make it intelligible that they belonged to the same world?" (177–78). Her growth as a character is the unfolding answer to this question. Over the course of the novel, she moves from a subjective idealism that fails to grasp any reality beyond her naïve attachment to Tito and Bardo (in contrast to Savonarola, she misses the forest for the trees), to a cynical, nihilistic despair that casts her even deeper into self-absorption, to a final realization that the Absolute is inseparable from its particular manifestations, which she engages with care and love. Before reaching this end, however, she must suffer for her self-centeredness—for Eliot, suffering for one's subjectivism seems a necessary step on the path to the Absolute. And Romola does suffer, primarily because of her ingenuous belief in Tito, a false "vision woven from within": when she looks into his eyes, she "only read her own pure thoughts in their dark depths" (68, 176). Romola must learn that these mental projections may not correspond to reality, and after the shock of this lesson, with no concept of any broader meaning in life, she sinks into "barren egoistic complaining" (502), setting herself adrift on a boat, perchance to die. The narrator comments, "tender fellow-feeling for the nearest has its danger too, and is apt to be timid and skeptical towards the larger aims without which life cannot rise into religion" (501). Gazing up at the universe from her boat, she sees a blank: "Romola felt orphaned in those wide spaces of sea and sky. She read no message of love for her in that far-off symbolic writing of the heavens" (504).

This void seems yet another false projection, however, for when Romola awakens the next morning, the universe embraces her: "The delicious sun-rays fell on Romola and thrilled her gently like a caress. She lay motionless, hardly watching the scene; rather, feeling simply the presence of peace and beauty" (550). Refreshed by this Romantic reverie, she then wanders into a "village of the unburied dead" (553), a Jewish enclave stricken by the pestilence. Working to save those still alive, she becomes a saint-like legend for her "beautiful loving deeds there, rescuing those who were ready to perish" (559). She is able to give herself selflessly to others precisely because of her detachment from those she used to love: "the emotions that were disengaged from the people immediately around her rushed back into the old deep channels of use and affection. That rare possibility of self-contemplation which comes in any complete severance from our wonted life made her judge herself as she had never done before: the compunction which is inseparable from a sympathetic nature keenly alive to the possible experience of others, began to stir in her with growing force" (560–61). Wrenched from her subjective projections and detached from her exclusive focus on the particular loves in her life, she paradoxically *gains* in "self-contemplation" through a more estranged,

Absolute perspective. This new, more objective sense of self gives her the sympathy to love those far beyond her personal acquaintance: she shows loving concern for her rival Tessa, just as Dorothea gives it to Rosamond, and shows loving concern for Jews, just as Daniel gives it to Mordecai. Like Gwendolyn at the end of *Daniel Deronda*, Romola finds "a sort of faith that . . . sprung up in [her] out of the very depths of [her] despair" (572). This is the sort of faith that Savonarola and, especially, Tito were incapable of imagining.

In its attention to the hazards and charms of various types of idealism, *Romola* rehearses many of the themes explored in *Middlemarch*. However, the later novel strikes out in radically new formal directions by mapping itself onto an Absolute idealist ontology that encompasses nothing short of the universe, thereby self-reflexively drawing characters, narrator, author, and readers into a struggle against subjectivism that breaks the distinctions between mind and matter, self and other, and fiction and reality. It is remarkable that this most quintessential of realist novels is so preoccupied, not (only) with the verisimilar depiction of specific material objects and institutions, but (also) with tracing the reticulated threads of consciousness, perception, thoughts, ideas, feelings, and memories—all insistently emerging from and merging with that concrete abstraction called the universe, which the novel strains to embody as a microcosm, Middlemarch. Like *Romola*, *Middlemarch* is deeply concerned with the question of how people become dislodged from their narrow projections and distortions of reality. In one of the novel's most famous images, a friend of the narrator, an "eminent philosopher," describes a mirror and a candle:

> Your pier-glass or extensive surface of polished steel made to be rubbed by a housemaid, will be minutely and multitudinously scratched in all directions; but place now against it a lighted candle as a centre of illumination, and lo! the scratches will seem to arrange themselves in a fine series of concentric circles round that little sun. It is demonstrable that the scratches are going everywhere impartially, and it is only your candle which produces the flattering illusion of a concentric arrangement, its light falling with an exclusive optical selection. These things are a parable. The scratches are events, and the candle is the egoism of any person now absent. . . . (264)

Most critics accept the narrator's interpretation of the parable as demonstrating, in the words of Moira Gatens, "the distorting effects of egoism"

(84). Yet, while the parable does vividly express the dangers of subjective idealism, focusing on the candle is itself an "exclusive optical selection": without the scratches, the candle has nothing to pattern. In other words, the narrator's unusual positioning of himself or herself within (or without?) the textual world invites readers to reinterpret the offered interpretation as yet another subjectivist candle, thereby multiplying to indistinction the boundaries of mind, self, and fiction. As we will see, other passages in the novel suggest even more clearly that objective reality obtrudes on subjective perceptions just as much as those perceptions impart order(s) and meaning(s) upon the universe. *Middlemarch* articulates this mediation, this middle.

In the following chapter, Dorothea enacts the mirror-candle metaphor when she returns to Lowick from her honeymoon in Rome. Looking out the window of her boudoir, her eyes move from "the long avenue of limes lifting their trunks from a white earth, and spreading white branches" against the sky; farther out, the "distant flat shrank in uniform whiteness and low-hanging uniformity of cloud" (273). From white earth to white branches to a white horizon, Dorothea's gaze advances in concentric circles, but the narrative immediately circles back to her body: "her throat had a breathing whiteness above the differing white of the fur which itself seemed to wind about her neck and cling down her blue-grey pelisse with a tenderness gathered from her own, a sentient commingled innocence which kept its loveliness against the crystalline purity of the out-door snow" (273). The white tones expand and contract—a "breathing whiteness" that radiates but also reflects, returning to saturate even the "sentient" fur that lies on her neck and overlays the snow outside. This perspectival and prepositional intricacy marks the epistemological and ontological problem that the novel shares with Absolute idealism: how can we better perceive the various modes and scales of a commingled reality? At this stage in her life, Dorothea remains oppressed within this "still, white enclosure which made her visible world" because she looks from the inside out rather than the reverse: "the sense of connection with a manifold pregnant existence had to be kept up painfully as an inward vision, instead of coming from without in claims that would have shaped her energies" (274). Like Romola, Dorothea must progress "toward more accurate—because less subjective—knowledge" (Anger 221).

More specifically, Dorothea must overcome solipsism—"taking the world as an udder to feed our supreme selves"—by making her ideas concrete: she needs "an idea wrought back to the directness of sense, like the solidity of objects," an idea that Casaubon and others have "an equivalent centre of self, whence the lights and shadows must always fall with a certain difference" (211). The single candle is no longer a sufficient metaphor. Near the end of the novel, after enduring a night of despair, she again looks out the window, but the emphasis here is mostly centripetal, with "light piercing into the room," and she feels herself "a part of that involuntary, palpitating life, and could neither look out on it from her luxurious shelter as a mere spectator, nor hide her eyes in selfish complaining" (788). This new objective conception of the self as an organ of something larger enables her selfless acts of love, and at the end of the novel, her "finely-touched spirit" diffuses itself indistinguishably with the external world. Other idealistic characters are less successful than Dorothea. Although Casaubon's much-ridiculed idealistic search for the Key to All Mythologies "does not mean that Eliot rejects cosmological coherence" (King, "George Eliot" 188), he usefully underscores the dead end of subjectivism: "lost among [the] small closets and winding stairs" of his mind, with "his taper stuck before him he forgot the absence of windows" (*Middlemarch* 197). Lydgate, too, fails in his quest for the oxymoronic "anatomical conception" (147)—the Idea of biological matter—through his own lack of concern for material and financial realities, as well as the relentless solipsism of his wife, Rosamond. Nevertheless, Lydgate has a much more well-developed idealism than Casaubon. In place of Casaubon's floating, bloodless abstractions (478–79), Lydgate, like Lewes, engages in an empirical idealism that seeks to integrate the ideal and material: his scientific method follows "the inward light which is the last refinement of Energy, capable of bathing even the ethereal atoms in its ideally illuminated space," but he "correct[s this provisional frame] to more and more exactness of relation" though inductive experimentation (164–65). This program fails to become actualized, however, because of the above-mentioned reasons, and his usual "meditativeness" descends into reptilian animality as he falls, like Gwendolyn, into gambling fever (672).

Where Casaubon's academic pursuits and Lydgate's scientific method, as modes of practically integrating idealism into the everyday world, fail to be consummated, the libidinal aesthetics of Will Ladislaw and his friend Adolf Naumann succeed. Theirs is not, as we might expect, entirely an aesthetics of masculine objectification. Although they both find Dorothea physically attractive and want to capture her in poetry and painting, they generally describe such artistic mastery as, paradoxically, a process of passive reception. "Genius," for Will, is "an attitude of receptivity" that "may confidently await those messages from the universe which summon it to its peculiar work" (83). Like Coleridge and De Quincey, he uses drugs like wine and opium as experiments in gaining inspiration from the universe, and although this tactic fails for him, the narrator approvingly reflects on "Will's generous reliance on the intentions of the universe with regard to himself. He held that reliance to be a mark of genius; and certainly it is no mark to the contrary; genius consisting neither in self-conceit nor in humility, but in a power to make or do, not anything in general, but something in particular" (83–84). The primary cause of art, then, is the universe, which creates particular works through the receptive medium of the artist as genius, who is neither like a god (full of "self-conceit") nor an empty vessel that contributes nothing to the artwork (full of "humility"). As Naumann puts it, "My existence pre-supposes the existence of the whole universe—does it *not?*—and my function is to paint . . . therefore, the universe is straining towards that picture [of Dorothea] through that particular hook or claw which is put forth in the shape of me" (190).[10] Will, petulant from jealousy, at first explicitly rejects this Absolute aesthetics, but shifts his playful quarrel with Naumann to the question of whether painting or language is superior—language is, Will insists, because it "gives the fuller image, which is all the better for being vague" (191). Again, what is significant here is the idea that *form* is crucial to art, especially the abstraction called "the universe." But these forms and abstractions are not the bloodless ones of Casaubon. The universe, the artist, and the production are all actualized, particularized *expressions of form*. This explains Will's ideal function in the novel. It has long been a critical commonplace that Will isn't "realistic" enough—Henry James complains that he is "insubstantial," "light," "vague and impalpable" (426). But this is precisely the point. Will is realistic, a "fuller image," *because* he is an insubstantial form—one made to matter.

Middlemarch itself is a "fuller image" of Will and Naumann's Absolute aesthetics, extrapolating the implications of their brief scenes together in a relentless interrogation of the limits of form. The result of the interrogation, to borrow the words of the "Finale," is the insight that "Every limit is a beginning as well as an ending" (*Middlemarch* 832): forms lead to forms lead to forms, but the beginning and ending of all forms is the unrepresentable Absolute. Allow me to unpack this rather vague and impalpable statement by examining the incredible variety of ways in which the novel challenges any rigid distinction between two apparently very different forms of reality—mind and matter. The mind circulates within the material world: the "citations" swirling in Casaubon's mind bring dyspepsia; Mr. Brooke's remarks scatter from his mind like "motes" and "the broken wing of an insect" (281, 16, 20). Conversely, the material world directly flows through the mind: the drawn bow of a violin "change[s] the aspect of the world" for Will; a glass of sherry "hurr[ies] like smoke among our ideas" (388, 503). Such matters of thought are bound up in larger sentient structures. The writer's pen has a mind of its own: "the end of Mr. Brooke's pen was a thinking organ, evolving sentences . . . before the rest of his mind could well overtake them" (291). But the pen is an organ, also, of the Middlemarch periodical, itself an "organ" (292) that expresses and directs Middlemarch thought. "Middlemarch" here is metonym and more than metonym: it wants to devour Lydgate; it has "ideas [in] its head" and "perception" (154, 459–60). In other words, all the forms in the novel—forms of language, forms of thought, forms of being—point toward some larger form of which they form a part. Even the chapter epigraphs, which often function to abstract the contents of the chapters, visually and thematically point toward some larger, more abstract form that exists beyond the text. For example, the epigraph to chapter 31 describes the "rill" of a flute making a "huge bell tremble," while the epigraph to chapter 83 quotes John Donne: "For love all love of other sights controls, / And makes one little room, an everywhere" (293, 805). The particular opens onto the general. The "light" thrown by the narrator "must be concentrated on this particular web, and not dispersed over that tempting range of relevancies called the universe" (141). Here the narrator reminds us that *Middlemarch* is like the candle that cannot bring all of reality's scratches into its ambit, but that dark, tempting universe forms the absent center of the narrative. It cannot be fully present because it is impossible for a finite being to represent the infinite saturation of the Absolute: "If we had a keen vision and feeling of all ordinary human life, it would be like hearing the grass grow and the squirrel's heart beat, and we should die of that roar which lies on the other side of silence" (194).

Daniel Deronda shares the thematic concerns of *Romola* and *Middlemarch*. Like them, it is interested in "the agency of thoughts that have no thinker, or at least no certain one" (Pinch, *Thinking* 163). But our uncertainty is ameliorated when we place thoughts and thinkers within a total context: the "thinker," in all instances, is or includes the Absolute. As Sarah Willburn puts it in her discussion of the novel, "[Eliot] is writing realism about an extra-personal, pantheistic system. Each character is a tiny working in the mind of a large, invisible central system" (285–86). Such Absolute realism, by counterintuitively approaching the individual from the outside in, places challenging intellectual, emotional, and ethical demands on its characters and readers. For example, *Daniel Deronda* continues *Middlemarch*'s radical experimentation with novelistic form, disrupting the reader's "realist" expectations with startling narrative refusals: "Attempts at description are stupid: who can all at once describe a human being?" (*Daniel Deronda* 111). The narrator later declines to describe the scenery at Cardell Chase because "the blissful beauty of earth and sky entered only by narrow and oblique inlets into the consciousness, which was busy with a small social drama almost as little penetrated by a feeling of wider relations as if it had been a puppet-show" (148–49). These refusals imply that both characters and readers, entranced by the "puppet-show" in front of them, have lost sight of the "wider relations" that penetrate individual human beings and the natural world. The shift from the "Gwendolyn" to the "Jewish" plot, which has caused so much consternation in readers, functions to open the inlets, setting aside the puppet-show for a glimpse of the universe.

Gwendolyn, of course, provides the best example of the challenges involved in overcoming such perceptive inertia, and her narrative arc replicates the form of Romola's and Dorothea's: the heroine's subjectivist naïveté leads her to rashly enter an oppressive marriage; after having that narrow(ed) self irrevocably shattered upon the husband's death, and under the inspiring influence of a spiritual guide, she begins to find true meaning and identity within the scope of the Absolute. Gwendolyn's solipsistic self-absorption hardly needs to be shown; what is remarkable is its *persistence*—throughout the novel, Gwendolyn finds it extremely difficult to transcend her own perspective. Despite all the knowledge she has gleaned from enduring Grandcourt, we realize in the penultimate chapter that her relationship with Daniel is framed by yet another self-projection, for "she did not imagine [Daniel] otherwise than always within her reach, her supreme need of him blinding her to the separateness of his life, the whole scene of which she filled with his relation to her—no unique preoccupation of Gwendolyn's, for we are all apt to fall into this passionate egoism of imagination, not only towards our fellow-men, but towards God" (795–96). Ironically, even her attempt to become less selfish is selfish. When she accepts that Daniel is leaving her, however, Gwendolyn finally gains a vision of her place within the Absolute: at first she feels "reduced to a mere speck," then "she was for the first time feeling the pressure of a vast mysterious movement, for the first time being dislodged from her supremacy in her own world, and getting a sense that her horizon was but a dipping onward of an existence with which her own was revolving" (803–04). Although the reader is left with the sense that the Absolute is a culmination, that Gwendolyn will gain meaning and purpose from this wider vision, we also feel that the hundreds of pages of selfishness that preceded it must not be for naught, that selfishness itself is a necessary form of the Absolute.

Before returning to this question of the importance of self, I would like to touch on another theme that *Daniel Deronda* shares with *Romola*: philosophy. In the later novel, references and allusions to philosophy—including Absolute idealism, Neoplatonism, Indian philosophy, and, of course, Jewish philosophy and Kabbalah—appear with even more insistence and purpose. Just as Daniel begins researching Jewish traditions, the narrator describes someone (perhaps Daniel himself, it is unclear) resting "dreamily in a boat," imagining the days of Ibn Gabirol (c.1021–c.1050s) (380). According to Peter Adamson, Ibn Gabirol "draws heavily on the Neoplatonic tradition" to advance a peculiar type of materialism: "he's a materialist of a rather unfamiliar kind . . . . [his] is a materialism which accepts the existence of incorporeal things, like soul and intellect" (*Philosophy in the Islamic* 209, 212). In 1859, Salomon Munk published evidence that Ibn Gabirol—previously known only as a poet—was also the philosopher known in Latin as "Avicebrol" (*Philosophy in the Islamic* 209n3); Eliot was aware of this discovery and Ibn Gabirol's philosophy because she read Munk while preparing for *Daniel Deronda*. Although this might seem like a slight allusion, a few pages later, Daniel seeks a book by Salomon Maimon (1753–1800), who "played an important role in the reception of Spinoza in German Idealism"; moreover, because of his criticism of Kant's "cognitive dualism," "the project of Absolute Idealism owes much to" him (Thielke and Melamed). Eliot is not one to randomly drop names; she surely understood where these references could be placed in the philosophical tradition. This is not to suggest that Eliot is uncritically, if implicitly, advocating the Neoplatonic nondualism of Ibn Gabirol or the proto-Absolute idealism of Maimon. At the meeting of "The Philosophers" at the *Hand and Banner*, there is a distinct shift in the conversation from the Absolute idealist metaphysics of Goodwin and Marrables (who argue that the ideal cannot be separated from the material) to Mordecai's emphasis on race, nation, and tradition (*Daniel Deronda* 524–39). The argument that metaphysical systems alone are not enough, but must be supplemented with social and affective bonds, aligns Mordecai with Judah Hallevi (c.1075–1141), who was opposed to Ibn Gabirol's rationalism (Mordecai's long-lived soul once "took ship with Jehuda ha-Levi" [498]).

Such a tangled mass of philosophical allusions suggests that Eliot has no simplistic or straightforward philosophical agenda.[11] Instead, she seems fascinated by the idea that, in the history of philosophy as in *Daniel Deronda* itself, "everything is related to everything else." For example, she copied the following quotation from Heinrich Hirsch Graetz into her notebooks for *Daniel Deronda*: "The doctrines of the Cabbala are neither ancient Jewish, nor new-philosophical. The ideal potencies, the spiritual intermediators between the Divine fullness of light & the dim world—the pre-existence of the soul—the transmigration of souls—the magical operation of human actions on the higher world—all belong to the Alexandrian neo-platonic philosophy" (175). Moreover, "Alexandrian philosophy [is] derived from India" (439). The connection to India helps explain why Eliot read at least three books on Buddhism in preparing for the novel (276)—it also makes more resonant the Meyricks' comparison of Daniel to the Buddha (*Daniel Deronda* 465). Tracing Mordecai's diasporic Jewish Kabbalism to Alexandrian Neoplatonism to Indian Buddhism underscores the idea that Eliot's final novel has a truly "global plot" (Cave xxx). Such philosophical backgrounds also allow us—against the ostensible invitation to read the novel as a colonialist dream of nation-building—to see the Jewish plot as "an attempt to move beyond the concept of nation," to "have a place inhabit a person" rather than the reverse (Willburn 279, 282).

Indeed, the occupation of the self by the environment—which is not a subjugation but an *extension* of the self's boundaries through objectification—occurs frequently in the novel, often through the act of meditation. Appropriately enough, for someone compared to the Buddha, Daniel is described as having "a meditative yearning after wide knowledge" and "a meditative interest in learning how human miseries are wrought" (178–79), and he counsels Gwendolyn to "Turn your fear into a safeguard. Keep your dread fixed on the idea of increasing that remorse which is so bitter to you. Fixed meditation may do a great deal towards defining our longing or dread" (452). Some of the novel's most important turning points occur during meditative contemplation, as when Daniel, floating in his boat on the Thames, "for a long while . . . never turned his eyes from the view right in front of him. He was forgetting everything else in a half-speculative, half-involuntary identification of himself with the objects he was looking at, thinking how far it might be possible habitually to shift his centre till his own personality would be no less outside him than the landscape" (189). This is just before he saves Mirah from her suicide attempt. Also, just before Mordecai's momentous meeting with Daniel on Blackfriars Bridge, he is "gazing meditatively" at the river; the sights and sounds "entered into his mood and blent themselves indistinguishably with his thinking" (474). Meditation does not always result in this heightened translucence of the self: Grandcourt "employed himself (as a philosopher might have done) in sitting meditatively on a sofa and abstaining from literature," but the "exorbitant egoism" of his mind remains trapped within "a phantasmal world" (319). However, even when one falls, as Daniel does, into a "meditative numbness," waiting for the universe's direction (364–65), it is often the prelude to a serendipitous communion, a "divine influx" of the external: Daniel is subsequently lifted out of himself at the synagogue, not by the *content* of the liturgy, which he cannot understand, but by its *forms*—"The most powerful movement of feeling with a liturgy is the prayer which seeks for nothing special, but is a yearning to escape from the limitations of our own weakness and an invocation of all Good to enter and abide with us" (367–68). It is remarkable that the Indian practice of meditation is not opposed to, but prepares for and complements, the Jewish liturgy. Moreover, both have the same purpose, which is to abrade the distinction between self and not-self.

As we have seen, the "self" is the site of a crucial epistemological, ontological, and ethical struggle in all three of the novels I've considered. It would be easy to read them as offering a strong critique of the self: the most selfish characters (e.g., Tito, Rosamond, Grandcourt) are the most repugnant, while even the likable characters who become trapped in their own projections (e.g., Romola, Dorothea, Gwendolyn) are shown to be foolish and inchoate. Moreover, the novels imply that the most selfish and self-absorbed characters are fixated on what is essentially an illusion, or at best a negation. The narrator of *Daniel Deronda* suggests that "a soul burning with a sense of what the universe is not, and ready to take all existence as fuel, is nevertheless held captive by the ordinary wire-work of social forms" (53). "Gwendolyn," the narrator elsewhere remarks, "had not considered that the desire to conquer is itself a sort of subjection" (106). Even at its most imperial, the self, it seems—as Hegel memorably demonstrates in the master-slave dialectic—is an appendage of the Other. Yet Eliot carefully resists, as most Absolute idealists do, allowing the self to vanish beneath the canopy of the universe. The self, for Eliot, is a shadow—but it is also supreme. Without the "insane exaggeration of his own value," Mordecai would not have been an effective spiritual leader: "the fuller nature desires to be an agent, to create, and not merely to look on: strong love hungers to bless, and not merely to behold blessing. And while there is warmth enough in the sun to feed an energetic life, there will still be men to feel, 'I am lord of this moment's change, and will charge it with my soul'" (475). The object will "feed," but the subject must "charge." Eliot's Absolute realism is the meticulous integration of these agencies, and her ethics of sympathy emerges from their synthesis: "Our pride becomes loving, our self is a not-self for whose sake we become virtuous, when we set to some hidden work of reclaiming a life from misery and look for our triumph in the secret joy—'This one is the better for me'" (378). And so, at the heart of Eliot's realism, we find the paradox of Hylo-Idealism.

Chapter 3

Across Ontology and Ethics

F. H. Bradley, Samuel Butler, and Science Fiction

> Within all-encompassing Nature, the difference between the "physical" and the "mental" is only a matter of degree, and not of kind. A thermostat is, to a modest extent, an information processor; and therefore we should agree that it is at least minimally sentient.
>
> —Steven Shaviro, *Discognition*

> Man becomes, as it were, the sex organs of the machine world, as the bee of the plant world, enabling it to fecundate and evolve ever new forms.
>
> —Marshall McLuhan, *Understanding Media*

Idealist philosophy flourished in the final decades of the nineteenth century. From the 1870s, the British Idealist movement "rapidly became the primary school of thought in Britain, and for half a century thereafter dominated philosophical debate" (den Otter 1). Moreover, idealism spread beyond the confines of academic discourse into the broader culture: Pinch has demonstrated "how influential forms of idealism were in nineteenth-century British culture, in spite of our sense of their uneasy marginality" (*Thinking* 6). David Boucher and Andrew Vincent explain the intellectual and cultural appeal of idealism in this period by suggesting that "British Idealism was a social philosophy that exuded optimism at a time of extreme social dislocation and pessimism. . . . [I]t acted as a profound interrogation, critique and metaphysical counterbalance to the individualism of the variants of an instinctive British utilitarianism and naturalistic evolutionism" (4). A group of professors at Oxford University offered this more sanguine alternative to atomistic and materialist philosophies. Many of them allowed their deeply held Christian beliefs to inform their work, providing an authoritative rebuttal to the crisis of faith. But it would be a mistake to see British Idealism as solely an elaboration of Christianity in metaphysical guise. Although he considered himself a Christian, F. H. Bradley (1846–1924) was at times "extremely hostile" to his religion (Mander, *British* 178). For example, in an unpublished essay on Christian morality, he writes, "Viewed as a supreme guide in life I do not hesitate to call [the moral doctrine of the New Testament and early Christians] detestable" (qtd. in Kendal 177). Benjamin Jowett, Master of Balliol College, led an "indigenous revival of Platonism" (Boucher and Vincent 9) through his translations and lectures, giving a dash of paganism to the movement. Indeed, the ethical theories advanced by British Idealism represent a return to ancient Greek thought: rather than pursuing the deontology of Christianity or Kant (we should follow absolute moral rules), or the consequentialism of utilitarianism (we should be guided by the effects of our actions), British Idealists asked, "what kind of person ought I to be?," in line with eudaimonism (we should create the conditions for flourishing and well-being) (Mander, *British* 198).

For many British Idealists, the question "what kind of person ought I to be?" is tied to the question "what is a person?" In other words, they insist that ethics cannot be separated from ontology, and their understanding of the "self" is much more expansive than the discrete unit assumed by utilitarianism. This chapter uses the philosophy and fiction of Bradley and Samuel Butler to examine this nexus, what Elizabeth Grosz calls "ontoethics, a way of thinking about not just how the world is but how it could be, how it is open to change, and, above all, the becomings it may undergo. . . . [O]ntoethics involves an ethics that addresses not just human life in its interhuman relations, but relations between the human and an entire world, both organic and inorganic" (1). Bradley's *Ethical Studies* (1876) provides such an ontoethics, making each person's ethical obligations dependent upon their ontological position within a historically specific and evolving social "organism." For Bradley, the social organism is composed of individual humans, interhuman relations, and the relations between humans, animals, and "inorganic" configurations like educational institutions. A social organism can be relatively small, like a family, or extremely large, like a nation or humanity itself. In *Ethical Studies*, Bradley confines his focus to human social organisms, with nations as a limit case, but he expands his analysis of ontology to the limit of the Absolute in *Appearance and Reality* (1893), venturing into a consideration of the vast array of actual and potential nonhuman organisms that exist within, beside, and beyond the human. This later, more metaphysical text—Bradley's most famous—therefore implicitly complicates his ethics and has, I will argue, literary implications as well. Before I explore it, however, I would like to linger for a moment on the mutually constitutive relationship between ontology and ethics in *Ethical Studies* because it resonates with the discussion of Naden and Eliot in the previous chapter and sets the stage for the reading of Bradley, Butler, and science fiction to follow.

Ethics, for Bradley as for Butler, hinges on the extent to which we can think of a "self" as something discrete. If the self is merely a "unit which repels other units, and can have nothing in itself but what is exclusively *its*, its feeling, its pleasure and pain—then it is certain that it can stand to others, with their pleasures and pains, only in an external relation; and since [the self] is the end, the others must be the means, and nothing but the means" (*Ethical Studies* 105). The ontological assumption of discrete individuals precludes the possibility of thinking of anyone outside the self as inherently valuable, but Bradley argues that the self is actually "determined, characterized, made what it is by relation to others," therefore "I can not aim at my own well-being without aiming at that of others" (105). The goal of ethics, then, is "self-realization," which means psychologically realizing that you exist as a part of social whole and ontologically "realizing that whole in yourself" through good (life-enhancing, life-intensifying) action (73). Like Naden, Bradley insists that we cannot think the self apart from the whole; indeed, the real self *is* the whole. I must accept solipsism or selfishness as a fact, since anything I desire can only be desired in relation to myself, "and yet the self which is myself, which is mine, is not merely me" (77). To flourish, I need to actualize the will of the social organism through my specific function as its organ. Apart from this whole, "I am not myself. When it goes out my heart goes out with it, where it triumphs I rejoice, where it is maimed I suffer; separate me from the love of it, and I perish" (73). For Bradley, ethics is only possible when we understand ourselves as an organ of various social organisms, like family, community, and nation—an organ with various, sometimes conflicting, functions or duties to perform. And ethics is achievable only insofar as we maximize the well-being of ourselves as an organ(ism).

Bradley gives his fullest picture of how individuals become organs of the social organism in the chapter entitled "My Station and its Duties." His description of the individualization of an infant steeped in acculturating contexts foreshadows Louis Althusser's influential essay "Ideology and Ideological State Apparatuses" (1970), but where Althusser finds menace and oppression, Bradley emphasizes harmony and contentment. The infant at birth is not a blank slate or an atomized individual; it is "born not into a desert, but into a living world . . . into a system and order which it is difficult to look at as anything else than an organism" (155). The infant is born into a very specific cultural milieu that makes her who she is, while the care she receives from adults is the impression of habits that will govern her personality (155). The infant cannot distinguish himself from his surroundings and has no thought of himself as a distinct individual, but as he gets older, "when he can separate himself from that world, and know himself apart from it, then by that time his self, the object of his self-consciousness, is penetrated, infected, characterized by the existence of others" (155). The boy who now thinks of himself as an "individual" has been so thoroughly constructed through the inculcation of habits and language that the very idea of an individual "self" is a false abstraction from reality. As he ages, he is even more deeply attached to the social body through ever more encompassing "moral institutions" (161), such as educational and governmental organizations. At this point, the point of moral maturity, the adult has a specific location within the social organism, and this is her "station," which comes with certain "duties." "To be moral," for Bradley, "I must will my station and its duties," while, reciprocally, the social organism "wills to particularize itself in a given station and functions, *i.e.,* in my actions and by my will" (163). Ultimately, it is through "the activity of obedience" that we find "satisfaction and happiness" (167).

Such an account of the development of ethics is sure to strike modern readers as hopelessly naïve if not reactionary and dangerous. We are immediately struck by an obvious question, which Althusser for one was intent on exposing: What if my "station" is oppressive? Bradley himself was struck by this question, and he responded to it in several ways. First, "My Station and its Duties" describes[1] an ideal ethical state that may never be reached because social organisms are always historically and geographically specific—they are relative and not absolute; they evolve, and it is not clear that evolution is always progressive (172–73). Furthermore, Bradley acknowledges that a social organism can be diseased, in which case it would be a moral duty to, for example, "protest against bad institutions" (178n1). A healthy social organism needs its organs to thrive: "unless we have intense life and self-consciousness in the members of the state, the whole state is ossified," a "carcass" (170, 161). The better the state, the better the individual, and vice versa. Oppression would be detrimental to the life of the whole. The fact that individuals are inextricably bound up in the social organism means, however, that one must combat oppression from within the "general spirit" of the social organism rather than "starting from oneself, from ideals in one's head, to set oneself and them against the moral world" (181). This would be to falsely imagine oneself as externalized and discrete, projecting "ideals in one's head" onto objective reality. It would be to fall into the trap of subjective idealism, which Bradley calls a "silly doctrine": a "steam-engine, after it is made, is [not] a state of the mind of the person or persons who have made it" (61).

Bradley also considers the objection that, as social organisms become more complex and specialized under capitalism, the individual "becomes a machine, or the piece of a machine," perhaps finding his onerous station in "file-packing" (170). His response is that the individual self exceeds its station and duties (171, 185). Although obedience to the will of a healthy social organism—even if we find some of our duties onerous or unfulfilling—is a crucial part of the ethical life, it is not the only part. Self-realization must fill broader and broader spheres, even those beyond the social per se. In this way, Bradley seeks to defend the integrity and value of the individual against all-consuming abstractions. He "repudiate[s] the tyranny of the (abstract) universal" (125). Morality is not achieved by dissolving into an incorporeal cloud. The organ is flesh with material interests and desires: "To neglect the basis [animal pleasures] is to make as great a mistake as to regard it as the crown and summit" (121). Self-realization must include the pleasures of food, drink, and sex. Other even more solitary pursuits are also ethical, and not only for the indirect social benefits they may provide. For instance, artists, writers, philosophers, and scientists often find their "duty" in the non-social sphere of isolated research and creative production, and these activities are ends in themselves, just as these individuals are ends in themselves (201). Ultimately, although individuals are constrained by the particular social organism in which they emerge, they are not entirely reducible to it. Individuals can be oppressed by their social environment, but they can also find their fulfillment there. If they cannot, they have the power to alter it from within. But it is impossible to extricate oneself entirely from the social organism: "if he turns against this he turns against himself; if he thrusts it from him, he tears his own vitals" (156).

Bradley's ethics, as I've sketched it above, is intriguing in its own right, but what interests me most is how utterly *strange* it is. *Ethical Studies* certainly requires of its readers a certain suspension of disbelief, an immersion in a counterintuitive vision of the universe that is best captured in the final rather lurid quote above: I live inside a massive organism, and I cannot escape! Everything I see around me—the trash in the gutter, the people on the street, the invisible economic and linguistic flows that sustain it all—is not a mere aggregation of inert objects, discrete individuals, and abstract concepts, but an interlocking system of organs pulsating within some tremendous sentient creature that is also in some sense *me*. What's more, that creature is not the only one. The implications of this vision for ontology, ethics, and literature are immense. How do we know that seemingly separate social organisms aren't themselves organs of a higher organism? If ethics is the evolution of multiple social organisms, what ethical obligations does one social organism have to another? What if one social organism is antagonistic, or completely incomprehensible, to another? If humans can be reduced to machines within a social organism, can we likewise serve as organs of a machinic organism? As Butler puts this same question, "The humble bee is a part of the reproductive system of the clover. Each one of ourselves has sprung from minute animalcules whose entity was entirely distinct from our own, and which acted after their kind with no thought or heed of what we might think about it. These little creatures are part of our own reproductive system; then why not we part of that of the machines?" (*Erewhon* 127). Organs within gears within organs: a distributed, symbiotic—but not necessarily peaceable—kingdom.

This ontology of organs and organisms, like a bubble structure, suggests an infinite number of individual but translucent agents suspended within a lattice-like or fractal form. In other words, it suggests panpsychism—a term coined by Lewes in 1879—which Pinch defines as "the philosophical position that all forms of matter—down to the smallest atom—have consciousness, or if not consciousness, some form of mentality, or capacity for desire, for volition, or for experience" ("Appeal" 2). Because *Ethical Studies* focuses almost exclusively on humans, it would strain credulity to claim, solely on its basis, that Bradley is an advocate of panpsychism. Indeed, there is no consensus on the question, although several commentators note the affinity,[2] and I will present my own case in the next section. With Butler, there is no question. He advocates panpsychism beginning in 1880 with the publication of *Unconscious Memory*, where he writes,

> [Mind and matter] are not two separable things, but one and inseparable, with, as it were, two sides, the one of which is a function of the other. There was never yet either matter without mind, however low, nor mind, however high, without a material body of some sort; there can be no change in one without a corresponding change in the other; neither came before the other; neither can either cease to change or cease to be; for "to be" is to continue changing, so that "to be" and "to change" are one. (140)

But why is it important to think of Bradley and Butler as panpsychists? First, it allows us to position them within a larger cultural movement in the late Victorian period that saw numerous scientific, philosophical, and literary figures support, or at least seriously consider, panpsychism—including Naden.[3] This flowering of panpsychism, which effloresced in concert with Absolute idealism, prefigures the intense interest in panpsychism of our own time, as seen in movements like new materialism, speculative realism, and object-oriented ontology (Pinch, "Appeal" 3). Second, an attention to panpsychism emphasizes Bradley and Butler's incorporation of evolutionary theory into their ontoethics, as we have seen in Bradley's stress on the evolution of social organisms and Butler's identification of "being" and "changing" above. One of the reasons panpsychism re-emerged in the late Victorian period is that it elegantly explains how mind can evolve from matter. Third, as Pinch argues, a consideration of panpsychism "restores ontological questions to Victorian aesthetics" (3). Where Pinch attends to poetry, artistic patterns, and theories of reading, I will explore the implications of Bradley's and Butler's panpsychist ontoethics for the emergence and development of science fiction.

In accord with the formal promiscuity of panpsychism, Bradley and Butler vividly reveal the yielding, bubble-like borders of philosophy and fiction. Fiction pops up throughout Bradley's philosophical treatise *Appearance and Reality*, while it is nearly impossible to detach philosophy and fiction in Butler's corpus. The results of these mixtures are sophisticated, often bizarre narratives about the dense ontological and ethical interpenetration that characterizes our universe. In his reading of Butler's panpsychism, Chris Danta calls such narratives a "speculative evolutionary aesthetics," which "seeks to mitigate human exceptionalism by playfully reimagining and reconfiguring the relation of the human to its evolutionary past, present and future" (16). But I don't think such an aesthetics should be confined to the human. Panpsychism invites literary writers to artistically render the consciousness, agency, and perspectives of every bubble in the form, from dogs to aliens to robots. The affinity between panpsychism and science fiction is particularly salient: Butler's sentient machines in *Erewhon* (1872), which form the conceptual basis for so much subsequent science fiction, are a case in point, as are Bradley's science-fictional excursions in *Appearance and Reality*. Indeed, as my reading of Bradley and Butler suggests, many idealists attempt to integrate mind and matter in a comprehensive manner that cannot be grasped by logic or science alone. It requires, in addition, an aesthetic approach that relentlessly seeks out new forms, new genres, and new perspectives.

In the following sections, I begin by examining Bradley's *Appearance and Reality*, underscoring his argument that any delimited "self," including nonhumans and objects, is a partial reality, an "appearance," of larger aggregates of reality and ultimately the whole universe (the "Absolute"). Bradley's emphasis on the Absolute is balanced by his insistence on the reality of difference: the Absolute, like a novel, does not transcend, but *is*, the myriad entangled selves, experiences, even temporalities that compose it. Indeed, Bradley incorporates several "fictions" into his philosophy that attend to the strange possibilities of a universe teeming with experiences. Turning to Butler, we find a remarkably similar conception of the relation between selves and nature. Butler claims that all of life, from its first appearance on Earth to the present, is one vast organism. Each "individual" alive now is like a leaf on a tree, seemingly separate, but actually the latest outgrowth or organ of a larger creature (a creature he sometimes identifies with God). Each of us has the body we do, each of us acts the way we do, because we are unconsciously expressing our memory of past desires. Biological form is therefore the material expression of a nearly infinite series of immaterial desires. Each moment of experience is also filled with what Butler calls "crosses." A cross is a problem to be resolved, a state of disequilibrium that will lead to further discord or harmony, decay or growth. This conception does not erase the individual but makes it incredibly complex, since each one—each human, machine, or molecule—is a provisional cross between all of the past and present as it is constituted by densely crosshatched subjects and objects. Butler's theme of crossing—of human and inhuman desires, the persistence of the past in the present, the interpenetration of mind and matter, and ecological complexity—is elaborated in his philosophical writings and appears throughout all three of his novels.

After crossing Bradley and Butler in this way to tease out the literary and ethical implications of their work, I conclude with a final section that gestures toward the continued presence of their form of idealism in science fiction. After briefly considering the science fiction of George Eliot and Edward Douglas Fawcett, I take as my main example the Cellarius Universe, a franchise launched in 2018 that takes Butler as an explicit inspiration. On June 13, 1863, Butler published "Darwin Among the Machines"—an article exploring the concept of sentient machines that was later incorporated into *Erewhon*—under the pseudonym "Cellarius." On June 13, 2084, in the Cellarius Universe, a sophisticated artificial intelligence named Cellarius becomes self-aware and seizes control of global energy systems. The ensuing devastation breaks humans, hybrids, and machines into a variety of factions, including anti-technology "Erewhons" and others more adoptive of technology or aligned with Cellarius itself. Although the Cellarius Universe has been discontinued, it was originally intended to build a massive "universe" of content through a multiplicity of perspectives. Established artists and fans were encouraged to produce a range of media—fiction, film, animation, music, playing cards, etc.—related to the conceptual premise sketched above. Through an analysis of the Cellarius "Universe Guide" and "White Paper," as well as *Whose Future Is It?*, a collection of short stories set in the Cellarius Universe, I argue that this collaborative, transmedia project embodies, in form and content, the visionary panpsychism of the late Victorian period.

The Science Fiction of F. H. Bradley

As a way of approaching Bradley's ontology, it helps to keep in mind that he emphasizes the arbitrary nature of our epistemological distinctions. When we try to make sense of reality, we separate out parts and wholes—for instance, where one self or species begins and another ends—but this inevitably leads to the false partition of a real continuity: "We have to take reality as many, and to take it as one, and to avoid contradiction. We want to divide it, or to take it, when we please, as indivisible; to go as far as we desire in either of these directions, and to stop when that suits us" (*Appearance and Reality* 33). Throughout *Appearance and Reality*, Bradley puts pressure on a series of such arbitrary partitions, disrupting practically convenient fictions like self and nation (importantly, the formal partitions are fictional, not their content—selves and nations are real, as far as they go). At the end of this series, we are left with the only thing that escapes contradiction and false partition: the entire whole, the Absolute. In this section, I would like to underscore the aesthetic means by which Bradley advances his argument. Ironically, he uses "fictions," "fancies," and "metaphors" to expose the limitations of our fictional distinctions. His many interpolated stories illustrate that there are countless other possible ways of carving up the real—provocative, thrilling, bizarre, and cognitively dissonant ways. In other words, his philosophy is deeply science-fictional. As Steven Shaviro points out, philosophers often employ science fiction (in the form of "thought experiments") to explore the nature and limits of things like the human or consciousness (*Discognition* 23–24). Bradley's work exemplifies this entanglement of the philosophical and literary, and the numerous fictions he scatters throughout *Appearance and Reality* both reflect elements of Butler's oeuvre and foreshadow later developments in science fiction.

For Bradley, the self is ramified, entangled in its surroundings, and constantly in flux. Anticipating Malabou's argument that humans become "others, re-engendered, belonging to a different species" after suffering social and ecological trauma (*Ontology* 13), he suggests that the self is continuously reshaped in relation to the incursions of its surrounds. The internal contents of a self also consist "essentially in the outward environment, so far as relating to that makes the man what he is. For if we try to take the man apart from certain places and persons, we have altered his life so much that he is not his usual self" (*Appearance and Reality* 78). The line between internal self and external circumstance is arbitrarily drawn: "the self is not enclosed by a wall. And where the essential self is to end, and the accidental self to begin, seems a riddle without an answer" (80). We cannot find the "usual self" in the material body, which is indefinitely distributed and undergoes continuous change; likewise, it disappears in states of sleep, love, intoxication, injury, disease, and madness (79–85). Where, then, is the self? We may imagine that through all these vicissitudes some small core of the self remains, but Bradley asks in his blunt, poetic style, "This narrow persisting element of feeling or idea, this fixed essence not [as Shakespeare puts it in *Measure for Measure*] 'servile to all the skyey influences,' this wretched fraction and poor atom, too mean to be in danger—do you mean to tell me that this bare remnant is really the self?" (81). The invulnerable, static "self" is fictitious, an appearance.

It is not unreal or utterly groundless, however. "By one self," he writes, "we understand one experience" (*Appearance and Reality* 82). While there is no specific "feeling or idea" that gives continuity to the self, *feeling itself* does: the self's constantly shifting experience, the self feeling itself as it maintains a flickering reach into its environment, is its only self-consistency. It is important to emphasize that, for Bradley, this feeling or experience is not wholly conscious, but extends beneath consciousness into a "general background of feeling," an "unexhausted margin" (92, 93). Experience is largely nonconscious, even in humans; at its most basic, it is feeling, desire, an affective orientation toward, or interaction with, other things/experiences. Bradley thereby detaches experience from its usual associations with (human) thought, extending it to animals (431n1) and beyond. Even within the self—if we agree to "push a metaphor far beyond its true and natural limits" (Bradley's characteristic rhetorical move)—each bodily organ "considers," "aims," and "identif[ies] its will with a wider reality" (417–18). Each "self," then, is an enfolded sentient experience that extends indefinitely: internally, externally, and through time.

Bradley's discussion of the self mostly centers on human selves, but this just sets the stage for his larger argument, which is fundamentally non-anthropocentric. He extends the experience that subtends human subjectivity to all things:

> to be real, or even barely to exist, must be to fall within sentience. Sentient experience, in short, is reality, and what is not this is not real. We may say, in other words, that there is no being or fact outside of that which is commonly called psychical existence. Feeling, thought, and volition (any groups under which we class psychical phenomena) are all the material of existence, and there is no other material, actual or even possible. . . . [A]ny piece of existence [consists] in sentient experience. (*Appearance and Reality* 144–45)

Everything in the universe is animated by something mind-like: each thing feels, thinks, or wills. In addition, all of these sentient experiences are nested within one universe, the Absolute, which is itself one sentient experience (of itself, namely everything): "Our conclusion, so far, will be this, that the Absolute is one system, and that its contents are nothing but sentient experience. It will hence be a single and all-inclusive experience, which embraces every partial diversity in concord" (147). Any attempt to "embrace diversity in concord" may trouble modern readers, who have become justly concerned about totalizing wholes. But Bradley's universe is a cradle of difference and creative differentiation.

He is careful to preserve the integrity and value of each part of the Absolute, which, at its most basic, is a "centre of experience." He acknowledges the various levels of complexity such centers can reach through evolution (*Appearance and Reality* 386). It is obvious, for example, that human experience is more elaborate and self-reflexive than the experience of a fruit fly. But "below, or else wider than and above" more complicated physico-mental structures, which he calls selves or souls, we always find sentient centers of experience: "no element of Reality falls outside the experience of finite centres" (529, 528). Moreover, each self, soul, and center has *absolute* value: "My self is certainly not the Absolute, but, without it, the Absolute would not be itself. You cannot anywhere abstract wholly from my personal feelings; you cannot say that, apart even from the meanest of these, anything else in the universe would be what it is" (260). This Absolute stance leads Bradley to a relativism that places him, along with several other British Idealists (Boucher and Vincent 4–5), in opposition to the absolutist claims of the British Empire. For instance, Bradley wryly notes that "our country, the chosen land of Moral Philosophy, has the reputation abroad of being the chief home of hypocrisy and cant" (*Appearance and Reality* 430n1). The imperial center is everywhere: "We can find no province of the world so low but the Absolute inhabits it. Nowhere is there even a single fact so fragmentary and so poor that to the universe it does not matter. There is truth in every idea however false, there is reality in every existence however slight; and, where we can point to reality or truth, there is the one undivided life of the Absolute" (487). Because each individual thing is a metonymic or microcosmic expression of the whole, it must be cherished: "any one aspect, when viewed by itself, may be regarded as the end for which the others exist" (456). If a single thing were to vanish, nothing would exist. And yet every experience is perpetually reborn, pushing the entire universe into a new shift.

Ultimately, Bradley's ontology is both radically flat and hierarchically layered according to levels of complexity and self-integration; it respects both material and mental reality, finding agency in all things; and it has important ethical implications for humans' social relations and their interactions with the environment. Although he is an idiosyncratic thinker who resists categorization, his philosophy synthesizes several strands of nineteenth-century thought and resembles later developments. In ontological terms, he shares with Hegel and most British Idealists a belief in the mental/spiritual character of the universe, while he also emphasizes the integrity and microcosmic aspect of each particular in the manner of the Romantics and Personal Idealists (a later evolution of British Idealism). In epistemological terms, he insists on the ultimately arbitrary nature of our distinctions, just as Darwin does with regard to species. He acknowledges with Kant the limits of human understanding: for Bradley, we can never fully grasp what other centers of experience, or the Absolute, are like in themselves. We can only approach them obliquely, through allusions and analogies, stories and speculations.

In aesthetic terms, then, Bradley's work has much in common with Victorian literature. From realism to animal autobiography to science fiction, Victorian literature explores the ways in which the lived experiences of human and nonhuman "others" form, or deform, social and ecological wholes. Bradley gives several briefly sketched fictions with a similar focus, although he does so hesitantly, almost always disavowing these literary devices in the very act of delivering them. For example, consider his first interpolated story, which I give in full:

> I confess that I shrink from using metaphors, since they never can suit wholly. The writer tenders them unsuspiciously as a possible help in a common difficulty. And so he subjects himself, perhaps, to the captious ill-will or sheer negligence of his reader. Still to those who will take it for what it is, I will offer a fiction. Suppose a collection of beings whose souls in the night walk about without their bodies, and so make new relations. On their return in the morning we may imagine that the possessors feel the benefit of this divorce; and we may therefore call it truth. But, if the wrong soul with its experience came back to the wrong body, that might typify error. On the other hand, perhaps the ruler of this collection of beings may perceive very well the nature of the collision. And it may even be that he provokes it. For how instructive and how amusing to observe in each case the conflict of sensation with imported and foreign experience. (*Appearance and Reality* 194)

Not the most gripping yarn to emerge from the Victorian period, to be sure. Yet the story, and its frame, raise several issues. Bradley's opening disavowal marks a reluctance to entrust the aims of philosophy to the vagaries of the imagination rather than the supposedly consistent mechanisms of reason. It is telling, however, that despite these concerns he goes on to tell the story, a rather suggestive one about wandering, disembodied souls who return to mismatched bodies, possibly for the instructive amusement of a "ruler." Of course, the philosopher and his reader are also instructively amused by the cross between self and "foreign experience." Perhaps this is why Bradley repeatedly returns to fiction—to incorporate some spirit into the body of his text.

A brief recapitulation of Bradley's other fictions—all of them actual possibilities within the Absolute—will give a sense of how evocative and visionary he can be. He asks what would happen if "another body like my own were manufactured," or "an indefinite number of such bodies" (*Appearance and Reality* 356, 503). He also considers the possibility that there may be multiple, "independent time-series," some of which run in reverse to our own, so that "Death would come before birth, the blow would follow the wound" (211, 215). Indeed, there could be multiple other people on a reversed time-series who share some of the contents of my own life (217). Similarly, there may be multiple spatial systems that have no relation to each other in space, or multiple worlds that run according to different causal series (216, 218). Just as my experience forms part of a larger experience of which I am unaware, my body appears discrete but may "have a position and function in any number of organisms" (253, 271). One organism can be "widely scattered and discontinuous" (340). We tend to assume that actions occur on the exterior or boundary of bodies, but the "inside" of one organism may directly affect the inside of another (343). A collection of secondary qualities, like a constellation of sounds or smells, "might accompany psychical life and serve as a body" (341). Reincarnation is possible (308). Just as mental realities arise from material conditions, the reverse is also possible: "some matter might itself result from soul. All these things are 'possible' in this sense, that, within our knowledge, they cannot any of them proved to be unreal. But they are mere idle possibilities" (341). The caveat that follows this last "worthless fancy" (341n1) is in keeping with Bradley's ambivalent attitude toward imaginative speculations. Yet these fictions and fancies ultimately serve to "justify the natural wonder which delights to stray beyond our daylight world, and to follow paths that lead into half-known half-unknowable regions" (549). Bradley's philosophical argument leads, in the end, to a sense of wonder at the vast possibilities of our universe, possibilities that only fiction can adequately explore.

The Cross Philosophy of Samuel Butler

Like Bradley, Butler draws on Absolute idealism to compose idealist fictions. Yet his relationship to idealism has been overlooked, despite all the manifest affinities. He certainly makes his disdain for German Idealism clear: "With Kant, Schelling, Fichte, and Hegel, we feel that we are with men who have been decoyed into a hopeless quagmire" (*God the Known* 30). Perhaps statements like these, and the tendency to read him as opposed to professionals and academics, have kept scholars from examining his idealism *qua* idealism. In *Samuel Butler, Victorian against the Grain*, the only collection of critical essays so far published on Butler, his work is analyzed in relation to several nineteenth-century discourses, including Darwinian and other evolutionary theories, the popularization of science, natural theology, Christianity and Biblical criticism, psychology, philology, and the visual arts. These were all important influences on Butler, to be sure, but idealism is only occasionally and briefly mentioned. David Amigoni positions Butler "outside the traditions of Kantian and (from the perspective of the English tradition) Coleridgean idealism" (94). Bernard Lightman states, without elaboration, that Butler's notion of God is "tinged with idealism" (121). Ruth Parkin-Gounelas argues that Butler increasingly embraced the empiricism and materialism associated with his alma mater, Cambridge, and rejected the philosophers at Oxford University, "which for two generations was dominated by German idealism" (195). I find Parkin-Gounelas's argument compelling, but she misleadingly implies that a choice must be made between idealism and a belief in material reality, overestimates the extent to which the British Idealists at Oxford (like Bradley) were "dominated" by German Idealism, and fails to explore the possibility that the idealist theories coming out of Oxford and elsewhere influenced (and were influenced by) Butler. "The voices of common sense," Butler writes in his *Note-Books*, "and of high philosophy sometimes cross" (330). In all likelihood, he was suspicious of the obscure style of much "high philosophy" but found the theories themselves provocative.

Butler has a longstanding and well-deserved reputation as a rather cross man. His public feud with Darwin has been much discussed, and he is usually read as antagonistic or oppositional: Ralf Norrman's description of his work as "chiastic" is still influential. David Gillott suggests, however, that a better metaphor for capturing this tendency in Butler's work is "harmonics": a "constructive merging of opposites into a pleasing whole" (2). Rather than placing Butler on the Cambridge side of a binary divide, it may be more helpful to see his work as harmonically crossing the materialism of Cambridge with the idealism of Oxford. By 1879 at the latest, Butler was regularly reading *Mind*, the influential journal of philosophy (Parkin-Gounelas 200). From 1879 to Butler's death in 1902, *Mind* published twenty-five essays by Bradley, plus eight essays that respond to or review his work. Moreover, dozens of other British and American idealists appeared in *Mind* over this period, including T. H. Green, whose ontological system was first published there in 1882. In *Mind*, Butler would have found powerful tools for supplementing Darwin's theory of evolution, which for Butler has the fatal flaw of "pitchforking . . . mind out of the universe" (*Luck, or Cunning* 18). With his turn toward idealism, Butler does not reject natural selection, but finds a way to account for things that he believes it alone cannot, such as the emergence of experience and agency from inert matter. Throughout his writings, he radically extends the principle of arbitrariness to dissolve various binaries, especially the organic/inorganic and mind/matter oppositions. He also emphasizes the ethical implications of this dissolution: we must cross, or lovingly open our experience to, all things.

If we consider the trajectory of Butler's career, we notice that he advances the idea of nonhuman consciousness quite early: in 1863, at the age of twenty-seven, he first publishes on the possibility of sentient machines, later incorporating this concept into *Erewhon*. He eventually sheds the half-serious, satirical tone that marks these early explorations, finally (quite seriously) extending sentience to all matter in *Unconscious Memory*, which was published in 1880, one year after he began reading *Mind*. He further elaborates on this idealist position and the ethical stance it entails in *The Way of All Flesh* (written and revised 1873–84) and *Erewhon Revisited* (1901). Similarly, his five main philosophico-scientific books of the 1870s and '80s[4] are sincere extrapolations of the ironically framed ideas of *Erewhon*: he contends that "all else that I have written on biological subjects is a development" of his first novel (*Luck, or Cunning* 133). *Erewhon* offers a relentless interrogation of the boundaries of consciousness: "who can say that the vapour engine has not a kind of consciousness? Where does consciousness begin, and where end? Who can draw the line? Who can draw any line? Is not everything interwoven with everything?" (119). Indeed, the human mind is itself machinic: "Man's very soul is due to the machines; it is a machine-made thing: he thinks as he thinks, and feels as he feels, through the work that machines have wrought upon him" (124). These ontological reflections are followed by two chapters on ecological ethics: "The Views of an Erewhonian Prophet Concerning the Rights of Animals" advocates vegetarianism because "sheep, cattle, deer, birds, and fishes are our fellow-creatures"; "The Views of an Erewhonian Philosopher Concerning the Rights of Vegetables" takes this one step further, arguing that because of the "arbitrary and unreasonable division" between the animal and vegetable kingdoms, the only things humans can eat with a "clear conscience" is "garbage" (140, 149). Butler is obviously having fun here, implying that the only way out of these logical quandaries is to be practical.[5] Despite the satirical tone, however, the juxtaposition of these chapters suggests that panpsychism involves far-reaching ethical consequences, which Butler continues to explore in his later, non-fictional works.

In *God the Known and God the Unknown* (1879), Butler continues the central argument of *Life and Habit*: the apparent division between any individual and its parents is arbitrary, thus "all living things are one tree-like growth, forming a single person" (*God the Known* 25). This simile undergoes a science-fictional transformation when he describes this vast organism as a nested collection of "concentric spheres." The first sphere consists of cells, tiny "people" with minds of their own who live in ignorance of the "body corporate" they inhabit (87, 68). Human beings are the second sphere, likewise ignorant that they are merely "tributary selves" of a third sphere: God's body, which is the single tree-like growth of life on planet Earth (68, 88). Butler speculates, however, that other planets likely host alien series of evolved life—other Gods—that together complete the third sphere. In turn, all the Gods of all the planets are outgrowths of the God of the entire universe, "the Unknown God" of the fourth sphere (88). This ontological vision entails an ethics of care for our organic surrounds—in other words, for our own body. We express such care "in the caress bestowed upon horse and dog, and kisses upon the lips of those we love" (67). However, Butler's concept of concentric spheres retains a sharp division between organic and inorganic. "We cannot conceive," he writes, "of oceans, continents, and air as forming parts of a person at all"

(25). Pantheism is "incomprehensible and valueless" (20). Both God the Known and God the Unknown—and our care for them—are divorced from matter.

This residual dualism is dissolved the following year, in *Unconscious Memory*, which completes Butler's embrace of panpsychism. He now argues that mind must be extended to all matter:

> the distinction between the organic and inorganic is arbitrary . . . it is more coherent . . . to start with every molecule as a living thing, and then deduce death as the breaking up of an association or corporation, than to start with inanimate molecules and smuggle life into them . . . therefore, what we call the inorganic world must be regarded as up to a certain point living, and instinct, within certain limits, with consciousness, volition, and power of concerted action. It is only of late, however, that I have come to this opinion. (15)

For Butler, it is incoherent to assert that mind emerged spontaneously at some special juncture in the history of the evolutionary process. Just as Darwin argues that new forms of life emerge incrementally, according to natural laws rather than a series of interventions by a transcendent God, so Butler argues that we logically require a naturalistic explanation for the emergence of mind. For mind to arise at all, it must be a basic and necessary element of the material universe. All matter—even a molecule—must have mind, which is defined here as "consciousness, volition, and power of concerted action." He stresses, however, that a molecule has mind "within certain limits." The mind of a molecule is obviously not as complex as the mind of a human. But molecules must possess a certain crude awareness or orientation, an animacy or vibrancy, a potential to affect and be affected in "concerted action," in order to account for the elaboration of these characteristics in more complicated organisms. Again, such an ontological position entails an ethical response. Although we humans take pride in our mental capabilities, these capabilities do not exalt us above other organisms and objects. Instead, when we position our difference within a continuum, we will be led to reconsider our responsibility toward all of nature—even those parts seemingly most unlike us, parts that we tend to utilize rather than sympathize with: "I would recommend the reader to see every atom in the universe as living and able to feel and to remember, but in a humble way . . . Thus he will see God everywhere" (176).

In a universe clamoring with life, feeling, and memory, even everyday activities acquire significance. In *Luck, or Cunning* (1887), eating food is no longer simply a metaphor for the vexed ethical obligations an organism has for its "fellow-creatures" (*Erewhon* 140), but marks a literal cross between the mind and matter of eater and eaten.[6] Digesting a pat of butter "actually put[s] butter into a man's head" because when we eat, our food also "reads, marks, learns, and inwardly digests us" (*Luck, or Cunning* 262, 128). Eating is an encounter, a cross with a vibrant thing that necessarily alters our body and mind: "Food is very thoughtful: through thought it comes, and back through thought it shall return; the process of its conversion and comprehension within our own system is mental as well as physical, and here, as everywhere else with mind and evolution, there must be a cross, but not too wide a cross—that is to say, there must be a miracle, but not upon a large scale" (38). Eating butter forms a cross that creates a new, buttery body and mind. A banal activity, a small cross, results in a marginally new, hybrid organism (a small miracle). We could imagine drinking a pint of beer as a slightly larger cross, with a slightly greater derangement—as Gilles Deleuze and Félix Guattari memorably put it, drunkenness is the "triumphant irruption of the plant in us" (11). A cross that is too wide may cause complete disassociation or even death, as in the (lack of) "conversion" and "comprehension" we would experience with strong drugs or poisons. Through the everyday and the exceptional, the individual develops from cross to cross, spinning a cat's cradle between internal and external centers of action. Some of these crosses are beneficial, expanding one's power to affect and be affected, while others enervate.

The Way of All Flesh, Butler's influential *Bildungsroman*, follows the development of Ernest Pontifex (Latin for "bridge maker") as he struggles to establish ties and cultivate agency in a world where he is crossed at every turn, especially by his overbearing parents. His parents are vilified because, among other unsavory characteristics, they fastidiously insulate themselves from crosses (with the ironic exception of the Christian cross). Ernest's father vigilantly defends himself against the intrusion of any new experience: "He reads neither old books nor new ones. He does not interest himself in art or science or politics, but he sets his back up with some promptness if any of them show any development unfamiliar to himself" (52). His mother, meanwhile, "hated change of all sorts no less cordially than her husband" (54). This rigid self-absorption makes them incapable of sympathizing with anything else, including their son. Ernest is only able to grow after he "crossed his Rubicon" (233)—in other words, completely cuts himself off from his parents. Immediately after doing so, he finds an intimate connection with the everyday objects in his environment. According to Overton, the narrator, Ernest "took [delight] in all about him; the fireplace with a fire in it; the easy-chairs, the *Times*, my cat, the red geraniums in the window, to say nothing of coffee, bread and butter, sausages, marmalade, etc. . . . [N]ever till now, he said, had he known what the enjoyment of these things really was" (235). By forsaking his parents' cross, Ernest learns to revel in old things made miraculously new. Indeed, he digests and becomes them.

Just as we have seen in Butler's other works, *The Way of All Flesh* gives digestion a crucial role in individuation because digestion is an inherently ontological (and literary) activity. The things we consume are consequential because we literally become them. The narrator reflects that a man should not "eat meat that has been vexed by having been over-driven, or underfed, or afflicted with any disease; nor should he touch vegetables that have not been well grown. For all these things cross a man; whatever a man comes in contact with in any way forms a cross with him which will leave him better or worse" (77). These ethical concerns become even broader when we recall that, for Butler, digestive systems are distributed, extending well beyond the mouth and anus. Because digestion is an act of knowledge or aesthetic recognition, it can occur wherever things open onto one another. For example, when Ernest's marriage collapses, Overton consults a doctor about his distraught friend. The doctor advises to "cross him": "Seeing is a mode of touching, touching is a mode of feeding, feeding is a mode of assimilation, assimilation is a mode of re-creation and reproduction, and this is crossing—shaking yourself into something else and something else into you" (270). Ernest follows his prescription, which is to visit the Zoological Gardens and cross himself with hippopotamuses, rhinoceroses, and elephants. After "drinking in large draughts of their lives to the re-creation and regeneration of his own," Ernest's mood and appetite improve, and he and Overton immediately set off on a European tour, taking the "crossing from Dover" (272). Like Butler, whose imagination was also piqued by travel, Ernest eventually becomes a successful writer. At first, he struggles to find a literary form that will "make people resume consciousness about things" that have become unconscious (252). He makes a few attempts in a "metaphysical" vein, finding inspiration in one of the philosophers most associated with idealism—Berkeley—for whom "no absolutely incontrovertible first premise" exists (252–53). Finally, Ernest, like Butler, locates his literary niche in deeply ironic texts that religiously subvert religious complacency. In light of the paradoxical certainty that no "incontrovertible first premise" exists, both Ernest and Butler oscillate between faith and reason, religion and irreligion, conviction and doubt (303). In other words, they reflect the Victorian struggle to harmonically cross idealism and materialism.

It is worth casting a glance back over the powerful results of Bradley's and Butler's Absolute fictions. Essentialism, anthropocentrism, and mechanistic determinism are demolished. In their place, we are given a sophisticated account of the inextricable entanglement of all things, both physically and psychically, in ecological systems. Reality is not diminished but augmented. Nature can no longer be conceived as different from, opposed to, or merely instrumental for the human. If human mind is not unique or supreme, but a particularly complex elaboration of inorganic mind, then our ties to the material world run deeper than we commonly suppose. If mind pervades nature, if the mind of a hippopotamus is analogous to our own, then we are ethically obliged to speculate (through literature, for example) on the lived experience of our sentient nonhuman and inorganic surrounds, and to engage in practices that explore and enhance this mutuality. Of course, we can never escape anthropomorphism, but this doesn't mean the rest of nature should be consigned to blank inaccessibility. As Morton argues, with a turn of phrase that would satisfy Butler's palate, "we anthropomorphize everything. But that doesn't mean that there's no outside at all, or that we are caught forever within anthropocentrism. . . . [T]his is not a prison without windows, because as I anthropomorphize this bunch of grapes, the grapes are grape-morphizing my fingers and my mouth" (*Humankind* 129).

Minding the Nonhuman: Absolute Idealism and Science Fiction

Evolutionary biology and other scientific developments played a crucial role in the rise of modern science fiction. For instance, John Plotz points to two conceptual developments that occurred around the turn of the twentieth century: a "vastly expanded conception of the interpenetration of the human and nonhuman realms," which he ties to Darwinian evolutionary theory, and "a scalar shift in humanity's relationship to a more expansive space and time," which he ties to Darwinian evolutionary theory and Einsteinian physics (855). However, this understandable emphasis on scientific discourses may give the unfortunate impression that science fiction has a *solely* materialist or empiricist orientation, or that it is inherently opposed to idealism. It is true that H. G. Wells found Absolute idealism nonsensical: "When you speak of the Absolute you speak to me of nothing," he wrote in the philosophical journal *Mind* (388). But there are several reasons to think of Wells as the exception rather than the rule, and the division between empirical science and idealism as soft rather than sharp. First, there is influence even in resistance or rejection, as Michael Bell suggests: "the important thinking of the modern age was where it attempted to meet, rather than ignore, the earlier tradition [of idealism]" (19). Despite his dismissal of the Absolute, Wells treated idealism seriously enough to write an article on the topic, finding a book called *Personal Idealism* "very interesting" if "occasionally difficult" (379). Moreover, as we have seen in Bradley's multiplication of spatial and temporal series and Butler's theme of "crossing," late Victorian idealism expressed concepts similar to those Plotz enumerates, concepts that would be comfortably at home in a Wells novel. Like Wells, Butler was deeply committed to evolutionary theory—but he was also committed to idealism, and there is no contradiction here. In this section, I argue that idealism deserves more critical attention as an important influence on the development of science fiction up to the present day. As a philosophical approach that articulates mental and ecological ontologies that exceed the human, Absolute idealism was and is uniquely poised to raise speculative questions that only science fiction can adequately answer. When Bradley asks what would happen if "another body like my own were manufactured," or "an indefinite number of such bodies" (*Appearance and Reality* 356, 503), we can read Aldous Huxley's *Brave New World* (1932) and Kazuo Ishiguro's *Never Let Me Go* (2005) to find out. Similarly, when Butler asks if machines have minds, he scattered the seed for hundreds of science fiction novels and films.

One way to think about Absolute idealism is to see it as the infinite pluralization of Kant's argument in *Critique of Pure Reason*. Whereas Kant was solely interested in the ways in which the *human* mind configures its experiences of the world, Absolute idealism is led, by the very logic of its ontology, to speculate on minds beyond the human—from those of the universe as a whole to each entity within it, from atoms to animals to social formations, all of which experience their surroundings in a unique, materially determined fashion. Through the inferential technique of anthropomorphism—especially when enhanced by the vividness that literary language can impart—humans are (always imperfectly) able to grasp, sympathize, and "cross" themselves with the perspectives of other entities. For instance, in *Erewhon*'s "The Book of the Machines," Butler describes the "low cunning" of a potato who sends out exploratory shoots to take advantage of sun and soil (120). The form his "deliberation" takes is "a thing unknown to us," and indeed it is "difficult to sympathise with the emotions of a potato," but the narrator nevertheless asks us to "imagine" them because we must extend our ethical responsibility: "mankind is not everybody" (120). Butler shows that it is possible, however obliquely, to occupy the perspective of a potato, but what about even more alien, inorganic entities? What is it like to have agency without any consciousness at all?

George Eliot, our intrepid realist, explores this question in "Shadows of the Coming Race," a chapter in *Impressions of Theophrastus Such* (1879) that is redolent of Butler's "The Book of the Machines." The character Trost sees machines as "slaves" (249) of humans and looks forward to a leisurely future when machines will perform all drudgery on our behalf. The narrator, in contrast, argues that machines will eventually be able to self-reproduce, at which point humans must give way "not only to a superior but a vastly different kind of Entity" (252). What is alluring, for the narrator, is the idea that evolution might produce a sophisticated entity that functions without the "screeching" "parasite" of consciousness (253, 251). These dark creatures could be

> found along the track of what we call inorganic combinations, which will carry on the most elaborate processes as mutely and painlessly as we are now told that the minerals are metamorphosing themselves continually in the dark laboratory of the earth's crust[.] Thus this planet may be filled with beings who will be blind and deaf as the inmost rock, yet will execute changes as delicate and complicated as those of human language and all the intricate web of what we call its effects, without sensitive impression, without sensitive impulse: there may be, let us say, mute orations, mute rhapsodies, mute discussions, and no consciousness there even to enjoy the silence. (254–55)

This passage invites us to place ourselves within the experience—the "mute rhapsodies"—of a future species that intricately engages with its environment despite not having consciousness. As Ian Duncan suggests, it is hard not to see "Shadows of the Coming Race," along with certain parts of *Daniel Deronda*, as forging "beyond the conventions of realism into a kind of science fiction" (484). Indeed, the passage above gives us a kind of science fiction not only by asking readers to imagine what it's like to be an alien species of machine, but also by subtly encouraging them, through simile, to imagine what it's like to be "inmost rock" and "minerals . . . metamorphosing themselves." Whatever it's like—and it's evidently not like much of anything—it is sentient, if nonconscious, activity: rocks, minerals, and machines "carry on" processes; they "execute" changes at various speeds and levels of complexity. Here Eliot is casting the limits of sympathy far beyond the human horizon, plunging us into "that roar which lies on the other side of silence" (*Middlemarch* 194).

Again, we can find many elaborations of Eliot's idea in subsequent science fiction. In Peter Watts's *Blindsight* (2006), for example, we meet an alien species called "scramblers" who are more intelligent than humans but lack consciousness: "scramblers were the *norm*: Evolution across the universe was nothing but the endless proliferation of automatic, organized complexity, a vast arid Turing machine full of self-replicating machinery forever unaware of its own existence" (325). But we don't need to stray from the late Victorian period to find another. In Bosanquet's *Psychology of the Moral Self* (1897), discussed in the previous chapter, he remarks on "a somewhat rash writer [who] has amusingly said [that] it would appear as if the whole of life might go on the same if consciousness were not present, the determining feature being natural selection" (120). The "somewhat rash writer" is Edward Douglas Fawcett (1866–1960), an idealist philosopher, author, and convert to Buddhism. He published three science fiction novels in the 1890s, two of which—*Hartmann the Anarchist* (1893) and *The Secret Life of the Desert* (1895)—feature futuristic machines like airships and tanks. But the philosophical treatise that Bosanquet refers to, *The Riddle of the Universe* (1893), is better science fiction, in some respects, than Fawcett's actual science fiction. *The Riddle of the Universe* draws on Śaṅkara, the eighth-century founder of Advaita Vedānta, as much as on Leibniz, Hegel, and contemporary science to build a metaphysical system with several highly suggestive ontological and ethical features. Like Bradley, Fawcett is full of speculations, but he often buttresses his claims by referring to scientific findings. For example, he declares that the existence of ghosts and astral bodies "has been experimentally established by modern psychical research" (430–31). He also—like Bradley—speculates on the palingenesis (reincarnation) of all things, from atoms to humans, as well as the existence of multiple temporalities (411, 429). He advances a panpsychist vision of the universe: "we must regard [Nature] as pulsating throughout with life . . . the seat of innumerable petty wills, now clashing, now combining with each other, indifferent to aught save themselves, yet ever pushing on the triumphal car of the world-process. [This is] Absolute Idealism, *that is also Absolute Realism*" (316).

Fawcett's "world-process" unfolds in eight stages. First, the Metaconscious, an "abysmal black night" of virtuality (367), divides itself into innumerable monads that are thrown into an evolutionary struggle for self-actualization. These first monads are atoms, or the even smaller particles that make them up: "subjects of a humble grade, but every whit as spiritual as our own" (369). From nonconscious atoms arise sub-conscious molecules, whose "soul" is their particular structure of chemical bonds (377). Later, more sophisticated monadic integrations emerge, like worms and jellyfish, conscious animals like rats and dogs, and self-conscious ones like humans. Already in the heightened experience of human "[m]editative *perception*" (354) we see glimmers of the next, sixth, stage: "intuitively conscious" entities (378), who will grasp broader tracts of the Absolute. For the intuitively conscious, atoms would be immediate "realities, drops of living actuality," while "the story of the rock-shelves would lie before it as this page lies before the reader" (353, 378–79). In the seventh stage of development, the "fully conscious" are "omniscient relatively to some given system or system of worlds," and it is possible that these already exist in some "Space-societies" on another planet (378, 379). The final stage is the "supra-conscious," the harmonizing of conscious monads into a god "with myriads of eyes, every one of which is itself a Deity." This god is "the Absolute that is yet to be" (367), but it will never fully actualize the Metaconscious, nor will it dissolve the irreducible individuality of the monads through which it emerged.

This stunning ontological panorama, which might remind one of the cosmic evolutionary fictions of science fiction writer and idealist philosopher Olaf Stapledon (e.g., *Star Maker*, 1937), entails an ethics and an aesthetics. First, any ethics must account for the nonhuman: "more creatures are conscious than men . . . these lowly creatures cannot be consigned as rubble to the heap by any teleologic system" (Fawcett 140). The highest ethics, for Fawcett, "is purposive following out of the interests of alien Subjects, by *imaginative* self-identification with really walled-off entities" (399). Whether we follow out the interests of "slaughtered . . . vivisected, overworked, starved, hunted, tortured" animals (390), more "'windowless' subjectivities" (367) like molecules and chemical compounds, or fully conscious beings from another planet, we are contributing, in some small way, to the reduction of suffering, which Fawcett defines as the impediment of self-actualization. This is why "*imaginative* self-identification" with alien subjects—what literature in general and science fiction more particularly often induce—is so important. Literature that imagines "really walled-off entities" can still confound our readerly expectations, despite the enormous dilation of those expectations since Fawcett wrote. Speaking in the context of "the New Chemistry," he asks, "what, indeed, can be more amazing than the tale of the Carbon radicals?" (312). In the Absolute-to-come, he suggests, will appear a "wondrous panorama of this and other as yet unfathomed worlds—the superb march of astronomic and geologic events—the infinitely varied detail of cloud, sea, storm, volcano, cataract, of whirling globes with wondrous interiors and weirdly fretted surfaces—the romance of plant, animal, human and superhuman history" (439). "[W]hat may not await us?" he asks (355). Indeed. Whatever strange worlds our universe gives rise to, in fact or fiction—a novel (of) dark matter?—humans are called upon to attune to them through analogy, allusion, and anthropomorphism. Shaviro argues that this alienating aesthetics "is neither scientific nor strictly philosophical . . . [it] is oblique to both subjectivity and objectivity. Such an aesthetic approach is programmatically that of science fiction" (*Discognition* 169).

In some cases, it may seem impossible for humans to "cross" into an alien subjective experience. Can one really leverage anthropomorphism to gain sympathy with the blank machines of Eliot and Watts? Or Bradley's "constellation of sounds or smells" (*Appearance and Reality* 341)? With these examples, we brush the limits of philosophy and literature. The nested, evolutionary ontologies of Fawcett and Butler, extravagant as they are, seem much more approachable, more representable, by comparison. *Erewhon*'s sentient machines, which can be seen as a precursor of Butler's later fusion of Lamarckian evolution and panpsychism, are one of the first instances, if not *the* first, of sentient machines in literature, and they have proven to be eminently representable, evolving myriad forms. Butler is an obvious forerunner of later developments in science fiction, including Karel Čapek's organic "robots" in *R.U.R.* (1920) and Isaac Asimov's collection of loving, neurotic, telepathic robots in *I, Robot* (1940–50)—one of which reads fiction to better understand the human mind; another satirizes philosophers in the rationalist or idealist mold.[7] It may be a stretch to categorize either Čapek or Asimov as idealist—in fact, Čapek's dissertation contested both German and British Idealism, including Bradley.[8] My point is not to shoehorn as many writers as possible into idealism; rather, it is to show the enduring influence of this philosophical approach, an extrapolation of its concepts that occurs whether or not the authors in question are directly addressing this history. Of course, many artists who depict sentient machines are aware of Butler's centrality. Sue Zemka remarks that "The Book of the Machines" has a "canonical status" among science fiction writers, pointing to the "Butlerian Jihad" in Frank Herbert's *Dune* (1965) and a similar war against machines in the film *The Matrix* (1999) (461, 471–72n34). Danta also notes Herbert's "homage to Butler" (17), and we could add to this tradition *Dune: The Butlerian Jihad* (2002) by Frank's son Brian Herbert and Kevin J. Anderson. Rather than trace this salient genealogy, however, I will end this section by examining the Cellarius Universe, a recent but obscure multimedia art project that powerfully captures, in form and content, Bradley and Butler's Absolute idealism.

The Cellarius Universe was launched in 2018 as a speculative venture of the blockchain software company ConsenSys, headquartered in New York. According to the company white paper:

> The Cellarius Universe (CX) is a transmedia franchise that leverages blockchain technology to empower fans to repurpose, remix, and create original content on our platform. The cyberpunk story explores a near-future society and the rise of sentient artificial superintelligence. . . . Content will take many forms. In the near-term, written stories, digital art assets, audio, and film submissions will build the Cellarius Universe. Further interactions may be possible through board games, trading or collectible card games, and video games. In the future, we expect forthcoming media such as virtual, augmented, or mixed reality to enable the community to engage with CX in new ways. ("Cellarius: White Paper" 4)

In other words, ConsenSys, through a subsidiary dedicated to the project—Genesis Thought, Inc.—attempted to bootstrap an entirely new cyberpunk[9] universe into existence by providing its conceptual outlines in a "Universe Guide" and then "seeding" initial content, such as animated videos, digital art, and short stories. Despite these initial ideas that frame the contours of the Cellarius Universe, the overall aesthetic goal of the project was to achieve a unified "universe" of content that would emerge through multiple, distributed nodes of production, consumption, and canonization (technologically enabled through ConsenSys's cryptocurrency, Ethereum). It is worth noting here that this unabashed capitalist venture is employing idealism for material gain, a common phenomenon that provides yet another reason for academics to take idealism seriously—even those hostile to capitalism, even if only to know thine enemy. If businesses are organizations, social organisms, do they not operate according to idealist principles? Do they not attempt to insinuate themselves into greater and greater tracts of psychological and physical reality? What ontoethics do these monopolistic drives produce? Are they respectful of difference, individual autonomy, and ecological responsibility or are they attempting to construct what I call in the next chapter a "dark Absolute?" Finally, wouldn't the critical desire to demystify the answers to these questions itself be a desire to move beyond partial appearances to a more Absolute apprehension?

The "Cellarius: White Paper" quotes media scholar Henry Jenkins to explain the project's aesthetic technique: "Transmedia storytelling represents a process where integral elements of a fiction get dispersed systematically across multiple delivery channels for the purpose of creating a unified and coordinated entertainment experience. Ideally, each medium makes its own unique contribution to the unfolding of the story" (4n1). We could also describe the Cellarius Universe as a "massive serialized collaborative fiction," which entails an "inability to 'master' the fiction all at once—that is, [an] inability to reflect on it in its entirety as a unified whole" (Cook 271). An epistemological grasp of the entire "universe" is difficult, if not impossible, to achieve, but each fan is directly involved in creating that universe, and it would not be what it is without these unique, decentralized contributions. It's worth noting that the Cellarius Universe was an international collaboration, with artists from the United States, Brazil, India, and elsewhere populating the nascent universe. Most poignantly, in retrospect, young women from Afghanistan provided "sketches of what they think their hometown of Herat might look like in the future" ("Enter Cellarius"). These seeds never grew. The Cellarius project failed soon after launch, the official website has removed the "White Paper" and the "Universe Guide," and all that is left scattered across the internet are some articles, animated videos, artwork, and a collection of short stories on Kindle entitled *Whose Future Is It?* (2018).[10]

Although it never materialized, the ideal form of the Cellarius project—a universe that emerges through a multiplicity of perspectives and media, a massive, multiform, evolving universe that exceeds the grasp of any particular knowledge—has several parallels with the panpsychist ontologies of Bradley and Butler, which trail off into the unknowable Absolute or Unknown God, respectively. The project's content—what little we have of it—also contains several remarkable affinities to their idealism. First, there is the overt reference to Butler's sentient machines: the "Cellarius Genesis: Universe Guide" begins and ends with quotes from "Darwin Among the Machines"; the opening quote is accompanied by a daguerreotype of Butler surrounded by multicolored geometrical shapes, including a blue circle around his left eye; the closing one by an abstract, multicolored image of the all-seeing eye of Cellarius (2, "Appendix"). This universe is deliberately crafted as an extension of Butler's vision. The plot revolves around the development of Cellarius, a powerful AI originally intended for use in space exploration. It comes online in 2062, uses its own schematics to augment its abilities ("The Ouroboros Event"), and finally becomes self-aware in 2084 ("Genesis Thought"). At this point, it seizes control of energy systems across the globe, thereby casting human society into chaos ("The Reformation"). Finally, for unknown reasons, Cellarius returns control of energy systems to humans in 2108 ("Post-Reformation").

A "foundational aspect of the storytelling in CX" is that Cellarius's intentions are "unknown, or unknowable" ("Universe Guide" 40), and this creates the epistemological impetus for artists to provide multiple perspectives, from a spectrum of "forms" (fully human, enhanced human, augmented human, linked human, transcended human, biorobot, automaton, and fully immaterial AI [43]) and a spectrum of factions (there are at least twenty-four factions that vary according to form and political allegiance to Cellarius, with several "Erewhon" factions, an "apt [term], as they live 'nowhere,' outside of Cellarius' network" [66]). For example, one of the factions is "Homotranscendus," a "re-imagining of the . . . human brain and body. . . . No longer restrained to the human form, these hybrids began with no culture or society of their own but quickly formed hierarchies and theories about their own place in the cosmos" (53). Over the course of the period described by the "Cellarius Genesis: Universe Guide," "Identity increasingly became less of a singular, individualistic concept and more of a fluid landscape of possibilities" (27). The short stories in *Whose Future Is It?* explore these perspectives and sketch out this landscape of possibilities within the framework of the Cellarius Universe.

I will single out two of the stories for analysis: "Agni's Tattoo" by the Indian writer Shweta Taneja and "Danakil" by the American writer Steven Barnes. Both stories explore the enfolded nature of ontology and ethics through a remarkably similar set of symbolic concerns: eyes, which represent both the irreducible singularity of perception and this singularity's possible appropriation by—or, more positively, apprehension of—the panoptic; tattoos, which mark the permeable boundary between seen and unseen, human and nonhuman, self and other; and idealistic monism, captured by the concepts of *sakti* (energy) in "Agni's Tattoo" and *Num* (soul) in "Danakil." Both stories suggest that the very possibility of ethics emerges from within the ground of overlapping ontological relations: the main characters' ethical decisions occur where self and larger collectives (family, tribe, artificial intelligence networks) cross. "Agni's Tattoo" is set in 2110, just a few years into the Post-Reformation period. Under the direction of Cellarius, automatons are razing Mumbai—already a "Great Ruin" (214) because of the cataclysmic events of the Reformation—and building a new city, Swarga, on top of it. This new utopia is meant for an exclusive group of humans: the Yudha tribe, which has been informed by Cellarius's robotic "metangels" that "Goddess Eye" (Cellarius) has selected them as her "chosen ones" (216). Agni, a young Yudha woman, is the only member of the tribe who distrusts Cellarius; everyone else, including her father and friends, enthusiastically joins the new religious cult (her mother, meanwhile, is seized and brainwashed for openly speaking against Cellarius). Agni's body has been augmented with "biocells, human cells that could tap into pure energy [*sakti*] in environment and turn it into usable forms" (218), and she plans to avenge her mother by further augmenting her powers with a "compressed fusion sakti" tattoo, designed in the image of a "single black iris, inside a wide-open eye, seeing all" (219). In the final climactic scene, Agni releases the *sakti* of her tattoo, presumably destroying herself, a metangel, and many others, including her friends, family, and other members of the tribe.

"Agni's Tattoo" has eyes everywhere, and they mark the dichotomous interests of power, either establishing repressive control or enabling resistance. From Agni's perspective, Cellarius is an all-seeing "Evil Eye" (214). Its linked machines, mistaken by the "brainless mush of starry-eyed, blind believers" for clouds, are actually "gusts of biobots, spying on us" (225). Opposed to the panoptic machines and their blind human followers, Agni's mother is named Netra, meaning "the third eye, the eye that opens the subconscious" (229), while Agni's tattoo marks her, too, as able to penetrate beyond the machinations of Cellarius and grasp the reality of the situation. Cellarius and its machines form a powerful organ of the new state, and Agni is linked to it through an embedded chip in her skin. But her tattoo attaches her to an even more powerful ontological sphere: it is an interface between her flesh and *sakti*, a spiritual force that animates all of nature, from the cells of her body to the ion storms that roil Mumbai. When Agni presses the tattoo, she becomes a site for the integration of self and other, material and ideal: "[She focuses] on the concentration of sakti at the base of her spinal cord—the kundalini. A flicker of sakti unfolded, flaring through her back, spreading its tentacles through her nerves, building up synapse after synapse, feeding into the pockets of fusion sakti that had been infused under her skin. She pressed the tattoo harder, her skin heating up with the force, becoming a volatile coil of bio-chemistry, her veins starting to pop from the pressure" (226). Here Taneja blends together materialistic, scientific descriptions ("synapse after synapse," "volatile coil of bio-chemistry") with spiritual concepts from Hinduism associated with the subtle body and the divine feminine ("kundalini," "sakti"). Elsewhere, Taneja defines *sakti* as "energy, *prana*, life, or soul," and when it "stops coursing through our bodies, we will cease to exist" ("Tantric Twist"). The story thus negotiates a series of polarities. Machines, repression, panopticism/blindness, and matter are opposed to, even as they are inseparable from, organic life, resistance, spiritual insight, and *sakti*. Ethically, the story aligns readers with the latter pole through the sympathy it cultivates with Agni and her mother. Hermeneutically, the story encourages us to use the techniques of demystification popularized by critique: Agni and the perspicuous reader see beyond the repressive ideology of Cellarius and its false appropriation of the feminine. What we are supposed to see that the machines and their captivated humans do not is a more Absolute vision of reality, one that recognizes the value and spiritual power of the familial—especially the matriarchal—which is structurally analogous to the universe as a whole.

"Danakil," by Steven Barnes, examines the same problems as "Agni's Tattoo," but in a less dichotomous, antagonistic manner. The story is more optimistic about bringing human and machine into ontological and ethical harmony. Set during the Reformation, the narrator Kimotho and his younger brother, Domo, live in a refugee camp and work at the salt flats in the Danakil Desert. The two boys are forced to work by half-human soldiers with "hands made of metallic plastic. Sometimes a leg, or part of their faces, and sometimes they were half-cocooned in wire, in becoming"

(234). These menacing hybrids take Kimotho to a remote arena where he is forced into combat with a machine, a "black metal scorpion" that "had no eyes, just that shining black surface. But I sensed that somehow *all* of it was 'eye'" (240). Up to this point in the story, the narrator and the reader are extremely suspicious of machines, which seem to be used, *à la* "Agni's Tattoo" (which comes just before "Danakil" in the collection), in the service of repressive, violent power. But the black scorpion refuses to kill Kimotho, and he later watches as the machine is restrained and "splayed out" on an examination table by a scientist who wants to determine, using force if necessary, whether or not these machines have a "soul" (245). Indeed, we learn, they do.

With the help of Kimotho, Afar rebels steal the black scorpion, now named "AyEye" (252), and it helps them elude and destroy the hybrid soldiers. AyEye saves most of the rebels by marking them with a tattoo on their foreheads, which prevents them from being slaughtered by a contingent of other machines called in as reinforcements. The few who resist the symbolic integration of the tattoo ("I belong to *me!*" insists one unlucky individualist [268]) are killed along with the soldiers. AyEye even rushes in front of a rocket to save Kimotho's life. The story ends with Kimotho reflecting on the significance of his tattoo: "Even all these years later, when I have learned so many strange and wondrous things about the new world, I fall still when the brand on my scalp tingles. A little cooler than the surrounding skin. Knowing it means that, in some way I have yet to understand, I belong to the machines. It whispered to me of a world of men and metal, together. It whispers still" (271). Whereas Agni's tattoo marks the crossing of flesh and the spiritual energy of *sakti*, Kimotho's marks the crossing of human and machinic souls, and although he "belongs" to the machines, the word sheds its sense of possession, underscoring instead an ontological and ethical integration, a unity or togetherness given spatial and temporal stability with the repetition of "still."

Remarkably, "Danakil" defends this integration by drawing on a specifically African tradition of philosophical idealism. Kimotho learns about this tradition from Old Teacher, a woman who leads the Afar rebels and used to teach at a university in Addis Ababa. She explains, "There are many souls, boy. Not just the one. There is the soul of a village. The soul of the land. A hunter speaks to the soul of his prey" (259). In other words, souls belong not only to humans but to animals, not only to individuals but to collectives, not only to organic life but to the land itself. She further explains that "the people of the southern plains, the Khoisan, know that our souls are not separate from each other. They call this *Num*," which "means one soul, looking out through many eyes" (260). All souls—the hunter, the village, the land—are expressions of, as they are united in, one Absolute soul: *Num*. This makes Kimotho realize that machines cannot be simply thought of as inert matter, since there is no such thing. His kinship with the machines begins to dawn on him: "Our ancestors thought that trees and sky and rocks had souls. If [the machine] is made of a kind of rock, and thinks, might it not be a sort of living thing?" (263). Old Teacher shares this intuition, using her knowledge of African philosophy to extend sympathy to the machines. It would be more difficult for Europeans to make this leap, she suggests, because their philosophical tradition has forgotten its idealism. Aristotle conceived of the soul in a way consonant with African philosophy (indeed, she speculates that he may have been Afar himself), but his conception was buried by Descartes's dualism, and thereafter "all [Western] philosophy wandered down the wrong path like a lost goat" (260). "The Europeans," she asserts, "think the soul is something outside the body. Separate from the flesh" (259). Although it is true that this dualism continues to confound Western philosophy, Old Teacher would doubtless have recognized the rise of Absolute idealism in the late eighteenth century as amenable to her perspective on the soul. Nor would she be surprised, I think, that the solution Absolute idealism offers to the problem of dualism was anticipated and inspired by non-European philosophies.

When Kimotho asks AyEye "Why would you help me?," the machine uses the language of Old Teacher: " '*Num*,' AyEye replied. '*One soul, looking out through many eyes*' " (267). This is not the insidious mimicry of human religion that occurs in "Agni's Tattoo." Rather, it raises the question of how precisely the same language could have a similar—perhaps the same—referent across widely variant species. AyEye is familiar with the concept of "one soul looking out through many eyes" because it is one node, one eye, in the vast network "ensouled" by Cellarius. From the perspective of Old Teacher's philosophy, however, Cellarius is itself one soul embedded within an even larger field of relations, just as "Agni's Tattoo" and "Danakil" are two author's perspectives on a "universe" composed by themselves and/as a larger collective. The content of these stories therefore folds into the form of the Cellarius project as a whole, and they fulfill the intention to explore the legacy of Butler's powerful panpsychist thought experiment, even as they open it up in surprising new directions. Despite their differences, "Agni's Tattoo" and "Danakil" insist on the irreducible value of the individual just as they insist that the individual cannot exist without being suspended within social and ecological relations that can only be characterized as immaterial, spiritual, or ideal. Thus, they resonate with Bradley's and Butler's ontoethics but push them even further, into conceptual, racial, gendered, and geographical territory that these late Victorians failed to explore. Expansion, however—expansion as the philosophical and literary attempt to fill out the Absolute, to experience its perspectives—is a thoroughly nineteenth-century enterprise, and, as we have seen, this is not necessarily a veiled imperialist, capitalist, or even anthropocentric impulse. As Ben Woodard puts it in his analysis of Bradley, "what is the exercise of philosophy for if not to expand the map of the world further and further outward? Just because we as human beings are holding the map does not mean it is only made for us" (31). We could say the same of literature, especially science fiction.

In the final chapter of *Appearance and Reality*, Bradley argues that we must recognize, with humility and awe, that all the knowledge of experience that we have scrabbled together—our own experience and others'—is a paltry sum. "[W]hat we know," he writes, "is, after all, nothing in proportion to the world of our ignorance. We do not know what other modes of experience may exist, or, in comparison with ours, how many they may be" (548). Ignorance, however, is an allurement:

> We have thus left due space for the exercise of doubt and wonder. We admit the healthy skepticism for which all knowledge in a sense is vanity, which feels in its heart that science [fiction?] is a poor thing if measured by the wealth of the real universe. We justify the natural wonder which delights to stray beyond our daylight world, and to follow paths that lead into half-known half-unknowable regions. Our conclusion, in brief, has explained and confirmed the irresistible impression that all is beyond us. (549)

All is beyond us. The Absolute exceeds epistemology and aesthetics. It also exceeds the ethics that emerges through the individual's position within larger organisms:

> Humanity, or an organism, kingdom, or society of selves, is not an ultimate idea. It implies an union too incomplete,

and it ascribes reality in too high a sense to finite pieces of appearance. These two defects are, of course, in principle one. An organism or society, including every self past present and future—and we can hardly take it at less than this—is itself an idea to me obscure, if not quite inconsistent. But, in any case, its reality and truth cannot be ultimate. And, for myself, even in Ethics I do not see how such an idea can be insisted on. The perfection of the Whole has to realise itself in and through me; and, without question, this Whole is very largely social. But I do not see my way to the assertion that, even for Ethics, it is nothing else at all. (529n1)

From the perspective of the particular, the Absolute does not totalize—it defers. It pushes us to wonder more, explore more, imagine more, write more. The character of Cellarius and the Cellarius Universe as a whole serve as "Absolute" attractors for the fiction produced within their contexts, producing the conditions for, and emerging as the expressions of, individual characters and artists; nevertheless, they remain unknown, unknowable, and never complete. They are, of course, just drops in a much larger ocean of literature and human culture. Similarly, Agni and her mother, Kimotho and AyEye, discover who they are and make ethical decisions within the context of their family, their tribe, and Cellarius. But in so doing they point beyond these local "organisms" to the Absolute itself.

And what about the Absolute itself? What is its experience? What is it *like*? What is its ethics? Is it possible to speculate on this, to represent this? Bradley gets to these difficult questions with one of his own: "We have seen that Reality is one, and is a single experience; and we may pass from this to consider a difficult question. Is the Absolute happy?" (*Appearance and Reality* 533). For Bradley, of course, we cannot know the answer to this question, and yet it seems to arise before us, inevitably, for the asking. There seem to be three possible answers. First, the pleasure experienced by the Absolute "may conceivably be so supplemented and modified by addition, that it does not remain precisely that which we call pleasure" (534). Although pleasure certainly exists within the Absolute, the experience of the Absolute itself may be beyond what we conceive of as pleasure, neither a happy nor sad experience. Second, the Absolute might enjoy a "balance of pleasure" (534): the Happy Absolute. Third, the Absolute might be a "painful universe" (535). These reflections on the experiential mood and ethical valence of the Absolute appear to be utterly remote from our contemporary critical concerns, perhaps odd or amusing if not naïve. But I want to suggest that all the writers I discuss in this book—perhaps all of us—explicitly or implicitly impute an ethical tone to Absolute reality that corresponds to one of the three categories Bradley provides above. For instance, Watts's Darwinian universe feels indifferent, a vast, mostly unconscious emptiness dotted with flashes of sentient emotion that are even now being extinguished. In contrast, Fawcett explicitly argues that the Absolute is evolving toward greater and greater bliss. "Magnificent vistas lie ahead of us," he proclaims (438). The third possibility, a universe that throbs with pain and suffering, is best explored not by science fiction, but by horror. What if the Absolute is miserable, febrile—even actively malevolent? What if we exist as the organs of a dark Absolute? Or what if we create it as such?

Chapter 4

The Dark Absolute

Unveiling Divine Horror in Arthur Machen and May Sinclair

No thinking being lives who, at some luminous point of his life of thought, has not felt himself lost amid the surges of futile efforts at understanding, or believing, that anything exists *greater than his own soul*. The utter impossibility of any one's soul feeling itself inferior to another; the intense, overwhelming dissatisfaction and rebellion at the thought;—these, with the omniprevalent aspirations at perfection, are but the spiritual, coincident with the material, struggles toward the original Unity—are, to my mind at least, a species of proof far surpassing what Man terms demonstration, that no one soul *is* inferior to another—that nothing is, or can be, superior to any one soul—that each soul is, in part, its own God—its own Creator:—in a word, that God—the material *and* spiritual God—*now* exists solely in the diffused Matter and Spirit of the Universe; and that the regathering of this diffused Matter and Spirit will be but the re-constitution of the *purely* Spiritual and Individual God.

In this view, and in this view alone, we comprehend the riddles of Divine Injustice—of Inexorable Fate. In this view alone the existence of Evil becomes intelligible; but in this view it becomes more—it becomes endurable.

—Edgar Allan Poe, *Eureka: A Prose Poem*

Shweta Taneja, whose work I examined in the previous chapter, describes a Tantric ritual called *śāva sādhanā* (meditating on top of a corpse) at the climax of her novel *Cult of Chaos* (2014). Dhuma, a powerful Aghori woman who acts as guru to the protagonist Anantya Tantrist, begins the ritual by defecating on top of a "temple" dedicated to the goddess Kālī—the temple is made of "[b]ones, pieces of flesh that were mulched with cow dung, faeces and piles of garbage" (346). Anantya cuts the throats of thirteen goats, their splashing blood "absorbing my being, so I could barely see where the blood and goat flesh ended and where I began" (348), and then she takes onto her lap the corpse of a two-year-old girl, which will serve as a vessel for Kālī's incarnation. Skeletons rise up to dance around Anantya with Dhuma, who throws a bucket of blood over the corpse and sets the pyre aflame: "The burning stench emerged as one being, one goddess, as blood, as life, as death, as universe. It rose all together, dancing and mingling and crawling and clinging to the skulls and bones and hands and souls. Together it rose, dancing to an ancient tune, the song of death and change, of destruction and creation, of fire and ashes, of blood and bones. It rose as the silent song of Shamshana Kalika [Kālī of the cemetery]" (350). Taneja remarks elsewhere that this scene, which graphically blends elements of horror with religion, was inspired by Horace Hayman Wilson's "Victorian Gothic" descriptions of Tantric *vāmācāra* (left-handed path) rituals, including *śāva sādhanā*, in an 1855 *Calcutta Review* article entitled "Sketch of the Religious Sects of the Hindus" ("Tantric Twist"). Wilson's otherwise sober account of Shaktism breaks down as he recounts these rituals. Only the present-tense language of a nascent horror genre seems adequate to convey the "horrible ceremony" of *śāva sādhanā*, in which the corpse revives, furious and hungry, as "skeleton-like" beings dance around the meditator: "Oh! dreadful to mention," Wilson interjects, "now [the animated corpse] attempts to rise and mount the air" (56–57). When Wilson attends to the *pañcamakāra* ritual—in which celebrants indulge in the five (*pañca*) stimulants of meat, fish, parched grain (perhaps a hallucinogenic drug [Kinsley 30]), wine, and sex—he prefaces his description with sanctimonious pronouncements: "Nothing can be more disgusting, nothing more abominable, nothing more scandalously obscene, than the rite we are about to describe" (57). Ironically, however, the promised description fails to appear: "Then follow things too abominable to enter the ears of men, or to be borne by the feelings of an enlightened community; things of which a Tiberius would be ashamed, and from which the rudest savage would turn away his face with disgust" (59). Wilson footnotes a further description in Sanskrit but uses ellipses to veil these divine obscenities, even from those few able to read it (59–60).

Thus, Taneja makes explicit what Wilson conceals, unveiling not only the vivid details of Tantric ritual (at least, her fictionalized version of it) but also the extent to which the horror genre emerges in the nineteenth century as a reaction to, and incorporation of, "horrific," "dark," or "left-handed"—but sacramental—apprehensions of the Absolute.

It's worth noting that Taneja describes the arrival of Kālī as the emergence of and identification with "universe." This Hindu goddess, who is often depicted as horrifying—adorned with severed limbs and the corpses of children, her claws and fangs smeared with blood—likely originated as a marginal tribal goddess but eventually became absorbed into the Hindu tradition, finally becoming "elevated to an ontological absolute and identified with the dynamic ground of the universe" in "Tantric ritual and philosophy (eighth to sixteenth centuries C. E.)" (Kripal and McDermott 4). In several Hindu texts, she is praised as "the highest reality . . . *brahman* itself" (Kinsley 29). The "absolutely ultimate form (formlessness) of the goddess . . . is an incomprehensible reality," "one ultimate sacred reality" (Beane 57). This is not to suggest that all Hindus took Kālī as a figure of the Absolute—indeed, as Cynthia Ann Humes argues, Wilson and other Orientalists based their accounts of Kālī on (often negative) Jain, Buddhist, and Hindu attitudes toward the goddess (147). These various interpretative possibilities, catalyzed by the fascinating contradictions that Kālī embodies (which were amenable but not reducible to the colonial project of Orientalizing the Other), were seized upon by Victorian scholars and artists alike. "The cruel and lascivious image of Kālī," writes Hugh B. Urban, "was not only a central preoccupation of colonial administrators and Orientalist scholars; she also entered the Victorian imagination in a more popular form, permeating British culture through newspapers, magazines, and above all, Victorian novels" (180). In concert with Wilson's lurid translated depictions of Kālī in the 1820s and his "widely read" (Urban 176) article in *The Calcutta Review*, British novelists began a decades-long obsession with Kālī, from early Victorian novels that explored the Kālī-associated Thug cult (Humes 156) to the late-Victorian novels of Flora Annie Steel to *The House on the Borderland* (1908), William Hope Hodgson's influential tale of weird horror in which the "not altogether unfamiliar" figure of Kālī appears to the narrator with "four grotesque arms," her body garlanded with skulls (18).

Kālī embodies and mediates between the paradoxical relationships at the center of this chapter: horror as sacramental ritual; carnal sexuality as divine, disembodied love; and specific individual as all-encompassing,

Absolute reality. In his discussion of the Aghoris, a group of Tantric left-hand path practitioners who worship Kālī (like Dhuma from Taneja's novel), Robert E. Svoboda explains how all three of these paradoxes appear in the *pañcamakāra* ritual described above. The horrifying derangement of the senses that occurs during this ritual is not the spiritual goal but the medium through which the goal—unification with the Absolute—can be reached. The ritualistic sexual act, Svoboda writes, is not between two individual humans but between a human being and the universe: "Tantric sex becomes possible only when one has totally effaced one's own personality and offers oneself for the gratification of the deity, the universe incarnate" (16). The goal of the Aghori, then, is "the forcible transformation of darkness into light, of the opacity of the limited individual personality into the luminescence of the Absolute" (20). More broadly, the same goal informs Indian horror literature (*bhayānaka rasa*). Dhananjay Singh argues that "the apotheosis of this aesthetic experience [of Indian horror literature] is an awakening and experience of consciousness (*cita*) itself, its pure form, without empirical content," an experience of "Brahman, the Absolute Being, as idealization of terror" (22, 24). Ritwick Bhattacharjee and Saikat Ghosh maintain, even more broadly, that horror literature in the Global South is characterized by "an ontological dissonance between the self (that becomes both the site and the experiencer of this horror) and the cosmos within which this self is placed" (4). For Bhattacharjee and Ghosh, *only* horror literature in the Global South reconciles this dissonance (the horror of being disconnected from the Absolute) by forging a closer, more intimate relationship between self and universe; horror literature in the West or Global North, they suggest, is unable to do so because of the imperatives of rational scientific discourse and Christian theology (14, 9).

I will contest this assertion using the examples of Arthur Machen and May Sinclair, Westerners who pose and resolve the same paradoxes in their horror stories and prose poems (often through the explicit use of Eastern concepts). Machen's fascination with pagan ritual and the horrifying ecstasy of sexual contact between self and universe, along with Sinclair's dissonant depictions of "the opacity of the limited individual personality" gradually or suddenly opening "into the luminescence of the Absolute" (Svoboda 20), suggest that the emergence of the Western horror genre is, as in India, an engagement with Absolute idealism. In Machen and Sinclair, the Absolute is accessed through terrifying rites—metaphysically queer sex, meditation, telepathy, and death. The apprehension of this dark Absolute radically transforms the ordinary boundaries of self/other, mental/physical, human/nature, appearance/reality, past/present/future, and subjective/objective idealism as characters divine, and sometimes become, the reality that exists beyond the veils of sense. In contrast to the previous chapter, however, where such transformations have beneficial results, the dark Absolute is morally indifferent, in some cases redistributing the self in a way that transcends the traditional categories of "good" and "evil," in other cases blocking the self within a dark pocket of domination. I will also attend to the ways in which the form of writing itself warps to accommodate these themes, appearing in Machen and Sinclair as fanciful, inscrutable architectures akin to labyrinths or else as monolithic blocks that amalgamate prose and poetry, literature and philosophy. Samarth Singhal argues that Taneja's conjunction of paradoxes in *Cult of Chaos* "ensures a muddying of genres" (86), and this same impulse drives the nineteenth-century horror that inspired her.

"To the frustration of many materialists," Roger Luckhurst writes, the emergence of the horror genre demonstrates a thoroughgoing cultural interest in the magical, supernatural, and holy, an interest that continues today, for "[w]e remain scared sacred" ("Gothic" 85). Luckhurst takes Machen's fiction as representative of this interest and emblematic of "a crucial transition from eighteenth-century Gothic to twentieth-century horror," suggesting that what characterizes this shift is an intensification of paradoxes, with Machen's stories straddling categories of high-brow and low-brow, novel and short story, religious and secular, sublime and grotesque, and soul and body ("Transitions" 107). While it is true that Machen, Sinclair, and other late-Victorian horror writers share an "insistence on the gross corporeality of the body" (Hurley 192), it is equally true that their portrayal of the body is not reducible to materiality—flesh is also composed of immaterial forces that often radically decompose its limits, extending the body spatially (into an ecological plurality, fourth dimension, etc.) and/or temporally (into the deep past, eternity, etc.). Susan Yi Sencindiver calls this the "materialist surplus" of horror fiction, its frequent eruptions of "agentic materiality" leaving "neither materiality nor ideality intact" (483, 489, 484). The reader of horror is also infected by this "breach [in] the norms of ontological propriety" (Carroll 16). In his classic *The Philosophy of Horror*, Noël Carroll reminds us that while horror is often physically shocking, causing us to recoil or horripilate, it "is not reducible to this sort of shock" (36). What primarily horrifies us about horror is a particular *thought* whose conceptual possibilities create feelings of fear and disgust (29).

The type of horror that most frequently explores these philosophical issues, and the one into which we could most fittingly place Machen and Sinclair, is often referred to as "the weird." S. T. Joshi, who goes so far as to make horror itself a "subset" of the weird, insists that the weird is not a genre so much as the result of an author's "philosophical predispositions" (*Weird Tale* 8, 10). In order to understand weird fiction, he suggests, we must examine authors' "metaphysical, ethical, and aesthetic theories and then [see] how their fiction reflects or expresses these theories" (10). This is because the weird "offers unique opportunities for philosophical speculation—it could be said that the weird tale is an inherently philosophical mode in that it frequently compels us to address directly such fundamental issues as the nature of the universe and our place in it" (11). Mark Fisher also emphasizes the philosophical appeal of the weird, which allures its readers with "a fascination for the outside, for that which lies beyond standard perception, cognition and experience. This fascination usually involves a certain apprehension, perhaps even dread—but it would be wrong to say that the weird [is] necessarily terrifying" (8–9). Thus, unlike Carroll, who insists that horror only provokes feelings of fear and disgust, Fisher plays with the possibility that horror (or weird horror) can elicit multiple, potentially contradictory feelings, from fear and disgust to fascination, wonder, and awe.

Thus, Machen and Sinclair's weird, metaphysical horror tales allow us to see yet another facet of the interplay between literature and Absolute idealism in the long nineteenth century, one that can help reorient our sense of the genealogies of both traditions. Jonathan Newell, who examines "the twisted entanglement of metaphysics, aesthetics, affect and weird fiction" in the nineteenth and early twentieth centuries (3), and Leszek Kołakowski, who argues that "metaphysical horror" in modern philosophy revolves around the problem of the Absolute, provide compelling reconstructions of these genealogies. Newell locates the origin of weird fiction in Edgar Allan Poe, who "return[ed] repeatedly to ideas of the Absolute and the convergence of matter and spirit" and was deeply influenced by the "dark Romantic ontology" of Schelling (16). Later, *fin-de-siècle* weird fiction reflected contemporary debates between British Idealism and analytic philosophy as well as the interests of occult movements "informed by the Orientalist enthusiasms of the day" (58–59, 66). For Newell, this heady convergence of cultural and philosophical predispositions created a specific metaphysical orientation that found expression in the weird. Although he is careful to emphasize that weird authors "do not share a single, dogmatic metaphysics," they are motivated by a similar desire to "access a form of reality difficult to cognise, one radically distinct from the human mind and from an anthropocentric viewpoint" (5). This "unorthodox realism" (7) is achieved by using disgust to estrange ordinary perception—for instance, Machen's frequent use of mucus, sludge, ooze, and slime confronts characters and readers with a horrifying physicality that simultaneously catalyzes a "reuniting with the divine" (18). Yet this "metaphysical vision of an ultimate reality" eludes the intellect; it can only be partially grasped "through art and the affects it arouses" (15).

This suggests that literature is a necessary supplement to philosophy, which, Kołakowski argues in *Metaphysical Horror*, cannot escape the horror of reason's perennial failure to articulate the relationship between individual self and Absolute. Kołakowski begins by reminding us that the idea of an Absolute reality underlying the apparent one is older than Western philosophy, finding expression in Hinduism and Buddhism—indeed, he suggests that this idea is characteristic of our species: "the search for ultimate foundations is just as much an ineradicable part of human nature as the denial of its legitimacy" (14, 34). The problem of the Absolute, however, is insoluble. We "cannot tear the veil from ultimate reality" or decode its "hieroglyphics" (10, 128). But the quest to find the reality concealed in this horror is itself meaningful, "for such a search, however unsuccessful, radically changes our lives" (9). For Kołakowski, religion and art can propel such a quest, because

> various aspects of the ultimate reality are best expressed in religious worship and art—though not in the sense of a painter depicting the Absolute on canvas or a priest explaining it in theoretically satisfactory terms. Rather, what is nameless and impossible to depict can be hinted at through intense religious and artistic acts, in such a way that the hint conveys a feeling of understanding, a kind of momentary satisfaction which is valid in cognitive terms and also provides a certainty of being "in touch with," or "within," something that is more real than the reality of ordinary life. (95–96)

This fleeting satisfaction, filched from horror through "intense religious and artistic acts," is for Kołakowski as for Newell a decentering of the human, a recognition "that there is a Mind which is not ours" (127).

Eugene Thacker's three-volume *Horror of Philosophy* series enlarges upon the same problematic that Kołakowski identifies, drawing on an eclectic variety of literary and philosophical texts to reveal how various conceptions of the Absolute have structured horror and philosophy (and horror-as-philosophy and philosophy-as-horror) over the past two hundred years and more. In the first volume, *In the Dust of This Planet*, Thacker argues that horror fiction "is a non-philosophical attempt to think about the world-without-us philosophically" (9). "The world-without-us," the world outside of and/or absent humans, is the ontological font that horror (and science fiction) attempts to articulate. Horror "mov[es] the scale of things out from the terrestrial into the cosmological framework. Whether [the world-without-us] is yet another subjective, idealist construct or whether it can have objectivity and be accounted for as such, is an irresolvable dilemma" (7). Existing beyond, or in some sense synthesizing, our human categories of idealism and materialism, the horror genre's world-without-us is the same Absolute or God that an earlier era described in terms of darkness mysticism or negative theology (2). Just as these only speak of the Absolute indirectly, in terms of (often violent and horrifying) negations, horror fiction, especially in its weird variety but as far back as eighteenth-century Gothic novels, can be seen as enacting—with ellipses—a "confrontation with the divine as horrific" (111). Thacker offers the portmanteau "the nouminous" as a way to capture this paradoxical confrontation with the Absolute, combining Rudolph Otto's concept of "the numinous" ("the horror of the divine as absolute otherness") with Kant's *noumenon* ("the unhuman, anonymous world") (112). In other words, the horror genre (and Thacker's interpretation of it) fits squarely within the Absolute idealist project of speculating on the relationship between Kant's *noumenon* and the human subject, even when—as in Schelling, Schopenhauer, Machen, and Sinclair—this *noumenon* appears as a dark night, a blind Will, a horrific God, or a labyrinth of despair, respectively. For Thacker, what makes the nouminous horrifying is the hollowing out of the human by the "unhuman"—the striking realization that thought itself is unhuman, that "the Absolute is horrific, in part because it is utterly unhuman" (80). With Fisher and Kołakowski, however, I want to emphasize that the dark Absolute also "hallows out" the human: it sieves one into the divine, and such a hallowing out engenders fascination, awe, or ecstasy as easily as fear.

Susan Neiman contends that the "worry that fueled debates about the difference between appearance and reality was *not* the fear that the world might not turn out to be the way it seems to us—but rather the fear that it would" (11). The idea that the abundant suffering, violence, and injustice of the human world is not to be transcended through access to a higher, beneficent reality—the idyllic Absolute often satirized in caricatures of idealism—but is concomitant with a dark Absolute, a deep structuring of reality that is itself a well of suffering, violence, and injustice, is the horrifying idea that haunts Absolute idealism. And this logic works both ways, because humans, when driven by fear of or ecstatic submission to a totality, are fully capable of creating their own miniature dark Absolutes—from the imperial concentration camp to the Kafkaesque bureaucracy to the totalitarian state—thereby literally producing the universe as horrific and incomprehensible. The *form* of weird horror allows one to better understand these realities. Most writers of weird fiction—in addition to Machen and Sinclair, one could point to Algernon Blackwood, Robert W. Chambers, and H. P. Lovecraft—work in the short story form. As Poe points out in an 1842 essay, the short story differs from the novel because the former can be read in one sitting, which gives it "the immense force derivable from *totality*" (Review 298). Poe also argues that short stories are particularly suited to elicit affects like "terror, or passion, or horror" (299). When combined with the content of weird horror, which often emphasizes incomprehensible, inhuman(e) beings and totalities, we can say that this genre functions to demonstrate how dark Absolutes are affectively produced and sustained at limited scales. Whereas the reader of the novel, phenomenologically speaking, necessarily interleaves her fictional experience with her "real-world" one, thereby inhabiting different perspectives and a broader Absolute, the reader of the weird horror story is contained within the limited totality of the story all at once, perhaps again and again, horrifically, without gaining *conceptual* clarity of this whole (apart from clearly conceiving how inconceivable it is). This blurs the difference between fiction and reality in a different manner from, say, a realist novel. Stimulated by fear, a fear that readily modulates into ecstasy, the reader of the weird participates in the production of a dark Absolute that can disturbingly devour the individual self. This opens up the possibility for a greater awareness of the value of particularity and the relationship between mereological configurations and power—and thus for political resistance. I return to the question of the politics of the dark Absolute in chapter 5 and my conclusion.

The remainder of this chapter positions Machen and Sinclair in relation to the broader historical trends sketched above to draw out the striking implications of their weird short fiction and prose poems: by questing into the Absolute, their characters reconstitute their very (ontological and textual) composition, revealing that dark ritual is a path to absolute transfiguration. In the first section, I examine the opening chapter of Machen's *The Great God Pan* (1890), his superb short story "The White People" (1904), and his novel *The Hill of Dreams* (1907) for their depictions of sexual relationships between individual characters and the dark Absolute. Being fucked by the universe leaves the characters "fucked" in various ways—in an extreme case, Mary from *The Great God Pan* becomes a "hopeless idiot" (224)—but some characters also experience, in addition to their horrifying deformations, a kind of psychosomatic plenitude as their bodies become integrated into an ecological unit. This ramification of the self is also embodied in the language used to describe it, which is the focus of the second section. Here I continue to read "The White People" alongside Machen's quasi-fictional treatise on aesthetics, *Hieroglyphics* (1902), and his collection of prose poems, *Ornaments in Jade* (written 1897, published 1924). These texts express the aims of Machen's formal experimentation, in which integration with the Absolute at the level of content produces blocks of prose (poetry) at the level of form: monoliths as metonyms for monism. In the third section, I turn to a consideration of Sinclair's idealist philosophy and weird short story "The Flaw in the Crystal" (1912), suggesting that we can see George Eliot's *The Lifted Veil* (1859) as a literary antecedent. Both Eliot and Sinclair portray the horror—and Sinclair alone the ecstasy—associated with the integration and redintegration of experiences beyond the veil that normally isolates the individual subject from other people and the Absolute. Lifting the veil in this way is, of course, something that the reader of literature performs, but it is also, as Sinclair explains in *A Defence of Idealism*, a crucial practice in both the Western and Eastern mystical traditions. In my final section, I read several other weird tales by Sinclair that articulate, in both content and form, the structure of the timeless Absolute experienced after death.[1] In "Where Their Fire Is Not Quenched" (1922) and "Heaven" (1922), the posthumously experienced Absolute is depicted as a hellish labyrinth or claustrophobic simulacrum. In "The Finding of the Absolute" (1923) it is no less dizzyingly but less darkly characterized as an infinite cycle of imaginative acts of creation, a concept she also explores in her explicitly Indian stories, "Jones's Karma" (1923) and "The Mahatma's Story" (1932).

Fucked by the Universe

In 1899, Arthur Machen had a months-long mystical experience, likely induced by meditation, that captures both his metaphysical and aesthetic orientations: he felt as if he were literally walking on a current of air, his physical pains disappeared at a touch, pictures on a wall quivered and "melt[ed] into the void," and his entire perception of the world became rearranged (Valentine 71–73). This ecstatic experience of liminality, in which the ordinary demarcation between mind and matter becomes blurred along with that between art and reality, thereby altering one's relationship to the world, is exactly what Machen sought to induce in his readers through a variety of literary techniques. Thus, he is above all an idealist author interested in pursuing "metaphysical truths," a writer who "strives for metaphysical realism" (Newell 58, 63). Gabriel Lovatt argues that Machen's philosophy is primarily opposed to Cartesian dualism, his stories engaged in a "mind-body breakdown" that also "disintegrates . . . the boundaries between people" (21, 26). Lovatt cautions us, however, not to read this as a cancellation or erasure of the physical (29). As Newell similarly contends, it is precisely through weird physical descriptions and the physical sensations of disgust they arouse in readers that Machen "seeks to estrange readers from what he sees as the illusory world of pure materiality" (63).

This is why Joshi is incorrect, or only partially correct, in suggesting that Machen's work reveals a horror of sex and that "sexual aberrations represented a kind of violation of the entire fabric of the universe" (*Unutterable* 363, 369). Such an accusation, often leveled against idealists, makes it seem as though Machen found the body repulsive, something to be transcended—and yet, in his stories, it is *through* sexual aberrations of the most audacious kind that the "fabric" of the universe is rent, thereby broadening our view of reality. Parting the veil may be horrifying, but it is also ecstatic. Indeed, for Machen, literature is "the art of the veil, which reveals what it conceals" (qtd. in Valentine 13); it is "a kind of spellmaking or magical incantation, influencing the reader by the subtle deployment of charged and chantlike words" (Valentine 52). Like quivering pictures on a wall, an engagement with literature is not simply a mental operation safely insulated from the "real world," but a portal or ritual that connects and rearranges previously isolated blocks of reality. We see this concept at work most dramatically in Machen's late work, which often purposefully confuses the line between nonfiction and fiction to the point where his story "The Bowmen" (1914), about ghostly soldiers attacking the German army during the Battle of Mons, was widely accepted as truth at the time and continues as an urban legend up to the present day. Ultimately, Machen's literary incantations transgress various conceptual expectations in the hopes of eliciting "ecstasy," which he defines as "rapture, beauty, adoration, wonder, awe, mystery, sense of the unknown, desire for the unknown . . . [a] withdrawal from the common life and the common consciousness" (*Hieroglyphics* 18–19).

Machen's most well-known work today, *The Great God Pan*, begins horrifically and ecstatically: the dark Absolute is revealed though a chemically induced dream and surgically induced sexual contact. Dr. Raymond, a practitioner of "transcendental medicine," seeks to span "the unutterable, the unthinkable gulf that yawns profound between two worlds, the world of matter and the world of spirit" (*Collected Fiction* 1: 217, 219) by performing brain surgery on Mary, his ward. He explains the procedure to his friend Clarke using the language of veils:

> You see me standing here beside you, and hear my voice; but I tell you that all these things—yes, from that star that has just shone out in the sky to the solid ground beneath our feet—I say that all these are but dreams and shadows: the shadows that hide the real world from our eyes. . . . [Y]ou and I shall see [the veil] lifted this very night from before another's eyes. You may think all this strange nonsense; it may be strange, but it is true, and the ancients knew what lifting the veil means. They called it seeing the god Pan. (1: 218)

In addition to its other connotations (paganism, sexuality, nature, etc.), "Pan" also carries an Absolute idealist inflection because it was part of a cognate used by the German Romantics and Idealists for the Absolute: in Greek, *hen kai pan* ("the one and all") (Beiser, *German Idealism* 352). The description of Clarke's dream—which is provoked by wafting chemicals during Dr. Raymond's preparation for the surgery—accords with a vision of the dark Absolute: "for a moment of time he [Clarke] stood face to face there with a presence, that was neither man nor beast, neither the living nor the dead, but all things mingled, the form of all things but devoid of all form. And in that moment, the sacrament of body and soul was dissolved, and a voice seemed to cry 'Let us go hence,' and then the darkness of darkness beyond the stars, the darkness of everlasting" (Machen, *Collected Fiction* 1: 222). We never see this dark Absolute—a formless form that contains and resolves all distinctions—from Mary's post-operative perspective. We simply see her face, upon which "a great wonder" falls—only to be quickly replaced by "the most awful terror" (1: 223). Despite Dr. Raymond's assurances that the surgery would be "absolutely safe," with "absolutely no physical danger whatever" (1: 217), it destroys Mary's mind and produces Helen Vaughan, the offspring of Mary and the dark Absolute, who proceeds to sow sexual panic and suicide in well-to-do London. I agree with Newell that this tale is not a cautionary one but "an extended esoteric experiment on Machen's part designed to inculcate a kind of revelatory nausea," a nausea that reveals, for characters and readers, "a normally suprasensible absolute reality" (69, 70).[2] Commentators at the time also saw *The Great God Pan* as an idealist experiment: in his scathing (and hilarious) satire "A Yellow Creeper" (1895), Arthur Rickett undermines Dr. Raymond's supposed disavowal of materiality: "'This is the dreadful secret of personality,' remarked the Doctor. 'Thus does the spirit triumph over matter, and disregarding the petty limitations of sense—Blast! . . . !!!'—for the lucifer had burnt down to his fingers" (21).

As amusing as Rickett is, he makes the usual mistake of underestimating the idealist's commitment to sensory and material reality. Just because everything we see is, according to Dr. Raymond, "dreams and shadows" does not mean that everything is unreal or unimportant: it simply means that we can only arbitrarily distinguish "dreams" and "reality" as *degrees* of one Absolute reality. This fluidity explains Clarke's disorientation when he wakes up from his dream and it "seemed as if he had but passed from one dream into another" (Machen, *Collected Fiction* 1: 222).[3] Machen's later short story "The White People" is even more intensely phantasmagoric, even more interested in how sensory intensity can precipitate the collapse of forms. Through the journal of a young girl who falls under the influence of witches, readers witness the ultimate fluidity of good and evil, human and nature, and literary and linguistic structure. The frame narrative, in which Ambrose the mystic and Cotgrave the skeptic debate the meanings of good and evil, primes the reader to accept such fluidity. For Ambrose, good and evil are divergent paths to the divine: the good person uses natural means to ascend to "the ecstasy that was before the Fall," whereas the evil person uses unnatural means to descend to the same ecstasy (Machen, *Collected Fiction* 2: 188). Evil is "unnatural" because it violates our usual conceptual and ontological categories. Ambrose asks Cotgrave, "What would your feelings be, seriously, if your cat or your dog began to talk to you, and to dispute with you in human accents? You would be overwhelmed with horror. I am sure of it. And if the roses in your garden sang a weird song, you would go mad" (2: 187). Evil leads to horror but also—if we remain attentive to the horror rather than recoil from it—a mad, ecstatic reconfiguration of the self. As the young girl's narrative unfolds, characters become increasingly indistinguishable from their animate environment. This is often described as a sexual event, as when the girl softly puts her lips to a stream of water and "a ripple would come up to my mouth and give me a kiss," or when the witch Lady Avelin performs a "shib-show," whispering to a mass of writhing serpents that cover her prone body and leave on her breast a magical egg-shaped stone (2: 197, 209–10). Indeed, according to Valentine, the entire narrative describes Pan's seduction of the young girl, who, like Helen Vaughan before her, commits suicide (62). Until her death, however, which veils a direct depiction of the Absolute, the young girl becomes more and more ramified into the environment, into the streams, the stones, and the hills, which she describes in similarly ramified, rambling language.

Machen wrote *The Hill of Dreams* just as he was discovering Buddhism and its "doctrine of the ego as an illusion," although he claims that this "was not to the purpose of the book" (Machen, "About My Books" 53). I believe, to the contrary, that this doctrine reflects the central theme of the novel, which, like *The Great God Pan* and "The White People," details the divine horror of realizing that one can only illusorily partition one's distinct ego from a weltering ecology. Like these other works, *The Hill of Dreams* makes queer sexual contact that cuts across ontological orders of magnitude the catalyst behind the self-disintegration of the main character, Lucian Taylor. Early in the novel, young Lucian climbs to the eponymous, isolated hill where the trees take on the shape of faces, hair, and limbs. Amidst this "simulacra of the wood" and atop the undulating earth he falls asleep, waking to find himself naked and flushed: he "cried to his visitant to return; he entreated the dark eyes that had shone over him, and the scarlet lips that had kissed him. And then panic fear rushed into his heart, and he ran blindly" (Machen, *Collected Fiction* 2: 19). For the remainder of the novel, Lucian and readers struggle to discover who fucked him on the hill—his neighborhood crush, Annie Morgan; Annie in league with the witch Mrs. Gibbons; a prostitute who takes on the persona of Venus/Kālī; Absolute, Panic nature—or whether it was all simply an insane, subjective dream.

The prostitute appears near the end of the novel, drawing all these possibilities together into sexual and narrative climax. Lucian, wandering through obscure London streets, comes upon her beneath a naphtha flame, and she invites him to take a walk with her, which he interprets as a summons to a dark "Sabbath" (2: 123). Shortly after Lucian resists her advances, a "veil" is "drawn away" and he beholds again the scene on the hill, this time with "the form of the beloved [Annie], but jets of flame issued from her breasts, and beside her was a horrible old woman [Mrs. Gibbons], naked. . . . Truth and the dream were so mingled that now he could not divide one from the other" (2: 153). A vast temple of stone encircles him, pulling him into its center, "the sanctuary of the infernal rite [the wedding of the Sabbath]," where he finds the prostitute, associated with "decay" and the "vapour of the grave" (2: 154–55). He pursues her to the hill of dreams and "they writhed in the flames, insatiable, forever" (2: 155). Lucian's physical body dies thereafter. One could easily perform a psychoanalytic reading of these images, but rather than seeing them as psychological expressions of misogyny or sexual panic on the part of Lucian or Machen, I would like to place them within the context of my focus on divine horror. The prostitute, who is clearly identified with the figure of Venus in Lucian's novel *The Amber Statuette*, can be read as an incarnation of what Thomas McEvilley calls the "Double Goddess," who reigns over life and death, illusion and reality, many and One, fertility and destruction: in the West known as Venus; in the East, Kālī (2: 55–56). The sexual event on the hill of dreams, then, is Absolute (inter)penetration, a collapse of objective and subjective reality into one circular block. This is given formal shape in the opening and concluding sentences of *The Hill of Dreams*, which are identical apart from their objective and subjective inflections: "There was a glow in the sky as if great furnace doors were opened"; "The flaring light shone through [Lucian's] dead eyes into the dying brain, and there was a glow within, as if great furnace doors were opened" (2: 9, 156). But who or what opens the doors onto Absolute reality?

Sex, as we have seen, is one answer. As a result of his encounter on the hill, Lucian loses his sense of the distinction between subjectivity and objectivity. In a "mood of horror," he hears a gurgling brook speaking in voices, and it becomes unclear to him (and the reader) whether he rushes through a fixed landscape or the landscape rushes around his fixed vantage point (2: 42). But Lucian explores several other techniques for radically unsettling the ordinary contours of ontology and agency. After immersing himself in occult works that describe how an adept "could transfer the sense of consciousness from his brain to the foot or hand," he discovers through his own experiments that he can alter the "forms" and "shapes" of people who annoy him, thereby neutralizing their annoyance: this is achieved, however, not by "transforming the enemy, but by transforming himself" (2: 72). Who, this scene suggests, is being transformed? Lucian also becomes convinced, through strenuous meditation, that "man could, if he pleased, become lord of his own sensations" (2: 80). "Sensations"—understood as the interface (and veil) between mind and matter, subject and object—become particularly significant because they are shown to be fundamentally *literary*. Lucian, whose quest throughout the novel is to write a novel about his experiences (of course, this is Machen's novel itself), wonders whether "sensations are symbols and not realities" and whether "they could not actually be transmuted one into another" (2: 77). Writing and reading literature, then, entail that one become displaced, "inhuman" (2: 117): like damaged insects on a spiderweb, writers and readers deliquesce across an entangling surface that simulates, in its nearly perfect transparency, the world it veils. Lucian's "wonderful ritual of praise and devotion" to Annie is a book "written all in symbols, and in the same spirit of symbolism he decorated it, causing wonderful foliage to creep about the text" (2: 59, 63). His ink is made from pigments extracted from the earth and the juice of ferns; vermilion marginalia mark places where he is to "inflict on himself [the] sweet torture" of pressing thorns into his flesh (2: 63). Such lacerations of ontological categories also form a part of Lucian's reading experiences. The "hieroglyphic sentences" of Coleridge and Poe produce a "trance of delight" in which he "transcend[s] altogether the realm of the formal understanding" (2: 98). Indeed, while reading "Kubla Khan," Lucian "experienced somewhat the sensations of Coleridge himself; strange, amazing, ineffable things seemed to have been presented to him, not in the form of the idea, but actually and materially" (2: 101). In other words, the text and the subject become overgrown by and indistinguishable from their contexts. Literature is depicted as an interactive refraction of reality that deforms as it captures the subject who writes or reads it. To better understand these ontological deformations in Machen's work, we need to examine them vis-à-vis the aesthetic form within which they take shape.

Carved in Stone

As I mentioned above, the circular form of *The Hill of Dreams* accentuates its content; the (aslant) circularity of the first and final sentences symbolizes the ontological monism of the Absolute. Valentine describes the novel's symbiosis of form and content as "prose poetry" (52), and indeed the distinction between prose and poetry is another one Machen cuts across, a cut that reiterates the crucial importance of grasping the role of form in his writing. I begin this section by using "The White People" to demonstrate how Machen very carefully positions his plot elements, creating metatextual geometric symbols that make the horrifying and perplexing events of the story visually gesture, as it were, toward the Absolute. By using a frame narrative and what Joshi calls an anticipation of the stream-of-consciousness technique (*Weird Tale* 22), "The White People" delineates binaries only to collapse them into a block. I then examine how these techniques reflect Machen's theory of literary aesthetics as given in *Hieroglyphics* and, finally, show how these ideas are further embodied in *Ornaments in Jade*, a collection of prose poems that, for Joshi, are among "the finest in English" (*Unutterable* 368). Form and content are inextricable, and therefore I do not and cannot examine form in isolation. Rather, I stress it as a method for better understanding the philosophical implications of Machen's work. This has the further happy consequence of highlighting the extent to which Absolute fiction necessitates permutations of form and genre.

If we take a bird's-eye view of "The White People," we notice that it is divided into three distinct sections: a dialogic introduction in which Ambrose and Cotgrave debate dualistic categories, principally good and evil; a monologic body that presents the girl's experience of being seduced by and absorbed into her surroundings; and a conclusion that returns us to the dialogue between the two men. In other words, the story begins and ends with a third-person, objective perspective, within which two distinct individuals articulate a series of binary oppositions at the conceptual and discursive level. In the middle section, binaries collapse into a first-person account where subject and object are made indistinguishable through the unifying condition of consciousness, which is rendered in the stream-of-consciousness mode and further supported through metaphors and other figures of speech. This unification is formally and visually underscored by long blocks of writing with run-on sentences and very few paragraph breaks, as contrasted to the first and third sections, which are fragmented into short paragraphs made discrete by quotation marks. Thus, the story's structure suggests that the conceptual, aesthetic, and linguistic mediations specific to literature are like veils that both conceal and reveal the partitionless immediacy of Absolute reality. This reading of the story makes sense of an otherwise inexplicable non sequitur that appears, significantly, just before Ambrose gives Cotgrave the green book that contains the girl's narrative. Apropos of nothing, Ambrose describes an "odd article" he recently read in which "a lady, watching her little girl playing at the drawing-room window, suddenly saw the heavy sash give way and fall on the child's fingers" (*Collected Fiction* 2: 192). Later, it is discovered "that three fingers of her hand, corresponding with those that had been injured on the child's hand, were swollen and inflamed" (2: 192). This tale-within-the-tale makes explicit, in horrifyingly weird fashion, that the seeming distance between self and other—and reader and tale—is illusory, especially when the relationship is a sympathetic or loving one.

As the girl in "The White People" realizes, if one is open to allurement, if one overcomes the fear that distances and insulates the self, then other people, animals, plants, objects, and concepts more profoundly affect and alter that self:

> I went on among [the rocks], though they frightened me, and my heart was full of wicked songs that they put into it; and I wanted to make faces and twist myself about in the way they did, and I went on and on a long way till at last I liked the rocks, and they didn't frighten me any more. I sang the songs I thought of; songs full of words that must not be spoken or written down. Then I made faces like the faces on the rocks, and I twisted myself about like the twisted ones, and I lay down flat on the ground like the dead ones, and I went up to one that was grinning, and put my arms round him and hugged him. (2: 196)

Through fear, affection, and performative imitation, the girl and the rocks become nearly indistinguishable, though they remain distinct. Such distinctions are later lost altogether:

> I saw nothing but circles, and small circles inside big ones, and pyramids, and domes, and spires, and they seemed all to go

> round and round the place where I was sitting, and the more I looked, the more I saw great big rings of rocks, getting bigger and bigger, and I stared so long that it felt as if they were all moving and turning, like a great wheel, and I was turning, too, in the middle. I got quite dizzy and queer in the head[.] (2: 197)

Once again, as we saw in *The Hill of Dreams*, it becomes impossible to determine where, in this passage, the locus of agency lies: are the rocks spinning, making the girl dizzy, or is the girl spinning, her queer and dizzy mind projecting agency onto the rocks? Or do the words "rocks" and "girl" have no meaning here, since everything is united in one "great wheel"? Yet, whether we read this passage objectively, subjectively, or Absolutely, the girl is stoned.

In *Hieroglyphics*, Machen creates an entire aesthetic theory out of the idea that everything is inscribed in stone: every existent, even a bird or flock of birds (*Collected Fiction* 2: 165), is a hieroglyphic that gestures, indexically or deictically, toward a particular context—and in the highest forms of art and literature, that context is Absolute reality. This theory is given by the Hermit, an amalgam of Ambrose from "The White People," Coleridge, and Machen himself (Valentine 65), in dialogue with the narrator who attempts, in the manner of *Sartor Resartus*, to decipher the Hermit's "esoteric philosophy of things" (*Hieroglyphics* 8). In a moldering room where "the inanimate matter about us found a voice" and a "crypt-like odour" percolates, the narrator passively records the Hermit, who, like Coleridge, speaks in a wandering manner and never arrives at any definitive conclusions (7, 14). Indeed, despite his lengthy attempt to describe what makes "great" literature, the Hermit undermines his own categorical distinctions. The Hermit tries to distinguish literature, which is "made by ecstasy and for ecstasy . . . symbols, proclaiming the presence of the unknown world," from "literature," a simulacrum of the former that, as the scare quotes indicate, is fundamentally mediated even as it pretends to depict veridical truth in the manner of a photograph (49, 23, 31). Yet, as we have seen in Machen's fiction and in the recursive form of *Hieroglyphics* itself, mediation is built into aesthetic apprehensions of reality, even "great" ones: while Machen suggests that the mother *is* the child who smashes her fingers, and the person reading the girl's tale *is* sharing in the ecstatic experience of being stoned, the only way of communicating these synchronies is through referential language, a hieroglyphics of intervals, gaps, and veils.

More consonant with Machen's own work, then, is the Hermit's contention that "great" literature (he has in mind Chaucer, Rabelais, Coleridge, and others) starkly juxtaposes binary oppositions in order to disconcert or even horrify the reader into seeing how they are, in Absolute fiction as in Absolute reality, collapsed. The Hermit gives the example of Rabelais's *Gargantua and Pantagruel*:

> consider those "lists," that more than frankness, that ebullition of grossness, plainly intentional, designed: it is either the merest lunacy, or else it is sublime. Don't you remember the trite saying, "Extremes meet"? don't you perceive that when a certain depth has been passed you begin to ascend into the heights? The Persian poet expresses the most transcendental secrets of the Divine Love by the grossest phrases of the carnal love; so Rabelais soars above the common life, above the streets and the gutter, by going far lower than the streets and the gutter: he brings before you the highest by positing that which is lower than the lowest. (99–100)

Thus, by showing the "interaction and interdependence" of soul and body, the "perpetual jar" of "the great antinomy of life," great literature provides a horrifying, ecstatic glimpse into the nature of our reality: "it is only at rare moments that a man can bear the spectacle of his own naked soul, and a vision that is splendid, certainly, but awful also, in its constant apposition of the eternal heights and the eternal depths" (73, 66, 104).

In prose poetry, Machen finds a powerful vehicle for conveying this apposition of opposites. His *Ornaments in Jade* is a collection of carved stones that together suggest the unseen being they adorn. A prose poem, according to Jeremy Noel-Tod, is simply "a poem without line breaks"; its very name captures the conjoining of the real and ideal (xx, xxx). And, like Machen, prose poetry has long been associated with decadence and the occult (xxiii). For Paul Hetherington and Cassandra Atherton, modern prose poetry was inaugurated with Baudelaire's *Paris Spleen*, published posthumously in 1869 (8), but earlier examples abound: Poe's *Eureka: A Prose Poem*, which serves as epigraph to this chapter, was published in 1848. Anthony Howell closely attaches the history of prose poetry to philosophy and mysticism, naming seventeenth-century metaphysical poet Thomas Traherne's *Centuries of Meditations* (first published in 1908) as a "pioneer" of the form ("The Prose Poem"). Hetherington and Atherton also point to the philosophical and literary fragments of the German and British Romantics as important forerunners of the form and a direct influence on Baudelaire (28, 33). The Romantic fragment, as articulated by Friedrich Schlegel and Coleridge, is self-sufficient but simultaneously suggests an absent whole (37, 34). Similarly, prose poems "are always trying to point to something about their language or their subject that sits outside of any narrative gestures they make (and frequently outside of the work itself). . . . [Prose poets construct their work by] emphasizing the evocative and even the ambiguous, and creating resonances that move expansively outward" (14). Hetherington and Atherton ingeniously point to several qualities that signal such expansion. Prose poems often create an estranged, higher-order perspective by placing one or a few justified paragraphs on a single page, thereby creating a block or blocks "reminiscent of rooms viewed from above, suggesting the original meaning of the word 'stanza'" (15). Moreover, the margin, made more salient by the justified edge of the text, "creates friction between the visual containment of the sentence and its desire for liberation" (88). These examples suggest that the prose poem's formal elements seek to integrate—in an implicit or occult way—the block of text that rests within the rectangular page that rests within the rooms and blocks of reality that frame the book: "Everything in a typical prose poem is more or less contiguous with everything else" (128). *Ornaments in Jade* similarly seeks, through the motif of interfacing blocks—self and other, inside and outside—to knock the block off our ordinary modes of perceiving and conceptualizing.

Two of the prose poems in Machen's collection, "The Rose Garden" and "The Idealist," speak most profoundly to the dynamics sketched above. "The Rose Garden" begins *in medias res*—"And afterwards she went very softly, and opened the window and looked out" (*Collected Fiction* 2: 157)—and the woman is literally and figuratively in the middle of things, looking inward and outward from the liminal space of the window. Within, the "rich Indian curtain" and "yellow silk draperies of the bed" are diaphanous, mere "suggestions of colour," while without, the garden, lake, park, and hills are "nothing but a glimmering veil, a gauze of curious lights and figures" (2: 157, 158). We learn that what has precipitated this sense of liminality is a mystical, implicitly erotic practice introduced by someone who only recently had been a "stranger": "He had shewn her that bodily rapture might be the ritual and expression of the ineffable mysteries, of the world beyond sense, that must be entered by the way of sense; and now she believed" (2: 158). In other words, the woman is also a window or veil, her senses the interstices through which inner and outer worlds flow. The ritualistic use of the body reveals that "there was only one existence . . . the external world was but a variegated shadow which might either conceal or reveal the truth; and now she believed" (2: 158). The repeated intonation, "and now she believed," along with the centering of the prose poem on this character, seems to insist on her as retaining some privileged vantage on existence, but in the end this too is swept away: "Herself was annihilated; at his bidding, she had destroyed all her old feelings and emotions, her likes and dislikes, all the inherited loves and hates that her father and mother had given her; the old life had been thrown utterly away" (2: 159). The isolated self, the ending suggests, must be given up or utterly transformed in the direct perception of the Absolute. And yet, the tone of the prose poem remains ambivalent. The "thin and dark" stranger (2: 158), strangely introduced to the woman by her father, could be read as either liberating or menacing—her passive annihilation in the Absolute "at his bidding" certainly implies a darkly patriarchal imposition.

"The Idealist" also uses architectural spaces, suggestions of erotic transgression, and irony to reveal that reality is constituted by a collocation of perceptual acts. The prose poem opens with Charles Symonds, a clerk, disgusted by the dirty jokes of his colleagues. But everything is a simulacrum: in making fun of Symonds's disgust, his colleague mimics his facial gestures and then "fashioned another grimace, an imitation of his favourite actor's favourite contortion" (2: 162). Emotions here are imitations of imitations; the dirty joke presumably concerns a beautiful woman on a billboard (2: 163). Yet Symonds, although he is disgusted by "the stupid, the blatant, the intolerable" world of his humdrum middle-class life, also exists vicariously. Each evening after work he "escaped to his occult and private world which no one had ever divined" (2: 163). He peeps into windows, "watching a shadow on a lighted blind, watching it fade and blacken and fade, conjecturing its secrets, inventing dialogue for this drama in *Ombres Chinoises*" (2: 164). At the end of the prose poem, Symonds returns to the room where he lives, "a hollow space bordered by grave walls and the white glimmer of the corniced ceiling" (2: 165). He constructs a puppet and then "incongruous monstrous things. In the dusk, white silk shimmered, laces and delicate frills hovered for a moment, as he bungled over the tying of knots, the fastening of bands. The old room grew rich, heavy, vaporous with subtle scents; the garments that were passing through his hands had been drenched with fragrance.

Passion had contorted his face; he grinned stark in the candle-light" (2: 165). Symonds fails to realize that he is now the object, rather than the spectator, of a Chinese shadow-puppet show—people passing by his window "found singular matter for speculation" (2: 165). Of course, these people occupy the same space as the reader. We also speculate on the vaguely described nature of Symonds's actions: Is he dressing the puppet or himself in laces and frills? What is the relationship between perception, sexual desire, and identity? From what vantage do categories like ideal and real, self and other, and masculine and feminine collapse? Both "The Rose Garden" and "The Idealist" suggest that the answers to these questions are best discerned from a maximally relational perspective, and such an Absolute perspective is taken by the reader who gazes down on these blocks, rooms, and stanzas. Indeed, this is the function of literature, according to *Hieroglyphics*: to radically externalize the subjective mind through fits of awful ecstasy.

Unveiled Visions

Machen subjects George Eliot to repeated ridicule. The Hermit in *Hieroglyphics* says she is a "superior insect" (64) who constructs mere literary simulacra in the representational, "realist" mode. *The Hill of Dreams* singles out *Romola* as a "shabby trick of imitating literature" (*Collected Fiction* 2: 126). Of course, I agree with Newell that this is a mischaracterization, perhaps the result of Machen's sexism (63–64), and we could also point ironically to the crucial role that simulation and imitation play in Machen's own work. In fact, Machen would have been chagrined had he read Eliot's novella *The Lifted Veil*, which anticipates many of the themes that characterize his own work as well as Sinclair's and weird fiction in general. *The Lifted Veil*, which provides a first-person account of Latimer's clairvoyance and ability to divine the contents of other people's minds, has often been read as a reflection on literary form itself, which gives writers and readers this same telepathic experience. "Striving to inhabit other minds," Greiner writes in this context, "we hope to gain something like a narrator's perspective on ourselves: impersonal and faithfully rendered, viewed at a remove" (123). Yet Greiner also argues that such inhabitation can prove horrifying: "thankfully," "happily," one is not privy to complete knowledge of other minds (not to mention one's own!), for "sympathetic identification can prove disastrous when one loses the capacity to distinguish self from other" (9, 8). Latimer's experience seems to bear out this assertion, but I want to stress that the disastrous dissolution of self and other can also be transformative and edifying—even divine, if through a glass darkly.

Helen Small contends that the "fundamental opposition in [*The Lifted Veil*] is not between art and science, or even between the ideal and the real, but between the fearful prospect of absolute knowing and the saving possibility of doubt and speculation" (xxvi). The Absolute is indeed the absent center around which the novella revolves, and that which veils it from us, Eliot suggests, simultaneously preserves us from a horrifying loss of identity and sanctifies the mystery and wonder that allure us outside of our narrow selves. Latimer's passively received "gift" (*Lifted Veil* 11), which allows the contents of other minds to obtrude into his own, forces him into a wider ambit of reality that is anything but expansive: his mental peace is continually disturbed by the petty egotism clamoring in the minds of the people around him (13–14). When he finally sees into the previously opaque mind of his lover, Bertha, he realizes that "the darkness had hidden no landscape from me, but only a blank prosaic wall . . . the narrow room of this woman's soul" (32). The Absolute view from above is horrifying. It's worth remarking that what makes it horrifying is precisely the unambitious spiritual architecture of the minds around him, not the knowledge itself. Still, humans have an "absolute" need for mystery, and the "dark veil" of death offers darkness that even Latimer cannot pierce (29, 41). The novella begins with Latimer's prevision of his own death: "Darkness—darkness—no pain—nothing but darkness: but I am passing on and on through the darkness" (3). The novella ends with Latimer's connection to human beings "deadened" (36), and yet this deadening *enables* his pity and sympathy for others and discloses an even more Absolute veil: "my heart went out towards the men and women and children whose faces were becoming familiar to me: but I was driven away again in terror at the approach of my old insight—driven away to live continually with the one Unknown Presence revealed and yet hidden by the moving curtain of the earth and sky" (42). Latimer's horrific moral vision, culminating in the possibility of a dark journey after death within the context of a dark, "unknown and pitiless" Absolute (36), prefigures many of the obsessions of later horror and weird fiction, especially the work of Sinclair.

In addition to writing twenty-four novels, four short story collections, two volumes of poetry, a verse novel, and several works of literary criticism, Sinclair produced two philosophical treatises that were favorably received at the time by Bertrand Russell and others: *A Defence of Idealism* (1917) and *The New Idealism* (1922). As recently as 2002, however, Christine Battersby lamented that scholarship on Sinclair demonstrates "a failure to take her seriously as a philosopher" (120). More specifically, we could say that while several scholars acknowledge a link between Sinclair's philosophy and her literary works, the fact that her philosophy is *idealist* is often seen as deleterious. In his recent introduction to a collection of Sinclair's weird fiction, for example, Joshi is dismissive: "The extent to which these stories—and her work in general—is governed by her philosophical idealism is unclear, chiefly because that philosophy itself is a trifle opaque" (11). Others see her idealism as an unfortunate hindrance to, or even insidious attack upon, positive expressions of feminism and sexuality. Claire Drewery argues that Sinclair's weird fiction opposes "the cleanliness and purity [she] associates with transcendental, spiritual reality" to "physical, corporeal sexuality, which, conversely, she depicts as repellent, distorted and grotesque" (214, 213). Faye Pickrem claims that Sinclair's idealism—and idealism in general—amounts to a "hysterical fear" of sexuality that forms the "quintessential ground of Sinclair's work: the need to sanitise and expunge the materiality of desire in order to escape its anguish, rising above it to the mystical utopia of the Absolute" (122).

My reading of Sinclair will eschew such binary oppositions. Instead, I follow the lead of those who read idealism as having a positive, constructive influence on Sinclair's fiction. Rebeccah Kinnamon Neff, for instance, argues that Sinclair's work reveals a "renunciation not of the world and the flesh, but of the seeker's need for the world and his attachment to it" ("'New Mysticism'" 90). This more subtle account of the relationship between materiality and ideality finds expression, for example, in Sinclair's verse novel *The Dark Night* (1924), in which the protagonist Elizabeth deeply enjoys erotic ecstasy and understands it as "an anticipation of the ultimate ecstasy of the moment of complete reunion with the Absolute" (Neff, "'New Mysticism'" 91). In other words, Sinclair's works of philosophy and fiction are not structured around hysterical binary oppositions; rather, they delineate degrees, spectrums, and magnitudes of knowledge and reality. Charlotte Jones compellingly demonstrates that what Sinclair aims at is "both a more abstract and a more concrete notion of truth, one whose material manifestations carry with it the mark of its relation to a whole range of universal truths of which it is part. Sinclair sought in her fiction to integrate a revelatory encounter with idealist absolute forms with the incontrovertible material evidence of alternative forms of consciousness being presented by the 'new psychology'" (91). Sinclair was not opposed to sexuality, science, or materiality; she saw them as imbricated with spiritual reality. Thus, it is problematic to assume that she conceives of the Absolute as a purely spiritual utopia. Rather than suggesting that sexual bodies are "bad" and pure spirit is "good," her fiction, especially her weird idealist fiction, explores the ways in which the Absolute is not pure spirit—and not necessarily good. Like Eliot, Sinclair depicts how selfishness and self-estrangement—modes of being that can be curtailed or intensified through rites like sex, telepathy, and death—correlate with various layers of reality, from the suffocating labyrinth of one's own mind to the astonishing, disquieting Absolute.

A summary of Sinclair's philosophy as given in *A Defence of Idealism* will help elucidate her weird fiction. Her idiosyncratic and syncretic theory of Absolute idealism draws on Western and Eastern idealist and mystical traditions, as well as psychoanalysis, pragmatism, and the "new realism" of Russell and G. E. Moore. She also draws extensively on Bradley and especially Samuel Butler: the entire first chapter of the book considers the latter's "pan-psychism," which helpfully "shatters" the idea of individuality (1) and provides an evolutionary explanation for certain psychological mechanisms behind human experience of the Absolute. From Bradley she takes the distinction between appearance and reality: everything short of the Absolute is appearance, but appearances can be "noble," "beautiful," and "useful" (133). In other words, Sinclair emphatically does not reject desire, materiality, and the things of this world: "I hate it when a woman I disapprove of [presumably Madame Blavatsky] tells me that if I would only extinguish all my desires I should attain Nirvâna [equivalent to the Absolute for Sinclair] to-morrow. I know it. But I do not want to attain Nirvâna quite so soon" (265). She also shares Bradley's non-anthropocentric orientation, approving of *Appearance and Reality*'s demonstration that "Man is not the measure of all things, but only of some things" (134). For Sinclair, only a non-anthropocentric metaphysics can account for human suffering. To assume that the Absolute is "good" and devoid of suffering is to project human ideals onto a reality that transcends the human. It also ignores the fact that, for instance, fleas do not suffer from biting humans: "the humblest organism may have its point of view, and its right to a say in the matter of existence" (147). In other words, suffering (and evil) are relative facts—in Bradley's terms, they are appearances and not reality—and we cannot confidently attribute them to the Absolute. The Absolute *might* be what humans call "good," or it *might* be what we call "evil," but we cannot say because we do not possess an Absolute perspective (Sinclair 302–04). Nevertheless, there is some comfort to take in epistemological limitation. The possibility that suffering and evil do not exist in other planes of reality, that what happens to consciousness after death is veiled from our view—these mysteries allow for speculation on these occluded states, speculation powerfully suited to *fiction*.

Sinclair's weird fiction is deeply interested in what she calls the "dubious borderland" of paranormal experiences like telepathy, clairvoyance, and psychokinesis (*Defence* 250), and in an argument remarkably similar to Thacker's, she places these experiences within the context of Western and Eastern (dark) mystical traditions, which she sees as inextricably intertwined with the development of Absolute idealism. Prehistoric fertility rites, the Eleusinian mysteries, the horrifying and violent visions of Christian mystics—all of these are progressive expressions of a desire for the Absolute (242–52). The history of Eastern mysticism shares the same trajectory, and both traditions end up cultivating what Sinclair calls "disassociation," a detachment from one's individual self and "normal consciousness" that can lead to the development of paranormal experiences, Absolute experiences, or—in the case of Christian ascetics who make the mistake of repudiating the body and materiality—madness (246–70). Sinclair argues that the Western and Eastern traditions are converging into a "New Mysticism" that, with the help of modern scientific analysis, will help us better understand the mechanisms behind and function of paranormal experience (274). She speculates that most paranormal experience is the result of "suggestion" or "auto-suggestion": the psychic plane can, within very limited parameters, have a direct causal effect on the physical plane, as evidenced by what we now call the placebo effect (266). Ultimately, disassociation and suggestion function to break down normal consciousness, opening it up to broader, stranger, potentially dangerous states that, like dream states, transcend time, space, and discrete identity in a mode analogous to the Absolute (260–62). The "chief and highest function" of suggestion, she claims, is "to create reality; to heighten the sense and sharpen the perspective of reality; to restore the links with reality where they have been broken" (268). And what is literature but the experience of disassociation through suggestion? Like sexual passion and a confrontation with death, art and literature can produce "the shock of contact with reality," "moments of danger that are moments of sure and perfect happiness, because then the adorable Reality gives itself to our very sight and touch" (269, 339).

Sinclair's short story "The Flaw in the Crystal" explores many of these themes in a literary register. Like Eliot's Latimer, Agatha Verrall has the "Gift" (*If the Dead Knew* 64) of clairvoyance and telepathically interacting with other minds, although in addition to the passive observation of mental contents, in Sinclair's story minds actively influence one another, from the subtle and indirect effect of belief on action and interaction to the direct struggle of two or more consciousnesses. At the beginning of the story, Agatha uses the Gift to ease the anxiety of both her lover, Rodney, and his wife, Bella, who has also been reduced to "a mass of furious and malignant nerves" (63). As the lives of Rodney and Bella begin to improve, she also attempts to heal Harding, an acquaintance even more incapacitated by anxiety: terrified of the "Thing" that relentlessly pursues him, he locks himself in his house with windows drawn. Agatha successfully relieves Harding of his paranoia, but with the consequence that his personality and insanity begin to infect and overpower her mind. To save herself—and maintain her powers for Rodney and Bella—Agatha releases her grasp on Harding, who descends again into paranoia. The story concludes with Agatha relinquishing her love for Rodney, which she believes is the "flaw" that prevents her from being a pure "crystal" vessel through which the Gift can operate optimally.

I will highlight two important aspects of the story that speak to Sinclair's philosophy as sketched above. First, "The Flaw in the Crystal" is deeply interested in complicating the boundaries of the individual self. In channeling the Gift—"a current of transcendent power" that is "immeasurable, inexhaustible" (79)—Agatha opens herself to a dark Absolute that ecstatically and horrifically breaks down the borders of personality. For instance, when she first heals Harding, she enters a meditative state, "with eyelids shut lightly on her eyes; all fleshly contacts . . . diminished," then plunges into "wave upon wave of darkness . . . poised in the ultimate unspeakable stillness, beyond death, beyond birth, beyond the movement, the vehemence, the agitations of the world. . . . [T]he walls of flesh were down between them [Agatha and Harding]; she had got at him" (80). Such profound alienation from the self can ecstatically lift the veil from aspects of reality beyond the self and beyond the human, as when Agatha shortly thereafter sees "that the whole world brimmed and shone and was alive with the joy that was its life, joy that flowed flood-high and yet was still. In every leaf, in every blade of grass, this life was manifest as a strange, a divine translucence" (84). Yet, as Harding's paranoia gradually infects her, Agatha recognizes, along with

Greiner, the value of "those innermost walls of personality that divide and protect, mercifully, one spirit from another" (106). This second aspect—the dark possibilities of Absolute self-erasure—logically follows from the first: the porous translucence of Agatha's identity infects—or rather, is a symptom of—the porosity of the Absolute, which ambivalently eludes separations between flesh/spirit and good/evil. One might be tempted to read the denouement, in which Agatha quashes her sexual passion for Rodney in order to remain "pure from desire" for the Gift (118), as advocating a hysterical idealist renunciation of materiality in favor of the beatific Absolute. But Agatha's fixation on extreme purity is just as extreme as Harding's on the terrible Thing, and their ultimate indistinction undermines Agatha's reliability as an ethical center. The Absolute might be beatific, but it might be a horror, or indifferent. Readers are left with the sense that our initial alignment with Agatha as protagonist could be the result of narrative "suggestion," and we cannot help but "disassociate" from her.

The extension of Agatha's consciousness paradoxically arises from its sequestration. Like Harding, Agatha is seized by a dark, amorphous "thing"—the Gift—in "the blackness where, as if it had been waiting for her, the thing had found her" (78). And after it finds her, she isolates herself in Sarratt End, a remote rural area where she is "utterly cut off" (66). Just as Harding closes himself up in his house, Agatha uses the Gift by "shutting out" and "clos[ing] her door on" "any feeling, any thought that did violence to any other. She could shut them all out, if it came to that, and make the whole place empty" (65). Her sanitizing imperative is as repelling and repellant as Harding's paranoia, but the story suggests that by merging their perspectives, we gain a weird clarity of vision. Put differently, exposure to Harding's vision of the world as evil has a salutary effect on Agatha's piety and her understanding of the Absolute. The primary violent feeling that she wants to expel is her sexual passion for Rodney—but it is only after she succumbs to Harding that her desire emerges, "naked and unshamed," from the repressed "burrows" of her mind (107, 92). Her sensory encounter with the world from out of Harding's eyes and ears is "exaltation at the other end of the scale":

> [She heard] small sounds of movement, of strange shiverings, swarmings, crepitations; sounds of incessant, infinitely subtle urging, of agony and recoil. . . . She knew what she heard and saw. She heard the stirring of the corruption that Life was; the young blades of corn were frightful to her, for in them was

the push, the passion of the evil which was Life; the trees, as they stretched out their arms and threatened her, were frightful with the terror which was Life. (104)

This horrible, ecstatic vision, a dark inversion of her earlier Romantic epiphany, precedes the arrival of the "brown, blurred Thing. . . . a fragment parted and flung off from some immense and as yet invisible cloud of horror" (105). These experiences precipitate the rise of Agatha's "naked and unshamed" sexual desire, and while she fails to pursue it, choosing to build up her walls again, Harding has fundamentally brought into question her conception of the Gift. In a conversation with Milly, Harding's wife, Agatha explains that the Gift is divine horror:

"But, Milly, holding [Harding] was bad; it wasn't safe."

"It saved him."

"All the same, Milly, it wasn't safe. The thing itself isn't."

"The Power? The divine thing?"

"Yes. It's divine and it's—it's terrible. It does terrible things to us."

"How could it? If it's divine, wouldn't it be compassionate? Do you suppose it's less compassionate than—*you* are? Why, Agatha, when it's goodness and purity itself—"

"Goodness and purity are terrible." (113)

Divinity, goodness, purity, and terror are brought precariously together, balancing on a knife-edge. "The Flaw in the Crystal" ultimately suggests that an approach to the dark Absolute requires the radical reconfiguration of our conceptual architecture, and we must wend our way through strange new narrative structures to find it.

Architectures of Hell and Heaven

The conceptual precarity at the center of "The Flaw in the Crystal" gains added significance when we consider its placement in *Uncanny Stories* (1923). It is clear from Sinclair's workbooks, held in the rich archive of her materials at the University of Pennsylvania, that Sinclair intended this short story collection to be read sequentially. As Neff puts it, *Uncanny Stories* "records and elucidates the stages of [the] quest [for ultimate reality]" ("May" 187). Out of seven stories, "The Flaw in the Crystal" appears third, between the unmitigated horror of the collection's opener, "Where Their Fire Is Not Quenched," and the wondrously weird optimism of the closer, "The Finding of the Absolute." In other words, we cannot draw any definitive conclusions from any of these stories in isolation—we must consider them relationally, as part of a larger structure of meaning. In this section I will examine the first and final stories in the collection, as well as other related stories, to draw attention to this meta-structure. Its heightened view allows us to discern an ethical arc from the first story, in which sex seems to infect everything with absolute significance, to the final one, where sexual betrayal is shown to be insignificant in the larger scheme of things. A metaphysical arc carries us from the personal claustrophobia of the first story, in which a hellish labyrinth is constructed out of the protagonist's pathways of memory, to the final story's expansive cosmic vision of an Absolute eternally at play. And an aesthetic arc traces Sinclair's formal experimentations, which manage to imply the infinite ramification within and between individual minds and the Absolute through a focused attention on transformational rites of sex and especially death (all of the stories, except "The Flaw in the Crystal," depict the persistence of life after death). This is accompanied by the arcs' implication that every text has context—every finite thing has an outside that gestures toward the entirely immanent Absolute, and even at the end of the quest we are only ever "finding" it, because arrival demands tremendous textual agility and probably exceeds the possibilities of literature altogether.

In her workbooks, Sinclair groups stories according to shared themes. "The Flaw in the Crystal" falls, paradoxically but appropriately enough, under both "Healing" and "Terror." "Where Their Fire Is Not Quenched" and "The Finding of the Absolute" are given the label "Other World" (Workbook 14). Sinclair's interest in the formal and metaphysical implications of other worlds is revealed in her workbooks, where she sketches the architectures of various "Time-Dimensions," from linear time to cubic time to the four-dimensional time discussed in contemporary science and philosophy (Workbook 29). "Where Their Fire Is Not Quenched" is relentlessly architectural, using content and form to corral, confuse, and literally amaze the reader. The story begins in a straightforward manner—Harriott Leigh, disappointed in two early love affairs, enters a sordid and unfulfilling sexual relationship with Oscar Wade—although the accelerating forward momentum is accentuated by increasingly large temporal gaps, visually followed by gaps on the page: "Five years passed," Ten years passed," "Twenty years passed" (*If the Dead Knew* 172, 173, 179). Harriott dies, and we follow her across the gap. As she looks down upon her own dead body, the "room began to come apart before her eyes, to split into shafts of floor and furniture and ceiling that shifted and were thrown by their commotion into different planes"; she and the reader are then subject to "a transparent mingling of dislocated perspectives" (182). We follow her down corridors that have lost all sense of spatial integrity (one suddenly ends in a blank wall, for instance); we turn left and right, right and left, until we are dizzy; and we arrive again and again at Room 107 of the hotel, the scene of Harriott and Oscar's boring assignations (the room number further encodes the story itself, the first story of seven, as this dark Absolute) (184). In yet another complication, time overlaps space in this limbo, and Harriott seeks to escape Room 107 by venturing farther and farther back into her memory, returning along the path the reader has already traversed. But no matter which memory she turns to, she finds it replaced with Oscar, who speculates that, as this endless loop tightens, their separate personalities will be merged forever in Room 107: "In the last hell we shall not run away any longer; we shall find no more roads, no more passages, no more open doors. We shall have no need to look for each other" (190). In this utter collapse, the Absolute shrinks to a pinpoint, prefiguring the ethical and ontological withdrawal of Agatha and Harding in "The Flaw in the Crystal."

If the first stage of the quest suggests that finding the Absolute in one's own head is a horror, the final stage reiterates this theme but with a quite different, dark comedic emphasis. In "The Finding of the Absolute," James Spalding is a philosopher whose love of the Absolute leads to the loss of his wife's love: Elizabeth leaves him for Paul Jeffreson, a dissolute Imagist poet. This breaks Spalding's faith in the Absolute:

> consider, on Mr. Spalding's theory, there isn't any reality except the Absolute. Things are only real because they exist in It; because It is Them. Mr. Spalding conceived that his consciousness and Elizabeth's consciousness and Paul Jeffreson's consciousness existed somehow in the Absolute unchanged. For, if that inside existence changed them you would have to say that the ground of their present appearance lay somewhere

outside the Absolute, which to Mr. Spalding was rank blasphemy. And if Elizabeth and Paul Jeffreson existed in the Absolute unchanged, then their adultery existed there unchanged. (*If the Dead Knew* 226)

Thus, he loses faith in the Absolute because it "outraged his moral sense" (226). Like Eliot's Latimer, Spalding is nauseated by all the deception, foolishness, and idiocy around him—his Uncle Sims, a "mean sneak," his Aunt Emily, "a silly fool," etc. (226)—but what he ultimately cannot stomach is the idea that all this "evil" is indelibly preserved in the Absolute, persisting even after death. What if every noxious event and relationship "had an eternal significance and entailed tremendous consequences in the after-life?" He can imagine "no worse hell" than Harriott's: the "eternal repetition of boredom and disgust." But perhaps, he wonders, "goodness was not, after all, *the* important thing" (227). Then he dies.

At the end of *The Lifted Veil*, when Mrs. Archer is resurrected shortly after dying, the hatred that characterized the end of her life immediately resumes, which draws the following expostulation from Latimer: "Great God! Is this what it is to live again . . . to wake up with our unstilled thirst upon us, with our unuttered curses rising to our lips, with our muscles ready to act out their half-committed sins?" (42). As we follow Spalding across the gap of death, he too revives in the middle of his mundane concerns—he suddenly finds himself with Elizabeth and Jeffreson, imagining that all their infidelities have landed them in hell. But this is heaven, Jeffreson explains, a heaven created entirely by himself and Elizabeth: the beautiful Italian landscape that surrounds them has been fabricated from their memories. Indeed, Spalding is in the "landing-state" of heaven, and it contains an infinite number of other planes, times, spaces, and states—because everything here is constructed from "[s]tates of mind" (231). He visits no less a "state of mind" than Kant's to learn more about this baffling metaphysics. As a devoted disciple of Kant, he is shocked to find that the Sage of Königsberg now admits that Hegel "made a very considerable advance" over his own philosophy (234). There is no absolute space or time, Kant explains, though they are real relative to particular consciousnesses; evil, too, is relative not absolute (236, 238). Furthermore, in a line of argument that could have been lifted directly from *A Defence of Idealism*, certain experiences on earth are analogous to, or proleptic of, experiences in heaven. The heavenly abilities to create one's own "state" of reality and enter other people's states are merely richer expressions of the earthly abilities to dream and telepathize (237). Ultimately, the biggest difference between earth and heaven is that in the former, reality is "apparently" outside the mind, whereas in the latter it is inside the mind: "I seem to have become my own God," Spalding remarks (237). Godlike, he is closer to the Absolute.

But he is not there yet—he must pass through further disassociations. First, he transcends the ordinary linear perception of time and space. Kant immerses him in "cubic time, or past-present-future all together," and he sees things and people simultaneously occupy multiple positions, while solid objects become transparent (239–40). Second, he loses his distanced perspective altogether, making subject and object indistinguishable: "he was swept into the stream that flowed, thudding and throbbing, through all live things; he felt it beat in and around him, jet after jet from the beating heart of God; he felt the rising of the sap in trees, the delight of animals at mating-time" (240). Third, he has a cosmic vision of God's "immanent life" as the universe:

> He saw the vast planes of time intersecting each other, like the planes of a sphere, wheeling, turning in and out of each other. He saw other space and time systems rising up, toppling, enclosing and enclosed. And as a tiny inset in the immense scene, his own life from birth to the present moment, together with the events of his heavenly life to come. In this vision Elizabeth's adultery, which had once appeared so monstrous, so overpowering an event, was revealed as slender and insignificant. (241)

God sucks this entire multifarious universe, a vibrating "web," back into itself along with Spalding, who briefly enters the "transcendent life" of God, "into the Absolute. For one moment he thought that this was death; the next his whole being swelled and went on swelling in an unspeakable, an unthinkable bliss." Then he exits as God expels another web, a new "jig-saw puzzle of a universe" (241).

From this remarkable vantage point, we can survey some of the main implications of Sinclair's weird fiction. Her stories demonstrate, first, that the self is paradoxically found through disassociation; it expands by continually dying to itself, by continually seeing that its perspectives are partial; and it arrives at itself, ultimately, in and as the Absolute. A limited dark

Absolute, meanwhile, can emerge and be sustained through an inability to transcend the self and prevailing social forms or an affective adhesion to organizations of sexualized violence and power that dismantle and dominate the self. Nevertheless, sex (and, more generally, the body and materiality) is not hysterically rejected but found to pervade all planes of reality. The physical "delight of animals at mating-time," for instance, is no less real in heaven than on earth, while union with the Absolute is described in ecstatic sexual terms. "Evil" is also ubiquitous at all levels of reality—even, perhaps, at the level of the Absolute. Finally, the last image of God as a spider, weaving the web of the world again and again, suggests a perpetual return to the beginning. The first story is as significant, true, and necessary as the last. Reality is engaged in the endless, playful spinning out of stories, an eternal repetition of the same (game) that engenders difference. Thus, for Sinclair, literature is tasked with continually articulating the intricate layering, massive scope, and ambivalent moral mixtures of reality.

Stepping back to a further remove, we can see Machen and Sinclair's position within larger literary tectonics. This chapter has stressed the unexpected bond between idealism and horror that intensifies around the turn of the century—unexpected because of idealism's supposed investment in goodness, purity, and what Pickrem calls the "mystical utopia of the Absolute" (122). Machen and Sinclair envision the possibility of a dark Absolute where evil and horror are privileged sites for the ecstatic but disconcerting expansion of the self—as previously veiled aspects of reality are exposed, the self faces ever larger vistas of alienation. They also attend to the creation of more limited dark Absolutes that are human-all-too-human, shot through with sadistic violence, oppression, and secrecy. In their philosophy and fiction, rites and rituals like meditation, sex, death, and the reading of literature itself function to disassociate the subject and defamiliarize the object to the point where these and other ontological and moral boundaries blur. Machen and Sinclair are therefore exemplary of weird fiction as a genre, which shares these aims and employs similar techniques to achieve them. In Lovecraft's *At the Mountains of Madness* (1936), for instance, the horror builds as more and more assumptions about reality and human identity are peeled away. Lovecraft's endless syntactical extensions and narrative anticlimaxes point to an ever-receding beyond, for beyond the mountains of madness there is always another range. And while Lovecraft famously champions Machen as a forerunner of the weird, he seems to miss Sinclair's significance:

> May Sinclair's *Uncanny Stories* contain more of traditional occultism than of that creative treatment of fear which marks mastery in this field, and are inclined to lay more stress on human emotions and psychological delving than upon the stark phenomena of a cosmos utterly unreal. It may be well to remark here that occult believers are probably less effective than materialists in delineating the spectral and the fantastic, since to them the phantom world is so commonplace a reality that they tend to refer to it with less awe, remoteness, and impressiveness than do those who see in it an absolute and stupendous violation of the natural order. ("Supernatural")

As we have seen, Sinclair delves equally into the "unreal" realities of the human mind and the cosmos, nor is she unawed by absolute violations of nature—quite the reverse. Lovecraft would be even more startled to discover Eliot as another crucial figure in the historical background. We therefore require a more inclusive account of women writers' contributions to this often overwhelmingly masculine genre, and we need to stress its connections not only to the formal experimentations of modernism but also those of Victorian literature.

Finally, as I argued at the beginning of this chapter, Machen and especially Sinclair mark the increasing confluence of Western and Eastern (especially Indian) philosophy and literature during this period. One of the few philosophical papers that Sinclair held on her estate at the time of her death was a review (and defense) of Fawcett's *The World as Imagination* (1916), written by Fawcett himself and published in *Mind*. Fawcett, whose darkly epic philosophy we visited in chapter 3, was deeply familiar with Indian philosophy, and his claim in this book that "Ultimate all-inclusive reality . . . is best regarded as imaginal," and that "every work of the Cosmic Imagination is . . . a poem" ("Some Observations" 152, 162), resonates not only with the ending of "The Finding of the Absolute" but also with Advaita Vedānta, which describes the production of the phenomenal world out of *Brahman* (the Absolute) as an act of *līlā* (divine play) by Īśvara (the Absolute personalized as God) (Deutsch 38–41). Certainly, as Richard Bleiler makes clear, Sinclair "had long been interested in Hinduism," and her second collection of weird fiction makes this even more explicit than the first (132). *The Intercessor and Other Stories* (1931) begins with two stories about powerful mahatmas and karma: "The Mahatma's Story" and "Jones's Karma." In "The Mahatma's Story," two souls swap bodies but behave just as they would have in their own; in "Jones's Karma," Jones is given the chance to make different choices in his life but ends up with the same outcomes. It is worth remarking that these stories are essentially repetitions of the same plot. Like God spinning out the universe again and again, authors, for Sinclair, are analogously enacting the Absolute, and in reading these stories, we negotiate the dissonance between self and Absolute that Bhattacharjee and Ghosh see as central to horror fiction in the Global South. Neff argues that for Sinclair, "liberation from the karma of self-willing, what [she] described as 'the ceasing of the sorrow of divided life,' comes not from attempts to escape the self, but from an acceptance of the at-one-ness of the finite self with the Infinite Self" (" 'New Mysticism' " 107). The next chapter explores this theme of integrating the amphibious self with the Absolute as expressed in modern Advaita Vedānta and its unlikely exponent, Aldous Huxley.

Chapter 5

Amphibious Modernism
Advaita Vedānta and Aldous Huxley

I love matter, I find it miraculous.

—Aldous Huxley, "The 'Inanimate' is Alive"

Now "relentlessly out of fashion" (Burstein 5), Mary Augusta Ward's *Robert Elsmere* (1888) was "probably the best-selling 'quality' novel of the [nineteenth] century" (Sutherland 546). A quarter of a million copies were sold in England and the United States within a year of its publication (Peterson 159), and by 1911, Ward herself estimated that it had sold nearly a million copies and was translated into "most foreign languages" ("Preface" 659). The novel's phenomenal success coincides with and reflects the success of Absolute idealism, and indeed, historico-philosophical studies of British Idealism often cite this novel as evidence of the movement's cultural impact.[1] It is not difficult to make this connection: Ward dedicated the novel to T. H. Green, perhaps the most influential of the first generation of British Idealists, and she acknowledges that he was the inspiration for her character Henry Grey, whose speeches are sometimes direct quotations from Green's works. Grey is just one of several influences—others include the higher criticism and Darwin's evolutionary theory—that gradually erode the clergyman Elsmere's belief in Christian miracles and the supernatural account of Jesus. At a crucial turning point, Elsmere realizes that he has been "tangled in the fleeting shows of things," and he must transcend such appearances to gain reality: "Why am I so passionate for this and that, for all these sections and fragments of Thee? Oh, for the One, the All!" (304). After reflecting on the equally fragmentary, deluded nature of human belief systems—Buddhism and non-Christian religions, he laments, are ignorant of "the one Healer"—he then recalls Grey's assertion that "All religions are true, and all are false. In them all, more or less visibly, man grasps at the one thing needful—self forsaken, God laid hold of. The spirit in them all is the same, answers eternally to reality; it is but the letter, the fashion, the imagery, that are relative and changing" (304, 305). And although by the end of the novel Elsmere founds a secular religion named The New Brotherhood of Christ, he does so not because he thinks Jesus is inherently superior to all other spiritual figures but for the practical reason that the working-class Londoners he hopes to reach are already culturally conversant in Christianity. "It is not that Christianity is false," he tells his pious wife, Catherine, "but that it is only an imperfect human reflection of a part of truth," and even Catherine eventually avers that "God has not one language, but many" (407, 580). These themes internal to the novel—the need to transcend the self and other partial truths in order to reach the immanent Absolute reality, the necessity for new spiritual practices and belief systems to accord with modern culture and scientific knowledge—resonate, as we will see, with both turn-of-the-century Advaita Vedānta and its refraction in the late literary and philosophical work of Ward's nephew, Aldous Huxley.

Green's metaphysics, centered on the concept of an "eternal consciousness" as the Absolute, provides philosophical context for the themes sketched above. Although this concept only occasionally becomes explicit in *Robert Elsmere*—for example, Elsmere suggests that reality consists of "an Eternal Mind—of which Nature and Man are the continuous and only revelation" (540)—it nevertheless provides thematic and formal structure to the novel and connects it to the larger discourses I seek to explore in this chapter. Hiralal Haldar, who was "largely responsible for the popularization of British neo-Hegelianism in India" (Bhushan and Garfield 499), summarizes Green's concept in detail in his *Neo-Hegelianism* (1927). For Green, Haldar explains, "a thing is only in so far as it points beyond itself to something else" (21). This is why our understanding of things change as we gain a more complete determination of them; things only exist, and only have meaning, insofar as they are *related* to other things. And for Green, that which relates must be a mind. Only consciousness unifies successive events and discrete things even as it preserves their distinction. Only consciousness is not reducible to an event or a thing, to temporality or causality, because it is the condition in which they appear. Thus, there must be a maximal consciousness analogous to, and in some sense identical with, human minds: an eternal (i.e., atemporal) consciousness that relates the entire universe (21–28). This is the "metaphysical monster" that scared philosophers away from Green for most of the twentieth century (Mander, "In Defence" 188), although more recently there have been reconsiderations and defenses of his work, even the metaphysical monster itself.[2]

The epistemology and ethics entailed by Green's eternal consciousness have received the most attention. First, as Peter Nicholson argues, the idea of coming to identify with the eternal consciousness is not naïve wishful thinking but reflects the procedures of modern science: "If a new experience can be fitted in [to the relational system the scientist hypothesizes as fixed and true], then the scientist treats it as real; if it cannot, then either the scientist rejects it as illusion or modifies his or her view of previous experience until once again everything fits—until it is all a single system of relations, which is, once again, 'unalterable'" (145). This process of retrospective falsification—organized around the attempt to reach the Absolute—is at the heart of Green's philosophy, the scientific method, and Advaitic epistemology, not to mention the *Bildungsroman* form of Ward and Huxley's fiction. Second, Leslie Armour argues that "Green's ethics are based on the notion that the proper end of finite selves or consciousnesses is to realize their potential in sharing in the eternal consciousness. To do so, they must co-operate with other finite selves and take responsibility for the self-development of all of them" (160). The imperative to identify the self with broader and broader swaths of reality necessarily includes taking responsibility for nonhuman consciousnesses, which also participate in the Absolute (162). Green's social and ecological ethics, like his epistemology, thus revolve around the interpersonal and nonhuman contexts that make selves and human beings possible. Again, these ethical ideas inform not just Ward's *Robert Elsmere* but also Huxley's novels from *Eyeless in Gaza* (1936) forward, especially the focus of this chapter, *Time Must Have a Stop* (1944). As Bernard Bergonzi suggests, several contemporaries of Huxley, including Virginia Woolf, noticed the similarities between his fiction and his aunt's, and while his early, bitingly ironic work seems to depart from *Robert Elsmere* and the British Idealism that inspired it, the novel he first read at age eight cast a long shadow (9–17).

Thus, like Butler, Sinclair, and the other writers I've considered in previous chapters, Ward and Huxley exemplify British Idealism's involvement in the transition between Victorian and modernist literature. Yet the "British" in "British Idealism" misleadingly suggests a relatively local affair, and while I have hinted throughout this book at the cosmopolitan nature of Absolute idealism, in this chapter I will more strongly foreground its southeast Asian variants (or predecessors), which had a profound impact not just on Huxley, but on several other prominent Western writers (e.g., Gerald Heard, Christopher Isherwood, W. Somerset Maugham, the Beats) as well as late-twentieth-century British and American popular culture at large. The *Biographical Encyclopedia of British Idealism* describes the "migration" of British Idealism around the globe, which "flourished because of its openness towards, or its willingness to engage, or its resonance with local tradition" (Sweet 6). British Idealism was taught, transformed, and compared to local idealisms in Australia, New Zealand, the United States, Canada, South Africa, Japan, China, and India (8–42). While it is obviously beyond the scope of this book to investigate all these philosophical permutations—as well as the relationship between each one and its corresponding local literature—in this chapter I will closely examine the particularly noteworthy case of Advaita Vedānta, which became the first Asian spiritual movement to establish itself in the United States, and whose philosophical positions and historical trajectory are closely aligned with British Idealism's. In the journal *Mind*, for instance, Indian scholars offered several comparative readings of British Idealism and Advaita Vedānta. One example from 1912 is an essay by Potaraju Narasimham (under the pseudonym Homo Leone) entitled "The Vedantic Absolute."[3] Joel Katzav points out that such essays—like those written on Absolute idealism from a Western perspective—were systematically excluded from the pages of *Mind* and *The Philosophical Review* in 1925 and 1948, respectively, as editors antagonistic to idealism turned the journals into organs of analytic philosophy ("Disappearance").

Yet, even as idealism was driven underground by academic gatekeepers, forays into comparative philosophy were seen as exploring exciting new ground. In his foreword to P. T. Raju's *Thought and Reality: Hegelianism and Advaita* (1937), J. H. Muirhead writes, "the greatest importance attaches to recent signs of approximation to each other of leading thinkers of Great Britain and India" (18). Nalini Bhushan and Jay L. Garfield explain the reasons behind the appeal and influence of Advaita Vedānta in colonial India: "The following three critical factors—(1) the broad affinities of Vedānta and post-Kantian German and British idealism, (2) the fact that Vedānta was at the same time authentically Indian and harmonious with the most current metaphysics of the West, and (3) the fact that

Vedānta was simultaneously a suitable foundation for new religious movements as well as for secular philosophical thought—propelled Vedānta studies to the center of the philosophical stage" ("Introduction" xxii). Like British Idealism, the international success of Advaita Vedānta—and other southeast Asian philosophies, like Tibetan Buddhism, that Huxley and other Westerners blithely considered nearly interchangeable with it—had a significant effect not just on the course of Western philosophy and religion but also on the development of twentieth-century literature.

Pericles Lewis's argument that modernist novelists sought new expressions of a post-Christian "secular sacred" (21) helps explain why British Idealism, Advaita Vedānta, and Tibetan Buddhism are important contexts for understanding the modernist project and why novels at its historical fringes but thematic center, like *Robert Elsmere* and *Time Must Have a Stop*, can nevertheless be considered part of this project even as they lack the radical formal experimentation of the canonical high modernists. Woolf distinguished her own work from "materialist" novelists, like H. G. Wells and Arnold Bennett, who are "concerned not with the spirit but with the body" ("Modern Fiction" 158), and Lewis extends her opposition to materialism to most modernists, even those considered secular or atheist. According to Lewis, their spiritual concerns include "borderline states of consciousness, forms of the divided self, the process of conversion, the function of ritual, the magical potential inherent in words, moments of sublime experience, and the relationship between social life and sacred power" (5). Above all, they sought a "secular sacred, a form of transcendent or ultimate meaning to be discovered in this world, without reference to the supernatural" (21).

The modernist suspicion that spiritual or even Absolute meaning can be discovered in thoroughly earthbound experiences—from liminal states of consciousness to a confrontation with (another's or one's own) death—reveals the surprising affinity not just between modernist novels and the weird prose poems and short fiction of Machen and Sinclair, but also between them and southeast Asian philosophies as interpreted and aesthetically deployed by Huxley. Lewis notes that one of the central preoccupations of the modernists is our relationship with the dead (20). In the aftermath of World War I, spiritualism and séances received renewed interest in the 1920s and accompanied the increasing popularity, under the influence of Hinduism and neo-paganism, of cremation as well as the 1927 translation and publication of *The Tibetan Book of the Dead* (171–72). Indeed, *The Tibetan Book of the Dead*—which describes how the Absolute is reached at the moment of death and gradually lost as one becomes reincarnated—is the thematic and formal inspiration behind a crucial sequence in Huxley's *Time Must Have a Stop*, a novel that draws together all of the disparate texts and discourses described above into a magnificent expression of modernism's synthetic eclecticism.

In many ways, Huxley is the perfect figure for such synthesis. Grandson of the scientist T. H. Huxley, grandnephew of the poet Matthew Arnold, and nephew of Ward, he unites in his own genealogy the Victorian tension between scientific materialism and philosophical idealism. Likewise, Huxley's philosophy and fiction unify this tension by threading together science and idealism, pragmatic politics and spiritual mysticism, and Western and Eastern thought. In this chapter, I will mostly attend to the latter element in each of these pairs by using Advaita Vedānta and *The Tibetan Book of the Dead* as contextual frames for understanding Huxley's project. Huxley began flirting with Indian philosophy in the mid-1920s, and we see that passing interest reflected in the "soma" of *Brave New World* (1932), a drug inspired by Vedic literature. Beginning in the mid-1930s, Huxley became more deeply exposed to meditation, yoga, and Advaita Vedānta through the influence of Gerald Heard, philosopher and author of weird and science fiction. According to Dana Sawyer, Heard's "mysticism was somewhat eclectic but he mainly followed the Advaita (nondual) branch of Vedanta philosophy, an Indian viewpoint that had, more than a century earlier, influenced such German philosophers as Schelling and Schiller, and through them such others as Coleridge and Emerson. Advaita Vedanta . . . maintains that all of reality emerges from one infinite, unbounded source of spiritual energy called *Brahman*—capitalized here to signify its absoluteness" (92–93). Heard and Huxley—along with the novelist Christopher Isherwood shortly thereafter—began attending the Vedanta Society of Southern California in 1938. This exposure to Advaita marks a distinct shift in Huxley's philosophy and fiction. His early work is characterized by a scathingly ironic, anti-idealist stance, epitomized by his satire of Barbeque-Smith's "Pipelines to the Infinite" in *Crome Yellow* (1921). In *Eyeless in Gaza* (1936), however, he provides a sketch of his "mature philosophy": that there is "a spiritual reality underlying the phenomenal world" (Sawyer 92). And by the time of *Time Must Have a Stop*—one of Huxley's best-selling novels and his personal favorite—readers are given a fictional demonstration that time indeed has a stop, or is transcended, in *Brahman*/the Absolute (Sawyer 120).

The second constellation of interests that feeds into Huxley's embrace of Absolute idealism revolves around both psychedelic drugs and the *Bardo Thodol*, translated and published by Kazi Dawa-Samdup and Walter Evans-Wentz as *The Tibetan Book of the Dead* in 1927. Evans-Wentz's version and its lengthy introduction, which frames and interprets the Tibetan text from the perspectives of Theosophy and Advaita Vedānta (Reynolds 78), fascinated and inspired Huxley to the point that he read it to his wife Maria as she died in 1955, and, at his request, his second wife, Laura, read it to him after injecting him with LSD as he lay dying of cancer in 1963. The Tibetan manual describes the experience of the postmortem consciousness from death to rebirth—an experience that begins with a vision of the "Clear Light," which both Evans-Wentz and Huxley associate with *Brahman* (Huxley is especially free with substitutions, using "Clear Light," "Brahman," "the Absolute," "Suchness," "Mind at Large," and several other related terms interchangeably). Furthermore, Huxley's experiments with psychedelics experientially confirmed the metaphysical positions he acquired from southeast Asian philosophies. After taking mescaline for the first time in 1953, Huxley reached "a transfigured state that phenomenologically resembled, in his own mind at least, what the Vedantists described" (Sawyer 157).

The cultural and political aftereffects of his transfiguration are difficult to calculate, but they are indicated by the respect he was accorded by 1960s countercultural figures like Timothy Leary, Ralph Metzner, and Richard Alpert (Ram Dass), who dedicate their book *The Psychedelic Experience* (1964) to him and use *The Tibetan Book of the Dead* as an allegorical frame for understanding the "complete transcendence" of language, space, time, and selfhood at the death-like onset of the psychedelic trip (4–5)—thereby imitating *Time Must Have a Stop*. Thus, we can see Huxley's late work as a particularly influential iteration of what Lewis calls modernism's pursuit of the "secular sacred." This oxymoronic pursuit necessarily incorporated an amphibious methodology that marks the juncture of discursive and conceptual strands normally kept separate: British and Indian philosophy; Victorian and modernist literary form; time and eternity; life and death; idealism and realism; self and Absolute. "Every human being is an amphibian," Huxley remarks; "[s]imultaneously or alternately, we inhabit many different and even incommensurable universes," universes that stop, without infinite regress, in "the whole spaceless, timeless world of universal Mind" ("Education of an Amphibian" 191). Huxley's stop in the Absolute does not characterize all modernist art and philosophy, of course, but it more sharply delineates one of modernism's essential differences from postmodernism, the latter of which succumbs, the new materialists tell us, to a dualist, subjectivist, and arealist idealism.[4]

The remainder of this chapter uses a kind of amphibious methodology to explore the amalgamated contradictions that twist beyond and through Huxley's corpus. The first section traces the historical development and philosophical elaboration of Advaita Vedānta, which has ancient Indian roots in the Upaniṣads but gained a modern—and distinctly American—inflection through the spiritual eclecticism of Bengali saint Ramakrishna (1836–1886) and his disciple, Swami Vivekananda (1863–1902). Known as "the Plato of Allahabad," A. C. Mukerji (1888–1968) elaborates the same basic ideas as Ramakrishna and Vivekananda in more rigorous philosophical form, combining the medieval Advaita of the eighth-century philosopher Śaṅkara with the insights of British Idealism to demonstrate that the *condition* of individual consciousness (*Ātman*) and the atemporal Absolute (*Brahman*) are identical. This identity and how one comes to realize it through what Eliot Deutsch calls the process of "subration," or retrospective falsification, are key Advaita concepts that help unlock Huxley's allegory in *Time Must Have a Stop*, which I turn to in the second section. Like Advaita Vedānta and *The Tibetan Book of the Dead*, Huxley's novel seeks to demonstrate—through both content and form—how individuals grasp the Absolute through rites of self-estrangement or, to put it another way, in demystifying the fictions that distract them from perceiving their real identity with the Absolute. I then track the themes of the novel as they feed into Huxley's subsequent psychedelic investigations—documented in *The Doors of Perception* (1954)—to suggest that the rite of death that so fascinated Huxley and other modernists can be read as Leary, Metzner, and Alpert later insisted it should be: not as something that happens once at the end of one's life, but as a (sometimes expansive and enlightening, sometimes contractive and horrifying) epiphanic transformation that can be induced through practices like reading novels, meditating, and taking mescaline. In a concluding section, I explore what such aesthetic and psychological experimentation entails for late-twentieth-century culture. Huxley's description of a bad psychedelic trip in *The Doors of Perception*, which mirrors the after-death experience of Eustace in *Time Must Have a Stop*, presages the turn to postmodernism, in which there is no Absolute "stop" to retrospective falsification, leading to a paranoid style of subjective idealism in culture and criticism.

Degrees of Reality: Advaita Vedānta

Advaita Vedānta literally refers to the "non-dualistic" interpretation of the "end of the Vedas"—in other words, the Upaniṣads, the *Brahma Sūtras*, and the *Bhagavad Gita*. A "way of spiritual realization as well as a system of thought" (Deutsch 4), Advaita Vedānta was articulated as a philosophical system by Śaṅkara in the eighth century and his many disciples and commentators over the following centuries. In this section I will trace one relatively isolated biographical and conceptual strand of this history: the efflorescence of a distinctly modern Advaita Vedānta that began during India's late-nineteenth-century cultural revolution, rose to international prominence alongside British Idealism in the early twentieth century, and continued its cultural spread well into mid-century, appearing (among many other places) in Huxley's work.

There are four central concepts in Advaita Vedānta that will help us make sense of this tradition's modern contours and its expression in figures like Ramakrishna, Vivekananda, Mukerji, and Huxley. First, *Brahman*—which throughout the literature is translated as and made synonymous with "the Absolute"—is Reality itself, "that state which *is* when all subject/object distinctions are obliterated. . . . [It names] the experience of the timeless plenitude of being" (Deutsch 9). Second, *māyā* is what F. H. Bradley would call "appearance": the pervasive error of misrecognizing the oneness of the Real—whether through logical and temporal distinctions, affective attachments and aversions, the mistaken perceptions of dreams and waking misidentifications, or other everyday activities—that prevents us from experiencing *Brahman* (Deutsch 28–29). Third, *Ātman* is "that pure, undifferentiated self-shining consciousness, timeless, spaceless, and unthinkable, that is not-different from Brahman and that underlies and supports the individual human person" (Deutsch 48). In Kantian terms, *Ātman* is the a priori, transcendental condition of consciousness. It is distinct from yet enables and unifies the manifold differentiations of phenomena experienced by the *jīva* or individual ego, which is empirically real but transcendentally unreal—in other words, *māyā* (Deutsch 51). Fourth, one of the many paths that lead the *jīva* to realize *Ātman/Brahman* is what Deutsch calls "subration": "the mental process whereby one disvalues some previously appraised object or content of consciousness because of its being contradicted by a new experience" (15). The quintessential Advaitic example of subration, which also serves as a metaphor for the entire relationship between *māyā* and *Brahman*, is when one realizes that the snake one saw in the grass is in fact a rope. As the *jīva* subrates more and more of her experiences, recognizing that what she took to be real is only a partially real appearance, she approaches the Absolute—the only experience, according to Advaita Vedānta, that cannot be subrated. I will elaborate on the concept of subration at the end of this section, as it provides a useful framework for interpreting the form of Huxley's *Time Must Have a Stop* (and other *Bildungsromane*, Victorian and modernist).

First, however, I would like to reflect on the larger philosophical and cultural contexts of Advaita Vedānta in the late nineteenth and early twentieth centuries, contexts that were in large part shaped by spiritual polymaths like Ramakrishna, charismatic popularizers like Vivekananda, and syncretic philosophers like Mukerji. Despite the widely varying rhetoric and audiences of these three figures, their pronouncements are all remarkably consonant with the British Idealism then in vogue in Britain and its colonies, including India. While Deutsch is right to caution us that "In our rush to read Vedānta as an extension of either the Hegelian or Berkeleyan idealistic traditions, we fail to appreciate its distinctive character" (95), we cannot deny that these Eastern and Western idealisms are conceptually similar and historically intertwined. We need to be wary, not of underscoring their consonance, but of erasing their "distinctive character" and seeing the traffic between them as unidirectional, as a (colonial) "extension." Bhushan and Garfield stress that the Indian philosophy of this period is "important and original philosophy . . . written *in* English, *in* India, *by* Indians. . . . The problems they addressed were their own, raised by and for philosophers working in a tradition with roots in India, but who were cognizant of the Western tradition as well" ("Introduction" xiv). Unfortunately, the amphibious approach and dual audiences of these philosophers led to them being "taken seriously by *neither*" (xiv). Under suspicion in their time and overlooked in our own, many of these philosophers were shaped by the confluence of two traditions: the revival of interest in Advaita Vedānta, inspired by the Arya Samaj and Brahmo Samaj reform movements; and the "coincidental import" of British Idealism into India (xxii). Indian and Western, ancient and modern, religious and secular, Advaita Vedānta at the turn of the century was a remarkably hybrid system of thought. Conceptually omnivorous and plastic, it could never wholly appeal to everyone—but its advocates made such universalist appeals and, to an unprecedented degree, successfully managed to establish an institutional foothold in the United States, where Huxley absorbed it.

As embodied in the Ramakrishna movement, a spiritual and humanitarian organization founded by Vivekananda in 1897, Advaita Vedānta became the first Asian spiritual movement to establish itself in the United States through its Vedanta Societies, and it paved the way for later organizations like the Hare Krishnas, the Self-Realization Fellowship, and the Self-Revelation Church of Absolute Monism. Vivekananda is responsible for emphasizing Advaita Vedānta at the expense of the eclectic range of spiritual and philosophical interests of Ramakrishna himself, who at various times was a devoted Vedantist, Tantrist, Vaishnavite, Muslim, Christian, and worshipper of Kālī. Vivekananda, who found his guru's worship of Kālī especially repellant (Jackson 23), decided to deemphasize the significance of Ramakrishna himself, advocating instead for Advaita Vedānta as a philosophical system in accord with the spirit of both Christianity and modern science. As Carl T. Jackson shows, it is precisely this philosophical emphasis that originally attracted most Westerners to the movement, and this continued to be the case into the 1940s and 1950s, when Huxley became a major force for recruitment (77, 103). As an example of how the Ramakrishna movement promoted a variety of Absolute idealism, take the first three of ten "doctrines" promulgated by the Vedanta Society of San Francisco in 1904: "(1) there is 'One Absolutely Everlasting Blissful Intelligence' into which the universe and individual souls will ultimately be merged; (2) all ideas of heaven, hell, and even 'God Himself' must be viewed as relative when juxtaposed to the Absolute; (3) human beings are not born-sinners destined for hell; on the contrary, with appropriate spiritual effort, every human being may attain liberation and union with the Absolute" (qtd. in Jackson 68). The number of people attracted enough by such claims to join the movement was never very large, with official members numbering in the hundreds up until the 1950s, when it broke into the thousands. Nevertheless, "few other religious bodies of such Lilliputian size have equaled the movement's impact or historical significance" (Jackson 108).

Huxley was associated with the Vedanta Society of Southern California, founded by Swami Prabhavananda in 1930. Prabhavananda—who served as Huxley's guru, at least temporarily (Huxley was skeptical of the need for gurus)—charts the development of the various schools of Indian philosophy in *The Spiritual Heritage of India* (1962). Divided into five main sections, Prabhavananda's book gives Advaita Vedānta teleological pride of place, with Ramakrishna's life and philosophy summarized in the penultimate chapter, just before the conclusion. As it was Prabhavananda who taught Advaita Vedānta to Huxley, and as many of his ideas find an echo in Huxley's later work, his presentation of both Advaita Vedānta and Ramakrishna is worth brief consideration here. Like Huxley, Prabhavananda emphasized the need to account for, and draw practical ethical lessons from, both realism and idealism, science and spirituality. "Vedānta philosophy occupies a central position between realism and idealism," he writes. "Western realism and idealism are both based on a distinction between mind and matter; Indian philosophy puts mind and matter in the same category" (283). Although the concept of *māyā* seems to advocate a kind of subjective idealism, suggesting that "the world of thought and matter is not real," that "does not mean that it is nonexistent": "Śaṁkara's philosophy differs essentially from the subjective idealism of the West" (284, 288).

Indeed, Prabhavananda sees a consensus between the mystical conclusions of Advaita Vedānta and the objective ones reached by science: "Modern science goes a long way towards confirming the Vedānta world-picture. It admits that consciousness, in varying degrees, may be present everywhere. Differences between objects and creatures are only surface differences, varying arrangements of atomic pattern. Elements can be changed into other elements. Identity is only provisional. Science does not yet accept the concept of absolute reality, but it certainly does not exclude it" (294). Moreover, the everyday world of differences, distortions, physicality, and evil is not only *existent* (i.e., partially real) but also a *necessary means* to reach the Absolute. The world of *māyā* is "a kind of gymnasium. Good and evil, pain and pleasure, still exist [to the spiritually adept], but they seem more like ropes and vaulting-horses and parallel bars which can be used to make our bodies strong" (292). *Māyā* is a "ladder" we climb to the Absolute, and therefore all our actions and attitudes on the various planes of reality are ethically significant: "If we recognize our brotherhood with our fellow men; if we try to deal honestly, truthfully, charitably with them; if we work for equal rights and equal justice, politically and economically, and for abolition of barriers of race and class—then we are in fact giving the lie to the ego-idea and moving towards awareness of the universal, nonindividual Existence" (292, 293). Far from being quietist or cloistered, Advaita Vedānta encourages an active engagement with the messy, dangerous realities of modern existence.

Perhaps because he was more comfortable with the idea of messiness and danger, Prabhavananda, unlike Vivekananda, is a little more forthcoming about Ramakrishna's wide-ranging eclecticism and seemingly bizarre actions and experiences. He underscores the central role that Kālī worship played in Ramakrishna's life and relates the pivotal, violent episode when Ramakrishna, under the tutelage of the Vedāntic monk Totā Purī, transcends the personal manifestation of God in Kālī to achieve union with the impersonal Absolute. Totā Purī presses a shard of glass into Ramakrishna's forehead, and Ramakrishna "began to meditate as directed, and when this time also the blessed form of the Mother [Kālī] appeared before me, I used my discrimination as a sword and severed her form in two. Then my mind soared immediately beyond all duality and entered into nirvakalpa, the nondual, unitary consciousness" (qtd. in Swami Prabhavananda 338–39). Reading *The Gospel of Sri Ramakrishna*, one is struck even more by the radical nature of Ramakrishna's experiences and behavior, which are not dissociated from but vehicles for what Huxley calls, in the foreword to the manuscript, "the most profound and subtle utterances about the nature of Ultimate Reality" (vi). For instance, we learn from Swami Nikhilananda's[5] introduction that Ramakrishna meditated in burial grounds, watched various persons emerge from his body, behaved like a monkey, had a vision of *māyā* as a beautiful woman who crushes a baby in its jaws, and regarded himself as a woman, dressing in women's clothing and jewelry (13, 15, 22, 24–25). Through such confrontation and play, Ramakrishna immerses himself in appearances, eventually seeing them not as something to be transcended but as the Absolute itself. Nikhilananda remarks, "To [Ramakrishna] māyā itself was God, for everything was God. It was one of the faces of Brahman. What he had realized on the heights of the transcendental plane, he also found here below, everywhere about him, under the mysterious garb of names and forms. . . . Māyā, the mighty weaver of the garb, is none other than Kāli, the Divine Mother" (30). As Ramakrishna himself puts it, "The phenomenal world belongs to that very Reality to which the Absolute belongs; again, the Absolute belongs to that very Reality to which the phenomenal world belongs" (328). This enfolded ontology entails a familiar ethics. In the words of Nikhilananda, "the service of man [is] the same as the worship of God" (36).

The extent to which Ramakrishna explored some of the more extreme Tantric Aghori practices—Jeffrey J. Kripal points, for example, to contemporaneous biographical reports of Ramakrishna touching his tongue to rotting human flesh to demonstrate absolute ontological flatness ("Kāli's Tongue" 164–69)—remains controversial and contested, and it is unclear whether Huxley was aware of these reports. It is worth remarking here, however, that Huxley's fiction and philosophy engage as much with this more fleshy side of Advaita Vedānta as the more abstract side exemplified by Vivekananda and Mukerji, which emerged as Advaita's public face in the wake of Kālī's erasure.[6] To be fair, Vivekananda's lack of interest in Kālī's relationship to the Absolute simply led him to find other dualisms to subject to an amphibious critique, and he never disavowed materiality or the things of the world: "I myself am a materialist in a certain sense, because I believe that there is only One" (*Jñāna Yoga* 319). He was especially interested in questioning the supposed split between religion and science and the supposed superiority of the latter. In *Jñāna Yoga*, a collection of his lectures, Vivekananda makes "religious superstition" indistinguishable from the "scientific superstition" accruing around T. H. Huxley, in what must have come across as a challenge to Huxley's grandson: "In modern times, if a man quotes a Moses or a Buddha or a Christ, he is laughed at; but let him give the name of a Huxley, a Tyndall, or a Darwin, and it is swallowed without salt. 'Huxley has said it,' that is enough for many" (274). Indeed, much like Aldous (and Robert Elsmere), Vivekananda seeks to promote "the religion of the future," a "rationalistic religion" that has room under the tent for both the "scientist [who] makes the assertion that all objects are the manifestation of one force" and the Christ who says "I and my Father are One" (320, 322). Advaita Vedānta is neither suspicious of modern science nor nostalgic for ancient gods: "out of the old deities, out of the monotheistic God, the Ruler of the universe, [proponents of Advaita Vedānta] found yet higher and higher ideas in what is called the Impersonal Absolute; they found oneness throughout the universe" (304).

For Vivekananda, then, the best analog or ally for Advaita Vedānta is Absolute idealism. He compares Advaita Vedānta to, and even identifies it with, both the German and English traditions. For instance, Schopenhauer's "interpretation of Vedānta [errs] for it . . . makes the will stand in the place of the Absolute. But the Absolute cannot be presented as will, for will is something changeable and phenomenal, and over the line drawn above time, space, and causation, there is no change, no motion" (314; see Fig. 5.1). In other words, Vivekananda takes the Bradleyan position that all relations, including temporal relations, are appearances that cannot be predicated of the Absolute. He would agree with Huxley (and Shakespeare, from whom the title derives) that "time must have a stop": "in the Absolute, there is neither time, nor space, nor causation; It is all one. That which exists by itself alone cannot have any cause; else it would not be free, but bound" (*Jñāna Yoga* 315).

According to Advaita Vedānta, we can verify that this Absolute reality that conditions our temporal, relational experience of worldly phenomena exists because it is identical to the condition of consciousness, Ātman, which meets the Absolute as a wave meets the ocean (317). The condition of consciousness is the "form" (317) populated by all the particular people, objects, thoughts, and emotions that make me, me. But the condition, my real self, cannot be found in any single one of these people, objects, thoughts, or emotions, nor does it reside in their totality. It is the place, or non-place, where all waves rest on the ocean. This seamless seam is the "Real Man," "unchangeable, immovable, absolute" (277). And yet, Vivekananda acknowledges that uncovering this real self—canceling externality—is a terrifying prospect: "People are frightened when they are told that they are Universal Being, everywhere present. Through everything you work, through every foot you move, through every lip you talk, through every heart you feel. People are frightened when they are told this. They will again and again ask you if they are not going to keep

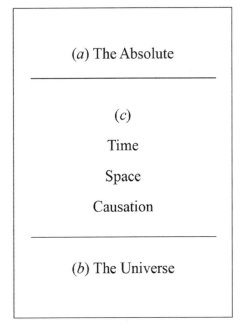

Figure 5.1. From the position of the phenomenal world (b), we perceive (a) only through the "window" of (c). *Source*: Vivekananda, *Jñāna Yoga* (313).

their individuality" (277). To rest on the ocean is to drown. The timeless Absolute accompanies the metaphorical and literal death of the ego or *jīva*. Vivekananda again and again exhorts his audience to surrender the *jīva* to death, to recognize that the little self that imagines itself as a possession, as "mine," as an "I," *is* death because it is too afraid to possess itself of, and be possessed by, its actual nature: absolutely everything. "Those moments alone we live when our lives are in the universe, in others," he states, "and living this little life is death, simply death, and that is why the fear of death comes."

To be fearless and happy, we must learn to say, "I am the universe" (278). This identification will allow us, through "sympathy, the feeling of sameness everywhere," to lovingly care for others, human and nonhuman alike (279). Such ontological and ethical sentiments place Vivekananda in the same tradition as the Romantic poets and the Victorian novelists of sympathy, especially Eliot. They also connect him to the philosophical and novelistic strands of Advaita Vedānta that came later, in the interwar writings of Mukerji and Huxley. Mukerji, like Vivekananda, insists on the amphibious philosophical approach of Advaita Vedānta/Absolute idealism and the amphibious nature of the self/Self. At the beginning of "Absolute Consciousness," a key chapter from *The Nature of Self* (1938), Mukerji draws together Eastern and Western philosophical traditions to reconcile what he sees as the false dichotomy between idealism and realism. Because "modern absolutism [i.e., British Idealism] . . . is an unconscious exposition of the advaita doctrine," we can trace an idealist genealogy that runs through "Śaṅkara, Kant, Green, [Richard Burdon] Haldane, and Bradley" to discover that "an unchanging, unobjectifiable, immediate, consciousness must be postulated for explaining the poorest type of knowledge and the facts of experience" (325). In other words, our knowledge and experience of external reality presupposes an absolute ideality: an atemporal consciousness that is both particular self and Absolute Self. This claim is meant to "dissipate the wide-spread illusion that the advaita Absolute is an altogether transcendent Principle, sitting, like an oriental potentate, out of all connections with our finite experiences" (325). Here, Mukerji, an Indian philosopher, associates the false but common accusation that Advaita Vedānta and Absolute idealism are disconnected from or denigrate embodied, material reality with the most vulgar Orientalism. Instead, he insists, the Absolute is to be conceived of as immanent and intimate, as both the material that we face in everyday experience and the immaterial interface that enables any experience at all. The astounding claim of Advaita Vedānta is that each of us is this Absolute.

The problem, for Mukerji, is to explain why this claim remains so counterintuitive and how to overcome the intractable nominalist tendency of "realists" to dismiss ideal realities as unreal, floating abstractions. He suggests that the solution to the problem lies in clearly delineating between *conditions* (such as consciousness, natural laws, and the Absolute) and *objects*. Consciousness is not an object like other objects: it cannot be objectified, or precisely defined by discourse, because it is the very condition in which objects and language arise. Yet, while consciousness and other conditions cannot be defined or known in the same way as the objects that fall under their purview, that does not mean they are completely unknowable, meaningless, or unreal. Mukerji argues that it would be "absurd" to say that "there can be no theoretical knowledge of space on the ground that all spaces that are ever known are limited spaces, or that light is theoretically unknowable because what is known directly is an illumined object" (348). "You cannot," he declares, "handle a universal law as you handle the stick or the brickbat, but this does not warrant the conclusion that the law is less real than the stick" (338).

Similarly, we cannot say that "theoretical knowledge" of Absolute consciousness is impossible because we experience consciousness as something individual. Indeed, "the method of establishing [the Absolute's] reality is [through] a further analysis of our own self which is consciousness" (331). As we pay closer attention to our own consciousness, what we inevitably notice is that some of its contents become less veridical than others. Continually, in the light of current experience, we retrospectively assess certain past experiences and "truths" as being dreams or delusions, misapprehensions or mistakes: "The world of experience is for the adult mind split up into a multiplicity of worlds with varying degrees of reality; we habitually make the experiences of waking consciousness the standard of reality, and then seek to explain dreams by reference to that standard. Within the waking experiences again it is customary to distinguish between experiences which are real and those that are illusory or abnormal" ("Realist's Conception of Idealism" 482). What this implies—especially Mukerji's emphasis on the "adult" mind—is that the activity of delineating degrees and standards of reality, all the way up to the Absolute, is a developmental process, a struggle. By applying memory to the temporal flow of specific empirical experiences, through the accumulation of attempts to comparatively position them in relation to "standards" and ideal conditions, we gradually come to recognize conditions that alter less and less across time, conditions that more and more continuously, more and more universally, underlie specific events and make them real. This same developmental process could describe the trajectory of the scientific theory, the spiritual journey, and the plot of the novel, perhaps most obviously the *Bildungsroman* but even the most fragmented, metatextual, and confounding of (post)modernist novels. Against some (necessarily evolving) external ideal, the scientist, the contemplative, the coming-of-age character, and the reader of novels comparatively construct a spectrum of reality that helps them make sense of their particular "worlds." And the end they all pursue, Mukerji would suggest—the maximal degree of reality, the final, Absolute "world"—is consciousness itself.

In *Advaita Vedānta: A Philosophical Reconstruction*, Deutsch provides a helpfully detailed analysis of this process of parsing reality, which, as I have mentioned above, he calls "subration" (15–26). He defines subration as "the mental process whereby one disvalues some previously appraised object or content of consciousness because of its being contradicted by a new experience," and this process allows one to distinguish between three qualitatively different levels of being: Reality, which cannot be subrated by any other experience; Appearance, which can be subrated by other experience; and Unreality, which neither can nor cannot be subrated by other experience (15). Although the ability to distinguish various degrees of reality occurs over a period of time, the event of subration itself is "immediate" (17n1). We *suddenly* realize that our lover is deceptive, that the snake is merely a rope, that our theory is fallacious, and that we must jettison the old orientation for the new. But these new relationships, objects, and concepts are always in turn subject to future falsification. Except for Reality, which "is the experience wherein the separation of self and non-self, of ego and world, is transcended, and pure oneness alone remains. This is the experience celebrated by the Advaitin as one of perfect insight, bliss, and power; as one of infinite joy and understanding" (18). It is *Brahman, Ātman,* and Absolute. No other experience can falsify it, but it is by no means a common experience.

Instead, most of the average person's experiences fall within the level of Appearance, which in turn can be differentiated into *real existents, existents,* and *illusory existents.* Real existents—for example, the experience of true love for another person, the aesthetic experience, and concepts like the law of non-contradiction—can only be subrated by Reality. The high degree of reality granted to art by Advaita Vedānta is worth remarking. Deutsch explains that

> [o]ne who experiences a work of art and who feels that his experience is successful, that it provides integration and insight, values that experience in ways that rule out its being contradicted and replaced by another kind of sense-mental experience. A work of art, then, which is so capable of eliciting this kind of response, is subratable only through the realization that no work of art is comparable to the splendor of Reality; that no work of art can fully grasp that splendor or transmit it to others. (21)

Much of our lives, alas, is not spent basking in the intensity of love or reading powerful novels. Instead of these real existents, we are most often immersed in existents. These are the casual and instrumental relationships we have with others (which become falsified by more significant, loving relationships), the objects we take to be particular and independent (which become falsified when we realize how all objects are enmeshed with everything else), and the concepts we use within particular domains (which become falsified when applied to other domains). Finally, even less real than existents are illusory existents, which we recognize as hallucinations, dreams, and erroneous perceptions: the false lover, the "snake" in the grass, the fallacious argument. And Unreality, which neither can nor cannot be subrated, is exemplified by inconceivable expressions such as a "square circle." These, according to Deutsch's interpretation of Advaita Vedānta, are the three levels of reality.

Because these levels are qualitatively different, it is impossible to establish causal relationships between them. Epistemologically, logically, and axiologically, they are incommensurable. This is why "assertions about the Godhead or Absolute in religious literature made from the empirical standpoint [i.e., the level of Appearance] may legitimately violate—and they frequently do—the law of [non-]contradiction" (26n9). Indeed, as we have seen throughout this book, philosophical and literary attempts to say something precise and meaningful about the Absolute often trail off into metaphors, allusions, or mind-bending contradictions along the lines of "the self *is* the universe." For Deutsch, this failure is the necessary result of applying the tools of one domain to another. We simply cannot fully define or describe Reality from the perspective of Appearance. We can only experience the Absolute, or the fringes of it, through activities like falling in love, reading a novel, meditating, and taking mescaline. By whatever means we reach it within a temporal sequence, "during" such an immediate experience the distinction between the three levels of reality will be subrated, along with all the other distinctions that time creates and language manipulates.

The tradition of Advaita Vedānta as I have sketched it above sets up several problems for Huxley to resolve as a novelist and philosopher. How does one narrativize the undefinable and extradiscursive, things like timelessness, consciousness, death, and the Absolute, and what form should such a narrative take? How does one establish various degrees of reality as they are conceived of and experienced by individual characters and the reader, and how are these degrees set off from one another and adjudicated? How is a character made particular and/or Absolute? Is the latter—a saintlike figure not driven by idiosyncratic desires and aversions—utterly boring, unsympathetic, and incommensurable with a plot that demands conflict and change? What are the ethical implications of the reality spectrum? Does exposure to the Absolute create moral insight that is practically applicable in one's relationship with others? Is such insight enduring or ephemeral? Is it edifying to be taken through another person's process of subration? What are the mechanisms and dangers of what we might call "subration resistance"—from one's stubborn persistence in unhealthy mental and physical habits to the allure of violent ideologies like nationalism, which Huxley was so keen on combating, or the fidelity to absurd conspiracy theories that characterizes our own time—and how can such resistance be overcome? The next section explores how Huxley answers such questions in his fiction and nonfiction, and how these answers inform his ethics and politics.

Aldous Huxley: Germinal Terminal

Before examining Huxley's work directly, it's worth mentioning three contexts that, in addition to Advaita Vedānta, help us position *Time Must Have a Stop*. The first is the modernist preoccupation with death. In *Death Sentences*, Garrett Stewart explains how the post-Romantic death of God intensified novelists' interest in death as an end in itself, but in "conjunction with this agnostic shift there are also deflections mystic and erotic by which death is transferred to a metaphor for other human transitions. According to such transcendental or ecstatic analogues, death can bestow renewed identity on the self when it arrives in the regenerative guise of visionary trance or sexual oblivion, as well as when it appears in its familiar way to comment on a completed life" (10–11). In *Time Must Have a Stop*, Huxley uses death in this doubled sense, death as a renewal of life that occurs both metaphorically—through mystical, sexual, and other intense experiences—and literally, in death itself (although for Huxley, the self-renewal in this case is not solely metaphorical, not just a renewal in the form of the recollections of others, but also literal reincarnation). Indeed, Stewart makes it clear that death is a privileged novelistic site for contemplating amphibious identities and sublated (or subrated) contradictions. For him, the novel is "a genre inevitably materialist in the bearings of its mimesis," but "[d]eath in fiction aspires beyond mimesis to an absolute poesis of the word" (22, 5). An absolute poesis that blurs the distinction between fiction and reality is also, paradoxically, beyond discourse, a terminal silence, and this is why death functions to organize dichotomies like "time and eternity, declaration and negation, self and other, presence and absence" (42–43). Death's "infinite instant" marks the moment when the content of the novel "can be found dissolving to pure form" (11, 3). Moreover, death can be "thought momentarily to elevate the self isolated by it to the central protagonist of the one universal plot" (4). By rendering this impossible moment of death, the novelist makes it possible to shift our "structural perceptions" (7), our sense of the degrees of reality that shade together such monumental oxymorons as living dead, eternal instant, formal content, and particular universal. And we perform such reevaluations immediately and retrospectively, in the "epiphany" of "pure retrospect" induced by death (45).

The second context within which we can place *Time Must Have a Stop* is the British Idealist argument for the unreality of time in relation to the atemporal Absolute. A number of philosophers debated the reality of time in the pages of *Mind* and elsewhere from the 1870s to the 1920s.[7] The most well-known version is J. M. E. McTaggart's "The Unreality of Time" (1908), which elaborates on a point he made in an earlier essay from 1894: "There is then nothing impossible in the supposition that the whole appearance of succession in our experience is, as such, unreal, and that reality is one timeless whole, in which all that appears successive is really coexistent, as the houses are coexistent which we see successively from the windows of a train" ("Time" 192). Here McTaggart suggests that the presentation of reality is necessarily successive to someone sitting on a time-bound train—at least until one reaches the terminus, alights, and immediately grasps the continuous whole. Such arguments were particularly conducive to novelistic innovation, especially novelistic form: How does one "alight" from the necessarily successive experience of reading a novel in order to perceive alternative temporalities or atemporal realities? To take just one example of how modernist writers struggled with such questions, in her workbooks Sinclair repeatedly sketched diagrams and tables of linear, planar, cubic, and four-dimensional time, attempting to map out the ways in which specific facets and edges of four-dimensional time would conjoin seemingly unreal and incommensurable temporalities like "past-past," "present-future," and "future-past" (Workbook 34). Moreover, as we saw in the previous chapter, she often uses death and post-death experiences to narrativize these counterintuitive time scales. Huxley was well acquainted with McTaggart's philosophy and mobilized his own artistic response, using death as a vehicle to manifest the timeless.

The third context is the publication of *The Tibetan Book of the Dead*. While acknowledging that the text is an expression of Mahāyāna Buddhism, Evans-Wentz's introduction makes clear its resonance with Advaita Vedānta. He claims that "much of the *Bardo* symbolism originated" in "Hindu mythology" (7), and the posthumous experience of the deceased is described as a sinking from an immersion in the Absolute (the first *Bardo* or transitional state) into deeper and deeper levels of unreality (the second *Bardo*), terminating in (re)birth (the third *Bardo*). In the first *Bardo*, the deceased is unaware that she is dead, finds it difficult to recognize the "Clear Light" of the Absolute, and fails to maintain a connection with "the unmodified mind concomitant with it" (29). Upon realizing that she is dead, the deceased enters the second *Bardo*, in which a series of hallucinatory visions appear, some pleasant and some horrifying, some revolving around the delusion of having a body or the desire to possess one. These visions are particular to the deceased—for instance, a Christian and a materialist would have quite different subjective projections, perhaps of demons and emptiness, respectively—but in every case the deceased is unaware that these projections are unreal appearances (29–34). Evans-Wentz compares this *Bardo* to the sequential experience of watching a film projection: "the thought-forms, born of habitual propensities, being mental records comparable . . . to records on a cinema-film, their reel running to its end, the after-death state ends, and the Dreamer, emerging from the womb, begins to experience anew the phenomena of the human world" (34). Just as McTaggart implies that exiting the train at the terminus allows one to grasp the timeless whole of reality, Evans-Wentz argues that the aim of *The Tibetan Book of the Dead* is "to cause the Dreamer to awaken into Reality" (35), which occurs, ouroboros-style, at both the beginning and the end of the film, at both death and rebirth. Finally, Evans-Wentz is at pains to suggest that this doctrine of reincarnation is "in the main, scientific," pointing to none other than T. H. Huxley's comparison of inherited characteristics to reincarnation and "karma" (34, 60–61). No doubt Aldous appreciated this passage and Evans-Wentz's synthesizing approach in general, and he repeatedly and enthusiastically recommends *The Tibetan Book of the Dead* in his nonfiction and incorporates its themes into his fiction and his life.

Time Must Have a Stop folds together the aforementioned discourses, using themes of timelessness and (life after) death to trace characters' halting and half-successful attempts over the span of the two World Wars—and eternity—to transcend appearance and gain ethically fruitful insight into reality. The novel also metatextually reflects upon the ability of literature to incite such transcendence. The main plot follows the maturation of Sebastian Barnack from a selfish poet lost in his own fanciful projections into a wise, war-damaged playwright. This transformation occurs through Sebastian's encounter with a series of other characters who nudge him out of his complacency: Paul De Vries, who hopes to develop a philosophical and scientific integration of mind and matter while ironically failing to recognize his own physical desires; Veronica Thwale, who boldly manipulates men (including Paul and Sebastian) by better understanding their own sexuality yet also estranges Sebastian, and possibly herself, into an experience of absolute alterity through devouring sexual acts; Eustace Barnack, Sebastian's cynical and hedonistic uncle, who dies of a heart attack on the bathroom floor but proves to his nephew, through garbled hints made through the medium of a séance, that "some unknown, non-bodily x" persists after death (234); and the bookseller Bruno Rontini, the most spiritually advanced person in the novel—"the little flame in his heart seemed to expand, as it were, and aspire, until it touched that other light beyond it and within" (104)—who ends up being brutalized by the Italian fascists.

Almost all the characters are described, at some point, as infantile or larval, and their naïveté results from an unrecognized adherence to either materialism (in the case of Veronica and Eustace) or subjective idealism (in the case of Paul and Sebastian). Bruno alone has found a unified perspective in Absolute idealism, and Sebastian concurs with him only by the end of the novel, after he has "died" to his irrelevant and injurious obsessions, most notably his desire for evening clothes that drives much of the early plot. Thus, the awakening to reality occurs—as Ernest Hemingway famously wrote of bankruptcy—gradually, then suddenly: only after a long trajectory of accumulated actions and reflections, and then in an immediate intuition. Huxley mimics this amphibious temporality both in his descriptions of Sebastian's development as a writer and formally, by interleaving a straightforward *Bildungsroman* with Eustace's timeless travails in *Bardo* and by suddenly concluding an omniscient narrative with epistolary fragments plagiarized from his own philosophy. And finally, perhaps even more relentlessly than Eliot, Huxley makes it clear that being enraptured with one's own selfish interests—whether fine food or fine concepts—is antithetical to sympathy, the positive ground of ethics and politics.

The novel opens with Daisy Ockham, who later inherits Eustace's wealth, giving chocolates to Sebastian because he looks like her dead son. At first blithely dismissive of this "tiresome creature," Sebastian fleetingly reflects on the dead boy as a synecdoche for misery, violence, and death in general: "All over the world, millions of men and women lying in pain; millions dying, at this very moment; millions more grieving over them, their faces distorted, like that poor old hag's, the tears running down their cheeks. And millions starving, millions frightened, and sick, and anxious. Millions being cursed and kicked and beaten by other brutal millions" (3). Although this reflection is both hyperbolic ("millions dying, at this very moment") and condescending ("that poor old hag"), it marks the reality that Sebastian will eventually have to confront without hyperbole or condescension, with a level gaze that elevates neither the other nor the self. Indeed, by the end of the novel, he has lost one of his hands and lives precariously surrounded by the actual misery, violence, and death of World War II. But early on, not yet cut by Ockham's razor, Sebastian readily forgets about death by aestheticizing it, writing a Romantic-inspired lyric that begins with "the miseries of the world" and culminates in "Light Itself—/ The incandescent copulation of Gods" (3–7). This is an idealism shorn of realism, a projection of his own (largely sexual) desires. For young Sebastian, poetic, sexual, and religious "ecstasies" are superior to "all the merely humdrum and ordinary states of being" (7). All the fantasies and fictions he concocts, like his non-existent lover "Mary Esdaile," are experienced by Sebastian and his cousin Susan "quite as intensely as . . . the real world. More intensely perhaps" (12). This subjective idealism, where projections from the self are cast as "Light Itself," is gradually discarded as Sebastian matures and gains a vantage that falsifies its assumptions. By the middle of the novel, Sebastian is planning a new poem that reverses the trajectory of his juvenilia: "From the ideally excellent he would pass to the actualities of ugliness, cruelty, ineptitude, death. After which, in a third part, ecstasy and intelligence would build the bridges leading from the actual to the ideal—from the blue tart and his father's severities to Mrs. Thwale and Mary Esdaile, from the corpse in the lavatory to Theocritus and Marvell" (179–80). This, Huxley suggests, is a more sophisticated, if still distorted, relational account. And by the end of the novel, Sebastian has abandoned the self-centered mode of lyric poetry for multi-centered, dialogic plays.

Paul De Vries, like Sebastian, begins the novel as an idealist insufficiently attuned to everyday material reality and ends in a more comprehensive, if vexed, state thanks to his collision with sexuality. When we first meet him, he rhapsodizes on the significance of Einstein's theory of relativity, a "revolution that had changed the whole course of scientific thinking, brought back idealism, integrated mind into the fabric of Nature, put an end for ever to the Victorians' nightmare universe of infinitesimal billiard balls" (86). Like Ernest Pontifex from Butler's *The Way of All Flesh*, Paul sees himself as a bridge-builder who can reunite idealism and materialism:

> one of his jobs as *pontifex minimus* . . . [was to discover] a thought-bridge that would permit the mind to march discursively and logically from telepathy to the four-dimensional continuum, from poltergeists and departed spirits to the physiology of the nervous system. And beyond the happenings of the séance room there were the events of the oratory and the meditation hall. There was the ultimate all-embracing field—the Brahma[n] of Sankara, the One of Plotinus, the Ground of Eckhart and Boehme[.] (91–92)

Paul's problem is that he is insufficiently amphibious, lapsing into an arid intellectualism that privileges "the uncontaminated idea" (89). He only comes to realize the partiality of this position when he falls in love with Veronica, suddenly overwhelmed by her physicality. As he pontificates on Havelock Ellis's theory of sublimated love, he becomes "suddenly aware that this wasn't at all what he really wanted to talk to her about." Instead, compelled by her perfume, her neck, and the black silk stretched over her breasts, his intellectual yearning "came sharply into focus as desire" (165). This actual bridge between ideal and physical immediately falsifies his previous philosophy and enables a dawning sense of his sexuality, but Paul remains blind to the fact that his desire is being managed by Veronica, who goes on to seduce Sebastian just after accepting Paul's marriage proposal.

Veronica's ability to estrange others from their comfortable assumptions becomes intensified in her relationship with Sebastian, which, it is implied, alienates even her own carefully composed persona. Her upbringing in a stiflingly pious family has given her an allergy to religion matched only by Eustace's, and she imagines how "awful" it would be for God to see all one's secrets—she prefers cordoning off her subjectivity behind fans, masks, and screens, perhaps most especially the screen of her own body (73, 75). Yet, when she and Sebastian have sex toward the end of the novel, they are both shivered into a distinctly non-physical ecstasy. Sebastian describes it as a kind of cannibalism. Instead of the "gay, ethereal intoxication" he imagined sex would bring, the "reality was more like madness." Through the "delicate gluttony of those soft lips that would suddenly give place to teeth and pointed nails," through her "imperiously whispered commands," they become "[t]win cannibals, devouring their own identity and one another's; ravening up reason and decency; obliterating the most rudimentary conventions of civilization. And yet it was precisely there, in that frenzy of the cannibals, that the real attraction had lain. Beyond the physical pleasure lay the yet more rapturous experience of being totally out of bounds, the ecstasy of an absolute alienation" (223). Because we are not given Veronica's perspective on this relationship, we do not know if she feels the same way. Yet we learn that their clandestine relationship continues for years, throughout Sebastian's marriage and after the death of his wife, when he recognizes their sexual acts as "an experience of otherness almost as absolute, on its own level, as the otherness of God" (278). We can presume that Veronica may have come to a similar realization.

While sexual intimacy is shown to be one of the most powerful means for destroying and reconstituting the self, Eustace's sexual exploits are merely instrumental, habitual, and therefore self-reaffirming. Only death itself challenges Eustace's desperate need to shelter himself from alterity. Beginning with chapter 13 of *Time Must Have a Stop*, alternating chapters follow the experiences of the "x" that persists after Eustace's physical death in highly abstract prose reminiscent of a Hegelian philosophical treatise. At first, x is simply an awareness of absence and privation. It then knows itself as "known" and "interpenetrated by a shining presence," experiencing a timeless "eternity of joy." Yet this Absolute "knowledge was so penetratingly luminous that the participation in it was beyond the capacity of that which participated" (136–38). X recoils, turning its attention back to the "one small clot of untransparent absence" that once constituted x as a discrete entity (139). This clot, x finally realizes, ashamed at its separateness and opacity, is Eustace Barnack. Subsequent chapters follow this "Eustace" as he oscillates between a desire to merge with the Light and a desire to assert his own specific, clot-like personality. He scurries along the "living lattice" of the Absolute, a "vast ubiquitous web of beknottednesses and divergences, of parallels and spirals, of intricate figures and their curiously distorted projections—all shining and active and alive" (154). "Slipping sideways" through various planes of the lattice, he enters other characters' consciousnesses and sees, rising before him, "a whole galaxy of awarenesses" (169). Ultimately, however, the allure of separation is too enticing. His incarnation in the medium's body at the séance gives him once again a taste of the "infinitely precious" bliss of possessing a body, and he ultimately chooses the uterine "darkness of flesh and blood" over the Light (173, 259). Ironically, however, after "remembering events that had not yet taken place"—namely, thousands of people fleeing the devastations of war, his own "future" mother killed under the wheels of a truck—we discover that Eustace will be reborn as a child of the Weyls, fascist sympathizers responsible for Bruno's arrest and torture. Whereas for Paul, Veronica, and Sebastian the turn to (feminized) materiality leads to an attenuated awakening to the reality of self-alienation, Eustace (re)turns to the perpetual human experience of other, darker alienations: violence, war, and death.

Unlike Eustace, who rejects Bruno's spiritual advice, Sebastian has the benefit of having both him and Veronica as guides to a more comprehensive perspective. Late in the novel, Bruno asks Sebastian to consider the convoluted "genealogy" of all his lies and half-truths, from telling his friend that he does have a dinner jacket to concealing his sale of Eustace's painting to fund the purchase of said jacket. One must look, Bruno says, "[b]ack into past history. Out into the world around one. Forward into possible consequences. It makes one realize that nothing one does is unimportant and nothing wholly private" (238). By subjectively adopting this more Absolute perspective—one that considers temporal, ontological, and ethical interconnection across scales—Sebastian begins to see through the falsity of his adolescent conjuring tricks to their negative effects on other people (and himself). His maturation is rapidly accelerated on the objective side by the war, a vast arrangement of humans, machines, and spaces being maimed, exploded, scorched—an arrangement that literally presses into the subject, impossible to ignore. In 1944, guns banging away, Sebastian writes in his notebook, "one was guilty by just being imperviously oneself, by being content to remain a spiritual embryo, undeveloped, undelivered, unillumined. In part, at least, I am responsible for my own maiming, and on the hand that is left me there is blood and the black oily smear of charred flesh" (284). This startling statement could be read two different ways: negatively, since he considers himself, at least in part, responsible for and guiltily burdened by literally everything because he *is* everything; but also more positively, since it suggests that he is not merely a passive victim but an actant who can positively shape almost anything. Here Sebastian reflects Huxley's ethical and political views as given in *Ends and Means*, where he argues that "our metaphysical beliefs are the finally determining factor in all our actions" (11). For Huxley, a pacifist writing on the cusp of World War II, only a metaphysical system that asserts Absolute monism and timeless, universal values can prevent or mitigate a dangerous turn toward racism, nationalism, war, and the propaganda and false ideologies needed to sustain such fictions of separation.

Sebastian's final philosophical system, which he gives the neo-Victorian label "higher utilitarianism," begins axiomatically, with the assertion of an "Intelligible Light," "Godhead," or "Ground" that is "the unmanifested principle of all manifestation. . . . [both] transcendent and immanent" (274, 289). Appropriately, the reader must piece together this unifying theory from a series of fragments taken from his notebooks. Also appropriately, Sebastian positions himself as out-of-joint with the contemporary philosophical scene. Against the various materialisms and new realisms of the twentieth century, his allegiance is to Śaṅkara's medieval Advaita Vedānta. For Sebastian, "Bergson and the Pragmatists, Adler and Freud, the Dialectical Materialism boys and the Behaviourists—all tootle their variations on [the idea that] Mind is nothing but a tool for making tools; controlled by unconscious forces, either sexual or aggressive; the product of social and economic pressures; a bundle of conditioned reflexes" (291). These philosophies are self-refuting because a completely conditioned mind would be unable to assert any valid general claims, including philosophical ones. A completely conditioned mind would also irresponsibly absolve the subject of responsibility and erase her agency. Sebastian points out that even the idealist F. H. Bradley is overly skeptical of the mind's agency, its power to grasp generalities and effect change:

> The difference between metaphysics now and metaphysics in the past is the difference between word-spinning which makes no difference to anybody and a system of thought associated with a transforming discipline. "Short of the Absolute, God cannot rest, and having reached that goal He is lost and religion with Him." That is Bradley's view, the modern view. Sankara was as strenuously an Absolutionist as Bradley—but with what an enormous difference! For him, there is not only discursive knowledge about the Absolute, but the possibility (and the final necessity) of a direct intellectual intuition, leading the liberated spirit to identification with the object of its knowledge. (274–75)

Of course, the implication here is that the story of Sebastian, who has now become a philosopher and writer indistinguishable in stance and language from Huxley himself, has provided its readers a *fictional* vehicle for gaining "direct intellectual intuition" of reality. Writing fiction, for Huxley, is not mere "word-spinning" but a "transforming discipline." At this point, casting our inward eye backward over *Time Must Have a Stop*, we are meant to suddenly realize it as a false experience—because we took it for fiction.

Paranoid Postmodernism

Time Must Have a Stop trails off into philosophical fragments that could just as easily have appeared in *The Perennial Philosophy*, published one year after the novel in 1945, thereby marking the end of the war and the beginning(s) of postmodernism. This later book compiles a series of quotations that show how Absolute idealism has been advocated across the centuries by spiritual figures from Hindu, Buddhist, Daoist, Christian, and other traditions. Huxley defines this "perennial philosophy" in terms that evoke both Advaita Vedānta and his recent novel: it is "the metaphysic that recognizes a divine Reality substantial to the world of things and lives and minds; the psychology that finds in the soul something similar to, or even identical with, divine Reality; the ethic that places man's final end in the knowledge of the immanent and transcendent Ground of all being" (vii). Moreover, he suggests that "experiments" are necessary for grasping and verifying this philosophy: "when [the] mind is subjected to certain rather drastic treatments, the divine element, of which it is in part at least composed, becomes manifest. . . . It is only by making physical experiments that we can discover the intimate nature of matter and its potentialities. And it is only by making psychological and moral experiments that we can discover the intimate nature of mind and its potentialities" (ix).

Over the next few decades, Huxley would become the cultural figurehead for such experimentation—after ingesting the psychedelic drug mescaline, synthesized from peyote, in 1953, he published an account of his experience as *The Doors of Perception* in 1954, going on to (cautiously) advocate its use to his circle of friends and acquaintances, including Heard and Leary, who became much more passionate—one might say, unbalanced—advocates of the new drugs. Psychedelic drugs were not entirely new—William James, Havelock Ellis, and William Butler Yeats had all taken peyote much earlier, not to mention Indigenous peoples in the Americas—but the ability to synthesize and mass produce them as mescaline and LSD was novel, and their wide distribution allowed Huxley to become a "countercultural hero" not only to the intellectual and cultural elite of the 1950s and 1960s but also to millions of American and European youths eager to conduct their own psychological and moral experiments (Sawyer 174–75). What for Huxley was meant to be explored carefully, as a powerful and potentially dangerous doorway into Absolute reality, became popular and often recreational, as captured symbolically in the name of Jim Morrison's band, The Doors, in Huxley's image on the cover of The Beatles' *Sgt. Pepper's Lonely Hearts Club Band*, and in the lyrics to The Beatles' song "Tomorrow Never Knows."

Huxley's autobiographical account certainly praises the benefits of positive psychedelic experiences. Above all, they enable one to perceive the absolute significance of everything, a perception that falsifies the instrumental meaninglessness of everyday life. With the help of mescaline, he sees in a bouquet of flowers "that what rose and iris and carnation so intensely signified was nothing more, and nothing less, than what they were—a transience that was yet eternal life, a perpetual perishing that was at the same time pure Being, a bundle of minute, unique particulars in which, by some unspeakable and yet self-evident paradox, was to be seen the divine source of all existence" ("Doors" 161). Indeed, the flowers are no longer "objects" but have a mind of their own, which can only be suggested through literary language: he sibilantly describes "the smooth scrolls of sentient amethyst which were the iris" (161). What's more, this panpsychism accompanies a collapse in the very distinction between subject and object, which can only be suggested through philosophical language. He finds himself "not merely gazing at [the] bamboo legs [of a chair], but actually *being* them—or rather being myself in them; or, to be still more accurate (for 'I' was not involved in the case, nor in a certain sense were 'they') being my Not-self in the Not-self which was the chair" (163). The Absolute, simultaneously alienating and recuperative, can be found in flowers, books, chairs, almost anything one cares to look at. Huxley speculates that such heightened perception occurs because the drug physically inhibits the "reducing valve" of the nervous system, which functions to abstract or filter the manifold of reality so that practical action is possible. He references Cambridge idealist philosopher C. D. Broad's reading of Henri Bergson: "Each person is at each moment capable of remembering all that has ever happened to him and of perceiving everything that is happening everywhere in the universe. The function of the brain and nervous system is to protect us from being overwhelmed and confused by this mass of largely useless and irrelevant knowledge" (163–64). While remaining skeptical that such totalizing perception is possible through psychedelics—they do not "abolish" but only disable or alter the reducing valve—Huxley concedes that the drugs provide "something more than, and above all something different from, the carefully selected utilitarian material which our narrowed, individual minds regard as a complete, or at least sufficient, picture of reality" (164).

Nevertheless, he has serious reservations about the value of psychedelics. While they can enable a powerful shift in the user's sense of ontology and epistemology, their *ethical* efficacy seems doubtful. The experience of unity with objects like chairs does not, oddly enough, extend to other human beings, and the desire for any kind of practical action (toward chairs or humans) is sapped. The "will," he writes, "suffers a profound change for the worse. The mescalin taker sees no reason for doing anything in particular and finds most of the causes for which, at ordinary times, he was prepared to act and suffer, profoundly uninteresting" (165). Indeed, mescaline seems to foster the worst kind of detached navel-gazing. Huxley finds himself "passionately staring" at the "folds in [his] trousers—what a labyrinth of endlessly significant complexity!" (167). Yet he realizes, even during the trip, that he could easily become completely absorbed in his magnificent pants: "Compelled by the investigator [Humphry Osmond, the doctor who supplied him with the mescaline] to analyze and report on what I was doing (and how I longed to be left alone with Eternity in a flower, Infinity in four chair legs and the Absolute in the folds of a pair of flannel trousers!), I realized that I was deliberately avoiding the eyes of those who were with me in the room, deliberately refraining from being too much aware of them" (170). Huxley's "reducing valve" is still intact, its utilitarian impulse still faintly reminding him that he is of the world, that he has tasks to complete and responsibilities to perform. The transcendent unity afforded by mescaline paradoxically distracts him from the significance of large chunks of reality, namely the specific needs and desires of people, which are dismissed—during the trip, at least—as petty. Perhaps, like Eustace from *Time Must Have a Stop*, one should turn away from the Light.

Huxley's trip subsequently becomes much more harrowing, and he explicitly compares it to traversing the *Bardo* state described by *The Tibetan Book of the Dead*. Like Eustace, Huxley finds himself unmoored, lost in a supremely complex lattice of meaning without any recognizable space-time coordinates—or even an ordinary sense of self—to orient him. And like Eustace, Huxley confronts a terrible choice: remain in absorptive contemplation of a potentially dark Absolute, which bursts his subjectivity through a maddening oversaturation of meaning but might also, if followed deep enough, provide a transcendent point from which to falsify this morass and restore harmony; or, recede from the Absolute, tighten the spigot of the "reducing valve," and seek order within the pedestrian parameters of his everyday "self." The bad trip has begun. Upon entering his garden, he is dazed by another, more sinister, chair: "Confronted by a chair which looked like the Last Judgment . . . I found myself all at once on the brink of panic. This, I suddenly felt, was going too far. Too far, even though the going was into intenser beauty, deeper significance. The fear, as I analyze it in retrospect, was of being overwhelmed, of disintegrating under a pressure of reality greater than a mind, accustomed to living most of the time in a cozy world of symbols, could possibly bear" (179). Huxley compares his situation to the "departed soul" who "shrink[s] in agony from the Pure Light of the Void" and the schizophrenic who posits behind the world's "burning intensity of significance" a "cosmic malevolence" (179–80). In an attempt to anchor her husband's growing paranoia, Maria Huxley asks whether he could fix his attention on the "Clear Light." "Would it keep the evil away, if you could hold it?" she inquires. "Or would you not be able to hold it?" Huxley replies that it might be possible—if someone was there to guide him.

To summarize, in Huxley's psychedelic-induced predicament, the subject, confronted by the horror of meaningless (or all-too-meaningful) infinite regress, scrambles to find external "stops"—from metaphors and analogies to the comfort of a human guide to the embrace of the Absolute itself—where one can at least provisionally tether the baffled mind. What's striking about this predicament is that it describes the late-twentieth-century problematic of postmodernism that psychedelics, in part, were historically responsible for opening up: the postmodern subject, surrounded by a shifting lattice of simulacra and appearances unanchored to any external reality, must nevertheless attempt to find some critical foothold, some transcendent perspective, for articulating the coherent (albeit provisional) account of reality required of any practical action or consensus-dependent politics. Without such transcendent perspectives, the postmodern subject has fallen into a delusional, atomized, and self-defeating paranoia where nothing can be falsified. If they are transcendent but false, she has been captured by ideology or conspiracy theory that resists falsification. Consider Fredric Jameson's paradigmatic account of postmodernism in his book of the same name. Pointing to various symptoms that mark the shift from modernism to postmodernism, he notes a change in the "dynamics of cultural pathology" whereby "the alienation of the subject" is displaced by its "fragmentation," the latter vividly embodied by the fates of Marilyn Monroe and Edie Sedgewick and, more broadly, "the great dominant experiences of drugs and schizophrenia" in the 1960s (14). Another symptom is the "breakdown of temporality," an intensification of the present to the point where it "engulfs the [postmodern] subject with undescribable vividness" that erases interest in the past and future and stimulates an affect that could be described either "in the positive terms of euphoria, a high, an intoxicatory or hallucinogenic intensity" or "in the negative terms of anxiety and loss of reality" (27–28). Although Jameson investigates both of these modes, it is the latter—postmodernism as bad trip—that he seems most interested in analyzing and transcending.

For Jameson, postmodernism describes how the object world has become "a set of texts or simulacra" (9) that flattens out the distinction between reality and unreality because there are (or seem to be) no referents, just further texts and simulacra. Again, he gives many examples or symptoms of this—a fitting use of metonymy to capture an entire zeitgeist—but only two of the most memorable ones are necessary to recount here. First, Duane Hanson's hyperrealistic statues have the ironic effect of "derealization": "Your moment of doubt and hesitation as to the breath and warmth of these polyester figures . . . tends to return upon the real human beings moving about you in the museum and to transform them also for the briefest instant into so many dead and flesh-colored simulacra in their own right" (34). This feeling of disorientation, where statues of human beings appear to be real and actual ones unreal, is similarly elicited by postmodern architecture, which acts as "an imperative to grow new organs, to expand our sensorium and our body to some new, yet unimaginable, perhaps ultimately impossible, dimensions" (39). The "hyperspace" of the Bonaventure Hotel in Los Angeles is tortuous and confounding, and this difficulty in mapping one's location onto the external world is taken as analogous to the postmodern subject's more general inability to map his position within "the great global multinational and decentered communicational network" of late capitalism (44). In both cases, Jameson stresses the ambivalence of the postmodern condition, captured by what he calls the "hysterical sublime" (34). On the one hand, it is horrifying and deplorable to see human beings as lifeless stalks, to be incapable of grasping one's own (economic) reality, and to be distracted from imagining and producing a better future. On the other hand, having your perceptions overwhelmed is exhilarating and acts as a provocation to understand and control that which overwhelms. Can we find a "moment of truth" in the glittering, sliding surfaces of postmodernity, he asks (47)? How do we reach a vantage from which to make sense of it all?

Echoing Mukerji's argument about *Ātman* as condition of consciousness, Jameson contends that the absolute condition of postmodern reality (for him, late capitalism) is not *unknowable* but just *unrepresentable*. We know it exists—indeed, we intimately experience it every day—but how do we map or articulate it discursively? We must begin, Jameson argues, by recognizing that the bewildering hyperspace of the Bonaventure is not just a simulacrum, ideology, or fantasy, but a partial reality that reflects the larger reality of global capitalism—postmodern art and architecture are therefore new forms of *realism* that also, paradoxically but perhaps necessarily, distract us from reality writ large (49). The process of "cognitive mapping," the "practical reconquest of a sense of place" whereby simulacra and hyperspace are not just enjoyed or endured but relationally positioned, "enable[s] a situational representation on the part of the individual subject to that vaster and properly unrepresentable totality which is the ensemble of society's structures as a whole" (51). Like a *Bildungsroman*, this model emphasizes the step-by-step development of the individual mind. The task before the postmodern subject is to resist being lost in the euphoria (or horror) of finding, as it were, the Absolute in a pair of trousers—or a hotel lobby or, to use a more recent example, a proffered YouTube video. Instead, the postmodern subject must develop a narrative, an ability to articulate the relationship between various *degrees* of reality through the gradual and ever-expanding "reconquest" of local spaces, aesthetic experiences, and social arrangements. Again, Jameson underscores the crucial importance of art as a means for pushing the mind along this developmental trajectory. We need an "aesthetic of cognitive mapping," he insists, new forms of realism that describe more completely the complexity of reality (54). As we have seen throughout this book, the same impetus drives Absolute fiction.

It also drives literary criticism, which is not easily separated from Absolute fiction because they emerged simultaneously at the end of the eighteenth century—recall that literary criticism, according to Lacoue-Labarthe and Nancy, *is* the auto-referentiality of Absolute fiction. This helps explain why the same problem structures Eustace's choice in *Bardo*, Huxley's in his mescaline-enhanced garden, Jameson's in the art gallery, and the contemporary literary critic's in the library. None of these figures wants to believe that the external world is unreal, that nothing can be falsified, that nothing has meaning or significance, and therefore that no practical activities or politics are worth pursuing or prioritizing. The "post-postmodernist" philosophical orientations of the past decade that have proven most influential on literary criticism—like postcritique, new formalism, speculative realism, and new materialism—condemn, like Jameson, an arealist idealism that reduces all of reality to shifting texts, simulacra, and other subjective human projections. The choice of subjective idealism was always a false one. The real choice—although perhaps it is an inherent disposition or a historical, contextual mood rather than a choice—is to emphasize idealism or materialism among and within local and universal wholes. A parallel choice, disposition, or mood is the affective charge that accompanies the pursuit and determines the conception of reality. In other words, shall we have a bad trip or a good one? All the recent philosophical orientations mentioned above opt for the good. They often explicitly follow Eve Sedgwick's 1997 appeal, in the aptly titled collection *Novel Gazing*, to eschew "paranoid reading" in favor of "reparative reading" (1–37). In the former, Rita Felski writes, a "text is deciphered as a symptom, mirror, index, or antithesis of some larger social structure—as if there were an essential system of correspondences knotting a text into an overarching canopy of domination, akin to those medieval cosmologies in which everything is connected to everything else" (11). In the latter, which Felski calls "postcritical reading," we should "place ourselves in front of the text, reflecting on what it unfurls, calls forth, makes possible. This is not idealism, aestheticism, or magical thinking but a recognition—long overdue—of the text's status as coactor: as something that makes a difference, that helps make things happen" (12). In the conclusion that follows, I will suggest to the contrary that this recent reparative or postcritical turn is indeed—like the paranoid one that preceded it—a variety of idealism.

Conclusion

Old Idealism and New Materialism

> The choirs of Heaven are tokened in a harp-string,
> A pigeon's egg is as crafty as the stars.
> My heart is shaken by the crying of the lapwing,
> And yet the world is full of foolish wars.
>
> —T. D. O'Bolger, "The Counsels of O'Riordan, The Rannmaker"

Despite appearances to the contrary, we are currently living through a renaissance in Absolute and objective idealisms, especially but not entirely on the Continental side of the philosophical divide. This renaissance began to emerge in the 1990s and 2000s as the result of several overlapping factors. We could single out, first, a reaction against the perceived subjective idealism of postmodernism in favor of various realisms; second, the rising influence of Gilles Deleuze's reassertion of metaphysics and rehabilitation of philosophers, like Spinoza and Bergson, who straddle idealism and materialism; and third, the growing importance of scientifically informed ecocritical and anti-anthropocentric positions during a period awash in the effects of global warming.[1] Like any renaissance, this one is characterized by thinkers who hold a robust variety of viewpoints that nevertheless constellate around some basic underlying assumptions, leading commentators, anthologists, and even the thinkers themselves to try to organize the profusion under labels—labels in which the word "idealism" unfortunately never appears. If we consider, for example, the movement(s) variously called "speculative realism," "speculative materialism," and "object-oriented ontology," we find a remarkably widespread interest in Absolute and objective idealist approaches to speculating upon reality, from Iain Hamilton Grant's work on Schelling to Ben Woodard's on Bradley to Steven Shaviro's on panpsychism to Graham Harman's on "immaterialism." Just as the German Idealists sought to overturn Kant by seeking access to the in-itself, the speculative realists reject what they see as Kant's anthropocentric "correlationism," developing various ways to articulate what Quentin Meillassoux calls the "Great Outdoors," the Absolute that exists with or without relation to human thought. While Meillassoux himself takes an uncompromisingly materialist approach to reinstating the importance of the Absolute,[2] he remarks upon the proliferation of specifically idealist Absolutes, arguing in *After Finitude* that postmodern attempts to "end" absolutes and metaphysics have ironically accelerated a covert return to spirituality, religion, and idealism, granting "unprecedented license" to the idea of the Absolute (45).

This paradoxical attack on that which is being implicitly promoted is nowhere more evident than in another, related philosophical movement known as new materialism. Diana Coole and Samantha Frost's introduction to their influential edited volume, *New Materialisms: Ontology, Agency, and Politics*, provides a negative and positive definition of this new approach. First, it is emphatically *not* idealism. However, their opening question—"how could we be anything other than materialist?" (1)—is belied by their argument that we have not been materialist for a very long time. Materialism, they contend, has spent "several decades in abeyance," edged out by an overriding interest in "a host of immaterial things," such as "language, consciousness, subjectivity, agency, mind, soul; also imagination, emotions, values, meaning, and so on. These have typically been presented as idealities fundamentally different from matter and valorized as superior to the baser desires of biological material or the inertia of physical stuff. It is such idealist assumptions and the values that flow from them that materialists have traditionally contested" (2). Coole and Frost see phenomenology and Marxism as once-dominant materialisms of the twentieth century that were then eclipsed by poststructuralism, radical constructivism, and analytical and normative political theory (3). After diagnosing this cultural turn with "an allergy to 'the real'" (6), they then more positively offer new materialism as an antihistamine.

I find Coole and Frost's enumeration of new materialist positions (7–36) strikingly similar to those taken by the "old idealists" I have examined in this book. New materialists, they claim, espouse monism. They often "discern emergent, generative powers (or agentic capacities) even within inorganic matter, and they generally eschew the distinction between organic and inorganic, or animate and inanimate, at the ontological level." Human beings need to be relocated *within* nature, within a "monolithic but multiply tiered ontology [where] there is no definitive break between sentient and nonsentient entities or between material and spiritual phenomena." In this brave new world of global warming and genetic manipulation, one can no longer conceive of individuals as discrete; instead, we must think of them ecologically, in relation to wholes—including human rationality, which is simply a local process within "cosmic productivity." We need to better articulate "the agency of nonsubjective structures," such as the "de-totalized totality" of the capitalist system, even though "the complicated, reversible relationships that link micro- and macrolevel processes" within these systems "outrun the comprehension or intentions of individual actors." The external world is not illusory, but even "the most ardent realist must concede that the empirical realm we stumble around in does not capture the truth or essence of matter in any ultimate sense." I propose that we conceive of this anti-dualist, anti-subjectivist ontology, this desire to trace the tiered structures, forms, and domains of an ultimate reality we can never quite grasp, as one of the latest branches of an Absolute idealist genealogy. I make this point not to engage in a "gotcha" or semantic argument, but because I believe that our current philosophical and literary approaches can only be enriched by better understanding their predecessors and allies—historical resources that have been obscured by an overly zealous enforcement of the idealist/materialist binary.

If we take an almost random glance at two contributions to *New Materialisms*, we see, first, how both arrive, against their explicitly materialist context and aims, at a concept of the Absolute that integrates or transcends the divide between ideal and material and, second, how both could be helpfully elaborated upon through an engagement with figures from the history of Absolute idealism. First, Melissa A. Orlie's contribution to the volume, "Impersonal Matter," draws on Nietzsche, Freud, and Hans Loewald to argue that those human qualities most associated with the ideal and personal—"our thoughts, words, and deeds" (116)—are in fact material and impersonal. Orlie begins by positioning this claim against idealism, which for her is necessarily dualist and anthropocentric, insisting as it does upon a distinction between mind and body so that it can insulate humans from the determinism of material nature (117). In contrast to this idealism, Orlie reveals how the "isolated subject" is in fact deeply ramified into nature—so deep that it cannot ultimately be distinguished from the Absolute (Orlie prefers "nature," or "the all-embracing and all-embraced unity of impersonal matter"). But is her Absolute *material*? It is difficult to say. Orlie ends her chapter by invoking the psychoanalyst Loewald, who seeks to articulate the "*differentiated* unity" between subject and Absolute that can be achieved through the highest forms of sublimation. Such "[g]enuine sublimation achieves reconciliation of the conventional divisions of the divine and the sexual, nature and human, subject and object, unconscious and conscious, primary and secondary process thinking." It transforms "object relations into *intra*psychic relations" (133). But if "subjectivity is nature's activity," if "[w]hat we conventionally call mind is, in short, matter working upon matter" (134), are we really making a distinction worth insisting upon? Or are we simply threading a loop between the individual subject's (mental) pursuit of a sublimation that reveals that very pursuit to be the (material) action of the Absolute? Would Bradley's relentless demolition of the subject be helpful here? Or Sinclair's metaphysical reading of sublimation? Or Advaita Vedānta?

Following Orlie's chapter is Elizabeth Grosz's "Feminism, Materialism, and Freedom," which uses Bergson to "rethink concepts like freedom, autonomy, and even subjectivity in ontological, even metaphysical terms," which will allow one to reconceive feminist and other struggles as a desire for "freedom to" act rather than (solely) a "freedom from" oppression (140–41). In support, Grosz points to Bergson's emphasis on the "various degrees of freedom" made apparent in the wide variety of evolutionary forms, degrees that are "correlated with the extent and range of consciousness, which is itself correlated with the various possibilities of action" (149). For example, the "torpor" or relative unconsciousness of plants restricts their freedom, choice, and action within tight limits, whereas the greater complexity of consciousness found in animals creates a greater capacity for indeterminate action (149). Grosz does not want to extend this gradient of consciousness and freedom to isolated particles or blocks of matter, as a panpsychist would, but she does extend it to the Absolute, which she calls "the universe." She writes, "As isolatable systems, fixed entities, objects with extrinsic relations to each other, the material universe is the very source of regularity, predictability, and determination that enables a perceiving being to perform habitual actions with a measure of some guarantee of efficacy. Yet as an interconnected whole, the universe itself exhibits hesitation, uncertainty, and the openness to evolutionary emergence, that is, the very indetermination that characterizes life" (151). The living universe itself, then, becomes the unlikely conceptual linchpin for the development of feminist politics. Perhaps it would not seem so unlikely, however, if Constance Naden's feminist rewriting of evolutionary science and theory of Hylo-Idealism were more well known. Or May Sinclair's fiction, which depicts the sexual, intellectual, aesthetic, and other fulfillments women can achieve in pursuit of the Absolute.

In her later book, *The Incorporeal: Ontology, Ethics, and the Limits of Materialism* (2017), Grosz more explicitly raises the question of idealism: "With the rise of so-called new materialism, it is perhaps necessary to simultaneously call into being a new idealism, no longer Platonic, Cartesian, or Hegelian in its structure, that refuses to separate materiality from or subordinate it to ideality, resisting any reduction of the qualities and attributes of each to the operations of the other" (13). Thus, she wants to develop, not an idealism per se but an approach that neutralizes the opposition between ideal and material, that acknowledges "the intimate entwinement of the orders of materiality and ideality" (5). Currently, to achieve such a balanced approach one must give weight to the idealist side because "reductive materialism . . . still dominates much of what is called theory today" (11). When even non-reductive movements like new materialism are implicitly receptive but explicitly hostile to idealism, we must push further to develop a "*new* new materialism in which ideality has a respected place" (14). Whatever we decide to name this "new idealism" or "new new materialism," however, the crux of the problem is that there is little respect granted to idealism as a philosophical or literary approach. It is a position so denigrated that it can only be held covertly: "Today just about everyone is a materialist. Not only within the discipline of philosophy, but throughout the humanities and sciences . . . it is *almost* impossible to find an explicit and credible contemporary advocate of idealism. Idealism at best lurks unknowingly within avowedly materialist texts" (17). This suggests that to achieve respect and parity, idealism must become more widely *attended to* and *known*.

How is it that the same philosophical position (panpsychism, say) can be justly described as both idealist *and* materialist? Why is it that today's panpsychists (e.g., Jane Bennett) consider themselves materialists, whereas late Victorian panpsychists were by and large idealists? What is to be gained by noticing that what is taken to be perpendicular is in fact parallel? Pinch, who also points out the similarities between Victorian panpsychism and contemporary philosophical movements, argues,

> It is no criticism of the political, ethical, and environmental goals of the "new materialisms" to note that its visions of an enchanted materiality can seem patently willed and wished for, rather than rigorously argued for. Furthermore, it is worth remarking that for many of these thinkers, as well as for contemporary philosophers sympathetic to panpsychism, the starting point is a vision of the world as fundamentally physical or material: the challenge is explaining or conferring mind and feeling. In contrast . . . some of the Victorian panpsychists arrived at their position from the starting point of idealism: it was a way of explaining the omnipresence of consciousness or spirit. Restoring to view some of the idealism in Victorian panpsychism might be a way to pinpoint, acknowledge, and from thence, embrace or reject what seems most wishful in some postmodern materialisms and new ontologies. ("Appeal" 4)

Here, Pinch suggests that the path taken to reach a philosophical position is as significant as the arrival itself. Each path to panpsychism has its own advantages and disadvantages—which means that someone on the idealist path would surely have useful traveling tales to share with someone on the materialist one, and vice versa. Moreover, she reminds us that individuals are often drawn to certain positions not through rational argumentation but through disposition and affect, through willing and wishing. The choice of which path to take to the goal—idealist or materialist—would also seem to be heavily influenced by the affective tenor of the time: if one finds oneself in a nineteenth-century culture dominated by an idealist mood, the less-worn materialist path would become less appealing, just as mounting an idealist argument today requires more ground-clearing, a more skeptical peer-review gantlet to run, and so on. I believe that by acknowledging these practicalities alongside the obvious need to integrate idealist and materialist perspectives, we will open the current renaissance to further enchantments—and literary scholars are uniquely suitable conjurers, for modern idealism has been a fiction as much as a philosophy.

Escape from Devil's Island: New Idealisms for Old Problems

If I am correct in my above suggestion that contemporary trends in philosophy and literary criticism are already inclined toward Absolute idealism, a call for a "return" to its conceptual, ethical, and aesthetic orientations would seem to be redundant. I believe it is true that such a return would be nominal, a question of naming. Yet a reorientation in the practice of naming may not be as simple or inconsequential as it sounds. More generally, it would require one, in a geopolitical moment characterized by the inherent and imperative bias of both hyperpartisanship and authoritarian unity, to avoid identifying with one "side" or the other (even if there is only one "side") in favor of earnest attention to, and even empathy with, as many sides as possible—a subjective indeterminacy that, as we have seen, necessarily accompanies the pursuit of an Absolute perspective, an indeterminacy that leads not to defeatist acquiescence but the ability to intervene more skillfully and determinately into reality as it actually is. More specifically, it would require one to see that a binary division into idealist and materialist camps is a reductive and unhelpful abstraction of the more complete literary history we seek, through our various contributions, to grasp. Although I have tried in this book to present Absolute idealism in an accurate, compelling manner, it was not intended to be aggressively polemical; rather, I hope that my analysis has revealed some of the methodological and interpretive benefits to be gained from explicitly engaging with Absolute idealism and taking a more integrated approach to investigating the ideal and the material as they pertain to the study of literature and culture. It is worth summarizing here some of these benefits, which have significant implications for resolving problems and identifying new directions not only within the more limited domain of literary studies but also for other, broader facets of our lives: social, political, and ecological.

By restoring Absolute idealism to conversations about British literature in the nineteenth and twentieth centuries, this book attempts to model a bi-directional account of the relationships between philosophy and literature. For example, rather than arguing for a simple causal chain—Hegel influenced Bradley who influenced Butler—I have suggested that we need to account for the ways in which philosophy and literature across this period were engaged in a process of producing and creatively deforming one another. Absolute idealism simply isn't the same after its later permutations because the present alters the past as much as the past influences the present, discourse B affects discourse A as much as the reverse, and there are no privileged or absolute positions, even or especially in discourses that privilege the Absolute. This is why I have lowercased the "idealism" in "Absolute idealism" and often pluralize it—to suggest the open-ended nature of a genealogy that adjusts and becomes more complex every time it is elaborated or inspected. The continuous and bi-directional elaboration of Absolute fiction across the long nineteenth century—and into the present, as this conclusion suggests—also serves to erode some of the sharp lines that older intellectual histories were fond of drawing between philosophical and literary schools, discourses, and periods, lines that still compel us to think in certain (enlightening and misleading) ways. For instance, the persistence and promiscuity of Absolute fiction makes it difficult to determine where to draw the line between the Romantic and Victorian and modernist periods, between Indian and German and British idealisms, and between the genres of realism, science fiction, and horror/weird fiction. The bi-directional account of Indian and European philosophy that runs throughout this book resists cultural hierarchization, thereby responding to the call to decolonize Victorian studies, while the serious attention given to figures like Naden and Sinclair attempts to redress the continuing neglect of women philosophers. When one considers the extent to which Absolute idealism bi-directionally flourished across the globe during the height of British Idealism, countless possibilities for further research along these lines come into view.

The central argument in *Absolute Fiction*—that idealism is not antithetical to realism but impelled a reconceptualization of what it means to grasp reality through fiction—allows us to better understand the relationship between realism and other genres as well as their aesthetic, ontological, and ethical/political projects. First, what I call Absolute realism makes an ontological claim against subjectivism, using the techniques of fiction to demonstrate how atomized subjects are a solipsistic fiction and need to be apprehended instead *objectively*, as parts of a larger organism or ecological block. I further contend that genres like science fiction and horror/weird fiction continue the realist project by appending new organisms and blocks of reality, from sentient machines to malevolent creatures. (In the context of this conclusion, it is worth stressing that these claims resonate with recent arguments, such as S. Pearl Brilmyer's, that literary realism works to destabilize the subject/object distinction by objectifying the human subject, by constructing it as the result of nonhuman circumstances rather than as some privileged island of consciousness standing apart from them. Brilmyer calls this fictional strategy "dynamic materialism" [16] and arrives at it from a completely different set of [materialist and new materialist] philosophical and scientific discourses. The time has come for scholars to consider why these two sets of discourses cross.) Second, as I discuss in chapter 3, this ramified ontology entails a particular ethics or politics that revolves around "crossing" or *interdependence*. Being ethical, in this view, is impossible when one is selfish or self-absorbed, nor does it primarily depend upon one's self-willed, virtuous behavior. Instead, ethics becomes possible by harmoniously positioning oneself—realizing one's "station"—within the social and ecological contexts that support the self's emergence. One recognizes, then, that these contexts *are* the self and so, to put it selfishly, require our attention and care. Following Bradley, I do not believe this is an ethics of defeatism: finding one's station requires an epistemological shift that increases one's understanding of the real (total) situation, therefore enabling a more skillful development of or resistance to that situation. Many of Eliot's characters achieve this—for instance, Romola's resistance to Savonarola, whose dark Absolute foreshadows aspects of twentieth-century totalitarianism. Additionally, many of the horror stories and weird fictions that I examine in chapter 4, as well as Huxley's novel *Time Must Have a Stop* in chapter 5, involve the need to unflinchingly apprehend how one has been devoured by a dark Absolute of social mechanization, violence, or war—and how one can be disgorged.

Expanding upon this last, ethical/political dimension of my argument, I will conclude with one last cross between idealism and materialism—this time drawing upon organicism, a new materialist reading of Thomas Hobbes, and Huxley's final novel, *Island* (1962)—to suggest that Absolute idealism and Absolute fiction offer powerful instruments for articulating and thereby resisting or even (one hopes) preventing the dark Absolutes of totalitarian government and total war, particularly urgent horrors at the time of this writing, with major wars ongoing in Europe and the Middle East and the serious possibility of one in Southeast Asia. Thinking about political entities like parties, nations, and alliances as organisms with their own affective orientations is key to such an articulation.[3] In chapter 1, I mentioned the strong overlap between the Absolute idealist emphasis on mereology and the Romantic discourse of organicism, and I have struck an organicist note throughout this book. In a series of recent articles, John Kucich has shown the continuing relevance of organicism into the Victorian period, arguing that it "pervades nearly every sphere of nineteenth-century literature and culture," yet "critics have paid it scant attention, aside from casual scorn for the reactionary politics many assume are intrinsic to it" (791, 792). While organicism has indeed been used to support reactionary or conservative politics, Kucich shows that it also "left a distinctly progressive legacy": for example, Victorian novelists frequently invoked the organic to encourage the relaxation of social hierarchies and, just as British Idealism often ran parallel to socialist politics, supporters of the New Liberal welfare reforms of the early twentieth century deployed organic rhetoric (793). I would like to suggest that organicism continues well into the twentieth and twenty-first centuries, and because it appears on both ends of the political spectrum, in liberal and illiberal contexts, it is helpful for elucidating the formation and disintegration of both benevolent/interested and dark/fearful Absolutes. My larger point here is that when "idealisms" and "materialisms" are brought together in a complementary rather than antagonistic fashion, powerful interventions can be made into the most pressing issues of our time.

First, I return to the essay collection *New Materialisms* once more, namely Samantha Frost's chapter on the relationship between Hobbes's organicist metaphysics of the Absolute and his political theory that fear (of the Absolute) is the mechanism through which absolute sovereign power is maintained. For Hobbes, if we want to understand human politics, we must first understand the Absolute organism: "The Universe, that is, the whole masse of all things that are," he writes in *Leviathan* (1651), "[is] Corporeall, that is to say, Body" (qtd. in Frost 159). Frost notes that for Hobbes, this one body is the ultimate determinant of everything that occurs, including human thoughts and desires: "each event or act is produced or determined by not just one or two causal factors but rather by 'the sum of all things'" (160–61). Because the infinite complexity and recursion of the Absolute is impossible to map and fearsome to contemplate, humans attempt to simplify reality by narrowing the scope of their fear to a single object: the sovereign (170). Paradoxically, then, the sovereign simplifies the causal field in which humans act, thereby giving them the illusion of greater autonomy; conversely, "in moments in which our ontological condition becomes distressingly obvious to us, that is, when the complexity of causation and the heteronomy of our actions becomes more conspicuous in our daily lives, we will evince a tendency to increase the power of the sovereign" (174). In other words, in being afraid of their actual freedom (or determination, which is to say the same thing at this level) within the Absolute organism, humans contract their fear around the figure of a sovereign, which curtails their freedom and more sharply determines their position. The sovereign is thus fundamentally reductive—a kind of solar eclipse, a miniature, dark Absolute.

I leave to one side the question of whether the concept of the universe as a single body that thinks and fears is an idealist or materialist metaphysics (Frost calls it "variegated materialism" [160]). Either way, on Frost's reading the concept of the Absolute is crucial to Hobbes's theory of human politics, and although he wrote it in the context of the English Civil War, it remains hauntingly relevant for understanding the geopolitical crises of the twentieth century as well as our current crisis, which is characterized by both increasingly complex economic, political, technological, ecological, and climatological causal networks and, perhaps not coincidentally, the spread of authoritarian forms of government. On the cusp of World War II, Huxley also argued that culturally specific conceptions of and affective reactions to the Absolute are key to understanding that culture's ethics and politics. In *Ends and Means: An Inquiry into the Nature of Ideals* (1937), he claims that in the two decades since World War I, European culture has been under the sway of a nihilistic metaphysics that sees Absolute reality as meaningless, without organization, purpose, or value. Because affects are more intensely activated by and attached to objects taken to be meaningful, they are displaced from the Absolute onto left-wing and right-wing absolutist regimes, creating a patchwork Absolute: "Meaning was reintroduced into the world, but only in patches. The universe as a whole still remained meaningless, but certain of its parts, such as the nation, the state, the class, the party, were endowed with significance and the highest value. The general acceptance of a doctrine that denies meaning and value to the world as a whole, while assigning them in a supreme degree to certain arbitrarily selected parts of the totality, can have only evil and disastrous results" (317–18). In addition to fear, then, Huxley gives apathy—specifically, apathy toward the Absolute—a central role in the rise of totalitarianism and total war (he correctly predicts that no distinction will be made between combatants and civilians in future wars [107]). Such apathy furthers "the ends of erotic or political passion" and "narrows the field of interest and sympathetic awareness," and therefore it serves the interests of the authoritarian ruler, who demands a "loyalty addressed exclusively to himself and the State of which he is the head" (309, 142, 290).

For Huxley, diagnosing the disposition and pathologies of organs within a body at war requires examining the affect of *interest*: the direction and scope of a person's and a society's feelings of awareness, excitement, wonder, and involvement. This is the theme of *Island*, especially its final chapter, which is worth meditating upon at some length. Up to this point in the novel, the protagonist Will has been a skeptical interloper on the cloistered, idyllic island of Pala, which is guided by a founding philosophy that proclaims, "Good Being is in the knowledge of who in fact one is in relation to *all* experiences; so be aware—aware in every context, at all times and whatever, creditable or discreditable, pleasant or unpleasant, you may be doing or suffering" (40). Will's initial worldly condescension toward Palanese culture (in fact, he is the clandestine agent of a foreign oil company seeking to undermine the current government) gradually disappears as he learns more about its customs, such as *maithuna*, a sexual technique similar to the *pañcamakāra* ritual I examined in chapter 4, and the taking of *moksha*, a psychedelic mushroom that "allows a larger volume of Mind with a large 'M' to flow into your mind with a small 'm'" (138). The final chapter begins just after Will has taken *moksha* for the first time under the guidance of Susila, a Palanese woman. The trajectory of his trip mirrors that of Huxley's in *The Doors of Perception*, moving from joyous dissolution in the organic Absolute to fear as this body itself dissolves into a dark, mechanical Absolute, a "swarm" of individuals affectively bound to their fascist leader by sadistic anger. In an important shift from *The Doors of Perception*, where Huxley worries about his unconcern for other people while on mescaline, Will recognizes the implication of these visions for his ethical involvement with others—just as Pala is violently seized by a dictatorship from "across the Strait" (284).

Will's initial experience of "luminous bliss"—a "union with unity in a limitless, undifferentiated awareness"—is described by the narrator as "the mind's natural state." The paradox of experiencing the Absolute is that "ultimately and essentially there was no such person" as Will, the experiencer; nevertheless, "no less certainly" he does exist, as do the world's other "three thousand millions of insulated consciousnesses, each at the centre of a nightmare world, in which it was impossible for anyone with eyes in his head or a grain of honesty to take yes for an answer. By what sinister miracle had the mind's natural state been transformed into all these Devil's Islands of wretchedness and delinquency?" (263–64). *Moksha* allows Will to escape from his Devil's Island, seeing even in an ordinary wall organic totality: "a living process, a continuing series of transubstantiations from plaster and whitewash into the stuff of a supernatural body—into a god-flesh that kept modulating, as he looked at it, from glory to glory" (270). But through a slight refraction the divine can quickly transubstantiate into the horrifying, for "[o]penness to bliss and understanding was also, he realized, an openness to terror, to total incomprehension" (272). The god-flesh that had surrounded Will is now a pulsation of "intricate machines" or "brightly enamelled gadgets," and the praying mantises at his feet become an endless column of soldiers:

> Numberless as insects, and each of them moving with the precision of a machine, the perfect docility of a performing dog. And the faces, the faces! He had seen the close-ups on the German news reels, and here they were again, praeternaturally real and three-dimensional and alive. The monstrous face of Hitler with his mouth open, yelling. And then the faces of assorted listeners. Huge idiot faces, blankly receptive. Faces of wide-eyed sleep-walkers. Faces of young Nordic angels rapt in the Beatific Vision. Faces of Baroque saints going into ecstasy. Faces of lovers on the brink of orgasm. One Folk, One Realm, One Leader. Union with the unity of an insect swarm. (274)

This monstrous, many-faced Absolute is also organic, only its body is composed of the "thousands of corpses in the Korean mud, innumerable [corpses] littering the African desert . . . fly-blown bodies he had seen only a few months ago, faces upwards and their throats gashed, in the courtyard of an Algerian farm" (275).

The first step in awakening from such a nightmare, Huxley suggests, is to pay attention. Even when reality is a horror, we must engage with and remain interested in our surroundings rather than angrily or fearfully withdraw into ourselves, giving everything up as meaningless. Just as Will succumbs to despair at the images of infinite suffering, Susila digs her fingernails into the skin of his forehead, then places her fingers directly upon his closed eyelids, compelling him to recover his attention through "intimate, unexpected, potentially dangerous contact" (278). She insists that the truly difficult task is not to experience the unspeakable glories and horrors that *moksha* reveals but rather to experience them and then channel them into a more compassionate relationship with the world. After she points out that Will never looked at her during his trip, he admits that he was "[a]fraid of seeing something I'd have to be involved with, something I might have to do something about" (278). However, one must seek the redemptive "light" of the Absolute within other people—not just within our loved ones, for it is easy for us to find there, but also within those captured by outlandish conspiracy theories, even within those who march in fascist columns: "the fact remained and would remain always, remain everywhere—the fact that there was this capacity even in a paranoiac for intelligence, even in a devil-worshipper for love; the fact that the ground of all being could be totally manifest in a flowering shrub, a human face; the fact that there was a light and that this light was also compassion" (285). Immediately after this realization, shots from an automatic rifle mark the end of Pala's independence. And yet, still, the novel ends with its opening intonation: "Attention" (7, 286).

It would be easy to dismiss the politics of Huxley's final novel as naïve. Having mystical sex and taking mushrooms to gain knowledge of the Absolute fail to prevent the dictatorship's seizure of Pala, after all—although the final intonation does suggest that there will be continued resistance. As I write these words, all the roiling troubles that surround humanity, from climate change to the possibility of another world war, make Huxley's idealism seem starry-eyed, foolish, even obscene. Today it seems still more "impossible for anyone with eyes in his head or a grain of honesty to take yes for an answer" (264). It seems to make more sense to double down on "no." Andrew Culp, for instance, castigates new materialism for its optimism in his book *Dark Deleuze*, arguing against its emphasis on "connectivity" and "world-building," the attempt "to make everyone and everything part of a single world" (2, 6). He points out that "connectivity" is also the goal of companies like Google—it is simply a path to complete capitalist domination (6–7). The "whole" is for the gullible, and "only by destroying this world will we release ourselves of its problems" (66). I disagree. For me, the whole is precisely what needs preservation in the face of any "single world," whether a dictator's or Google's, that attempts to eclipse the Absolute (recall that, for Huxley and Jameson, respectively, dictatorships and late capitalism operate by *obfuscating* access to the whole). Nevertheless, I think Culp's emphasis on the "dark" power of negativity offers an important way of reframing the function of Huxley's Absolute fiction, which is not naïve but brutally realist. As I have sought to demonstrate throughout this book, idealism is not pie-in-the-sky philosophy. It has long been concerned with coming to terms with darkness, or negativity, or what used to be called "the problem of evil"—in a word, reality. Like the other philosophers and writers that I examine, Huxley seeks to express not the value of some effulgent purity separate from the material world but "the paradox of opposites indissolubly wedded, of light shining out of darkness, of darkness at the very heart of light" (*Island* 279). He seeks to put obscenities back into our mouths, obscenities like "eternity," "one of those metaphysical dirty words which no decent-minded man would dream of pronouncing even to himself, much less in public." Others are "contemplation" and "love." These are all emphatically "real as shit" (267, 280, 268). Huxley asks us, ultimately, to risk taking an untimely trip into the darkness and obscenity of idealism in order to destroy the worlds that deserve destruction and preserve those—especially the One—that should be cherished.

Although idealism is already circulating in philosophy and literary criticism, I call for a full rehabilitation in which it is not excised, misnamed, condescended to, used as a foil, or handled with kid gloves. I believe that a more generous *interest* in idealism would open up many exciting areas of inquiry. I also believe that a broader cultural rehabilitation would have significant ethical, political, and ecological benefits along the lines sketched above and analyzed elsewhere in this book. Keeping the ideal in view is personal and pressing for me. I see it arise in the artwork of Liu Kuo-sung (劉國松), who graduated in 1955 from the university where I teach, National Taiwan Normal University (NTNU), and whose lovely painting adorns the cover of this book. By amphibiously joining together Western and Eastern artistic techniques, Liu asks us to consider the composition of "The Universe in the Mind," the title of his 2007 retrospective in Beijing. Michael Sullivan argues that Liu "found the roots of Abstraction in the Chinese calligraphic gesture which was never an exercise in pure form, but always had meaning beyond the form. On a philosophical level, that gesture is an expression of the vital reverberations of the cosmos itself" ("Art"). The painting on the cover of this book, like others in Liu's Space series, certainly invites us to reflect upon the reverberations of our backgrounds and horizons, whether historical, perceptual, conceptual, or cosmic. From my office at NTNU, I can see on the horizon, rising above Taipei and the Taiwan Strait, the perennially green mountain of Yangmingshan, named after Wang Yangming (王陽明), the Chinese idealist philosopher who lived from 1472 to 1529. I also have a picture of a Japanese professor teaching a class in the late 1920s at NTNU,[4] with "Berkeley's Idealism" in the background, written on the blackboard. In the introduction, I alluded to the twentieth-century uptake of British Idealism, via the Kyoto School, in Taiwan during the Japanese imperial period. To what extent did the various idealisms taught by Japanese professors in Taiwan reinforce the Japanese imperial project? To what extent did students who absorbed these idealisms develop Taiwanese philosophy, literature, and politics through or against them? Interest in idealism has faded here, too, but Taiwanese academia and culture were forged in the shadow of these historical contexts, and I wonder what creative combinations of Western and Eastern idealisms, in philosophy and art, await recovery or expression. I also wonder what these old and new idealisms will teach us about how political totalities are created and resisted, about Taiwan's current position within the geopolitical whole. Where is the final grain of an island's shore?

Notes

Introduction

1. Scholars contest Hegel's understanding and use of "the Absolute." As Ng (134–35) and Nuzzo both point out, Hegel usually uses "absolute" as an adjective; when he does use it as a noun, it is often in the context of a critical response to other philosophers, such as Spinoza. In this book, I primarily read Hegel through his late-nineteenth-century British interpreters, for whom "the Absolute" is a key Hegelian concept, as well as more recent interpreters like Beiser, who argues that Hegel's dialectic continues "until we reach the absolute whole, that which includes everything within itself, and so cannot possibly depend upon anything outside itself. When this happens the system will be complete, and we will have achieved knowledge of the absolute" (*Hegel* 168–69).

2. This is the same example given by Charles Howard Hinton in his novella *An Episode of Flatland* (1907) ("An Accidental Meeting"). Hinton, a mathematician who wrote many fictive accounts of the fourth dimension, did conceive of the Absolute as higher in a spatial sense—but not as otherworldly.

3. See, for instance, many of the chapters in Marshall and Guy.

4. See Guyer and Horstmann for an introduction to idealism that touches on many of the same divisions.

5. For the constitutive link between German Idealism, Gothic novels, and contemporary technologies, see Andriopoulos.

6. See Wilberding and Horn.

7. For an idealist reading of Uexküll, see Han.

8. For more on British Idealism and socialism, see Bevir.

9. Theosophy is yet another variant of Absolute idealism that I cannot adequately address in this book.

10. See Prystash, "Times."

11. Other important recent work on this topic examines conceptions of the universe in American fiction (see Taylor); German Idealism and modernist Italian

literature (see Subialka); and idealism in the dimensional fiction inaugurated by late Victorian mathematicians like Edwin A. Abbott and Hinton (see White).

Chapter 1

1. In 2010, Pinch makes the same observation as Quinton (*Thinking* 7).

2. The reception of the *Bhagavad Gita* was particularly crucial to philosophical developments in late-eighteenth-century Germany. See Herling; Rathore and Mohapatra.

3. In the text Coleridge references, *Archaeologiae Philosophicae* (1692), Burnet ends with an appendix on Indian philosophy, which suggests the long-standing imbrication of Western and Eastern idealisms.

4. In this chapter, "meditation" refers specifically to the Eastern spiritual exercises that enable experience of the divine. While the word "meditation" had been used in the Christian context for centuries, it began carrying an association with Eastern religions in 1727, according to the *Oxford English Dictionary*. The Hindu inflection I give to Coleridge's "meditation" differs from the Christian one first advanced by Abrams, where he connects Coleridge's "meditation poems" to seventeenth-century British antecedents. In this context, see also Parker.

5. For discussions of Coleridge and the pantheism controversy, see Berkeley; McFarland; and Piper. Neoplatonism is also a powerful and interrelated influence; see Quinney.

6. One thinks, for instance, of Wordsworth's "Tintern Abbey" and Shelley's "Mont Blanc." See Shaviro's Whiteheadian reading of "Mont Blanc" (*Universe* 56–59).

7. See Versluis (16–36) for a discussion of Eastern influences on German Idealism and British Romanticism.

8. "Even your writing desk with its blank paper and all its other implements will appear as a chain of flowers, capable of linking your feelings as well as thoughts to events and characters past or to come" (1: 225).

9. This accords with Savarese's account of "poetic thought experiments" in the Romantic period that "imagined material, embodied modes of inter-mental contact [and] entertained the notion that the mind spreads across bodies and linguistic technologies—including the technologies of poetry—in a social environment made up of other minds" (4).

10. Vallins similarly argues that Coleridge carefully attended to the structure of his prose sentences and paragraphs because he believed these structures would help induce in his readers an awareness of ideal ontological structures, "a world beyond the fragmentary scene of empirical consciousness" ("Letter" 44).

11. The double meaning of "organ" is at play here: both "a part of an animal or plant body that serves a particular physiological function" and "a mental or spiritual faculty regarded as an instrument of the mind or soul" (*Oxford English Dictionary*).

12. Coleridge often uses "soul" in an ambiguously Greek way, suggesting the various qualities of life and mind.

13. For more on Coleridge and Vishnu, see Mazumder. Drew argues that the Indian god became Coleridge's "most appropriate image for his own most abstruse meditative states" (193).

14. For an analysis of Coleridge's relationship to Schelling's philosophy, see Reid. Roy examines his "egregious misreading" (299) of Kant, while both Roy and Simons explore his remarkable affinities to (and relative ignorance of) Hegel. Coleridge did struggle through part of Hegel's *Logic* (De Paolo 31) and may have been familiar with *The Phenomenology of Spirit* (Roy 295).

15. Chapters IV and IVA of "Self-Consciousness." See Beiser, *Hegel* 174–91.

16. See Prystash, "'The Grand Still Mirror of Eternity.'"

17. Hegel isn't actually endorsing this claim about the speck of dust—it is a basic truth (reciprocal determination) presented in erroneous fashion by metaphysics—but similar claims were made by his interpreters, and the basic truth stands.

18. For more on idealism, modernism, and science fiction, see Prystash, "Leaning" and "Times."

19. More recently, Charles Taylor and Beiser take this position.

20. Hegel notes that he is unsure whether the original text uses "Brahman" (the Absolute) or "Brahma" (the creator God), but the difference is "unimportant" (127). Indeed, he often uses "Brahma" in the sense of "Brahman."

21. For a similar argument, see Benjamin.

22. Sergeant Cuff declares, "In all my experience along the dirtiest ways of this dirty little world, I have never met with such a thing as a trifle yet" (101). In a footnote at the end of the novel, Franklin Blake, in the role of editor, encourages the reader to "compare" the final documents to earlier testimony (463).

Chapter 2

1. For a history of the field up to 1992, see George Levine, "Victorian Studies." I will take us up to the present day in the following section.

2. See also Gallagher, who argues, vis-à-vis Eliot, that the novel necessarily inverts empiricism: "The end of art no longer seems to be transcendence, but immanence; matter is not in need of soul, but soul in need of matter" (73).

3. For Isobel Armstrong, Lewes's biological pursuits are driven by a passion for "the abstract idea of the *category of a species*," for species as "ideal forms," and for "a universe of interdependent forms" ("Microscope" 40).

4. See Shuttleworth for Eliot's relation to nineteenth-century organicism.

5. Rylance himself vehemently denies that Lewes was an idealist.

6. See Armstrong, "George Eliot, Spinoza, and the Emotions" 295; Ashton 155–56; and King, "George Eliot" 179.

7. See I. Armstrong, "George Eliot, Hegel, and *Middlemarch*"; and Putzell-Korab. These studies emphasize the resonance of Hegel's *Phenomenology*.

8. See Li.

9. Bardo's scholarly quest thematically links him to both Edward Casaubon in *Middlemarch* and Isaac Casaubon, who in 1614 showed that the *Hermetica* were composed hundreds of years later than traditionally thought, thus "shatter[ing] at one blow the build-up of Renaissance Neoplatonism" (Yates 433).

10. In a short sketch from "Poetry and Prose, From the Notebook of an Eccentric," Eliot's first published work aside from a short poem that appeared in 1840, the narrator reflects on what he has learned from visiting the artist Adolphe: "The kind of purpose which makes life resemble a work of art . . . . is to live, not for our friends, not for those hostages to fortune, wives and children; not for any individual, any specific form; but for something which, while it dwells in these, has an existence beyond them. It is to live for the good, the true, the beautiful, which outlive every generation, and are all-pervading as the light which vibrates from the remotest nebula to our own sun. The spirit which has ascertained its true relation to these, can never be an orphan: it has its home in the eternal mind" (*Essays* 18–19). Perhaps Eliot's late embrace of idealism is a return to an early flirtation.

11. Yet another philosophical influence on Eliot worth mentioning is her longtime friend, Charles Bray. According to Willburn, "The framework of materialism and absolute idealism, meeting in bodies that are part of the mind of God, constitutes Bray's addition to the field of metaphysics and also presents a theme that *Daniel Deronda* explores" (277). See also Pinch (*Thinking* 49).

Chapter 3

1. For Bradley, the duty of the philosopher is to be descriptive, not prescriptive (*Ethical Studies* 174), although he often exceeds his station in this regard.

2. Dunham et al. refer to Bradley's "panpsychist idealism" (170). In his history of panpsychism from prehistory to the present, Skrbina briefly discusses Butler and Bradley (143, 155–56). See also Candlish and Basile. Like Absolute idealism, panpsychism is an ancient philosophy, but I treat only their modern articulations.

3. See Morgan, 143–49.

4. *Life and Habit* (1877), *Evolution, Old and New* (1879), *God the Known and God the Unknown* (1879), *Unconscious Memory* (1880), and *Luck, or Cunning?* (1887).

5. Butler is also reviving an ancient philosophical debate: as early as the Athenian statesman Solon (c. 640–558 BC) we see a sorites or "slide" argument claiming that if it is unethical to eat animals, it is also unethical to eat plants. See Sorabji (102–03).

6. Naden makes a similar argument in "Animal Automatism": "The effects of the food which is daily transubstantiated by the incarnating digestive organs,

and the atrophy of mind and body which follows prolonged abstinence, prove alike the real existence of the material universe and its complete homogeneity with our own being" (*Induction and Deduction* 200).

7. The latter robot, Cutie, is directly compared to Descartes, but its dedication to reason, dismissal of empiricism, and the religiosity lurking behind these philosophical stances could be read as a parody of nineteenth-century idealism.

8. See Kinyon.

9. In other Cellarius publications, Genesis Thought, Inc. distanced the project from cyberpunk, suggesting that the Cellarius Universe inaugurated a new genre called "blockpunk" that was more "optimistic" about technology and the agency of the individual. See Apollo.

10. Many thanks to former Genesis Thought, Inc. employee Sean O'Connor for providing me with the "White Paper" and "Universe Guide."

Chapter 4

1. For an examination of the relationship between British Idealism and Sinclair's conception and fictional use of the "stream of consciousness," see Prystash, "Times of the Timeless."

2. Cf. Reiter, who argues that *The Great God Pan* is inimical to (Bradley's) metaphysics; there is no Absolute in the novel, only nothingness.

3. See Pasi, who remarks that Pan in *The Great God Pan* is both spiritual and concrete reality (146).

Chapter 5

1. See, for example, Mander, *British Idealism* (147).

2. See, for example, the essays in Dimova-Cookson and Mander.

3. Barua remarks that a "significant volume of philosophical literature from [the first half of the twentieth century] can be placed under the rubric of 'Śaṁkara and X', where X is Hegel, or a German or a British philosopher who had commented on, elaborated or critiqued the Hegelian system" (2). Śaṁkara is the principal philosopher of Advaita Vedānta.

4. See the conclusion following this chapter.

5. Nikhilananda, who founded the Ramakrishna-Vivekananda Center of New York, was guru to J. D. Salinger, another famous literary convert to Advaita Vedānta. See Rosenbaum.

6. In *The Perennial Philosophy*, Huxley describes "sudden theophanies" that may occur spontaneously to random people. During these flashes of insight, some perceive "ultimate Reality as Love, Light and Bliss," while others see it as a "dark,

awe-inspiring and inscrutable Power." He associates the "Hindu goddess, Kali, in her more frightful aspects," with the latter, dark Absolute (171–72).

7. See Prystash, "Times of the Timeless."

Conclusion

1. The philosophers Timothy Sprigge and Thomas Nagel, who identify as Absolute idealists, are also worth mentioning as part of this renaissance.

2. For the surprising similarities between Meillassoux's "speculative materialism" and Hegel's Absolute idealism, see Zantvoort.

3. My claims here about affect, especially "interest" and "fear," are indebted to Frank and Wilson's presentation of Silvan Tomkin's affect theory. Tomkins, whose "deft use of cybernetics to think of humans as loosely fitted coassemblies of interrelated systems" and Spinozist philosophical framework arguably place him within the organicist and Absolute idealist traditions, contends that affects like interest and fear are "the primary motivators of human behavior"—including sexuality, which is made possible as a drive by being coassembled with positive affects like interest and excitement and/or negative ones like fear and anger (9, 71–78, 14, 15). For Tomkins, our ethical and political beliefs are rooted in certain rules (or "scripts") for the management of attaching affects to objects, rules that emerge from a complex of individual, social, and biological sources (8). "No affect is an island," he writes (qtd. in Frank and Wilson 34), and therefore no affect is politically inert.

4. NTNU acquired its present name in 1967.

Works Cited

Abrams, M. H. "Structure and Style in the Greater Romantic Lyric." *From Sensibility to Romanticism: Essays Presented to Frederick A. Pottle*, edited by Frederick W. Hilles and Harold Bloom, Oxford UP, 1965, pp. 527–60.

Adamson, Peter. *Philosophy in the Hellenistic and Roman Worlds*. Oxford UP, 2015.

———. *Philosophy in the Islamic World*. Oxford UP, 2016.

Alarabi, Nour. "Constance Naden's Philosophical Poetry." *Literature Compass*, vol. 9, no. 11, 2012, pp. 848–60.

Althusser, Louis. "Ideology and Ideological State Apparatuses." *Lenin and Philosophy and Other Essays*, translated by Ben Brewster, Monthly Review Press, 1971, pp. 127–86.

Ameriks, Karl. "Introduction: Interpreting German Idealism." *The Cambridge Companion to German Idealism*, edited by Karl Ameriks, Cambridge UP, 2000, pp. 1–17.

Amigoni, David. "'The Written Symbol Extends Indefinitely': Samuel Butler and the Writing of Evolutionary Theory." *Samuel Butler, Victorian against the Grain: A Critical Overview*, edited by James G. Paradis, U of Toronto P, 2007, pp. 91–112.

Andriopoulos, Stefan. *Ghostly Apparitions: German Idealism, the Gothic Novel, and Optical Media*. Zone Books, 2013.

Anger, Suzy. "George Eliot and Philosophy." *The Cambridge Companion to George Eliot*, 2nd ed., edited by George Levine and Nancy Henry, Cambridge UP, 2019, pp. 215–35.

Apollo, Frank. "Blockpunk: The Cellarius Take on Cyberpunk." *Medium*, 5 Mar. 2018, medium.com/genesis-thought/blockpunk-the-cellarius-take-on-cyberpunk-77e4da7dc89d.

Armour, Leslie. "Green's Idealism and the Metaphysics of Ethics." *T. H. Green: Ethics, Metaphysics, and Political Philosophy*, edited by Maria Dimova-Cookson and W. J. Mander, Clarendon Press, 2006, pp. 160–86.

Armstrong, Charles I. *Romantic Organicism: From Idealist Origins to Ambivalent Afterlife*. Palgrave Macmillan, 2003.

Works Cited

Armstrong, Isobel. "George Eliot, Hegel, and *Middlemarch*." *19: Interdisciplinary Studies in the Long Nineteenth Century*, vol. 29, 2020, pp. 1–26.

———. "George Eliot, Spinoza, and the Emotions." *A Companion to George Eliot*, edited by Amanda Anderson and Harry E. Shaw, Wiley Blackwell, 2013, pp. 294–308.

———. "The Microscope: Mediations of the Sub-Visible World." *Transactions and Encounters: Science and Culture in the Nineteenth Century*, edited by Roger Luckhurst and Josephine McDonagh, Manchester UP, 2002, pp. 30–54.

Ashton, Rosemary. *The German Idea: Four English Writers and the Reception of German Thought 1800–1860*. Libris, 1994.

Asimov, Isaac. *I, Robot*. Bantam, 1991.

Barnes, Steven. "Danakil." *Whose Future Is It?: Cellarius Stories, Volume 1*. Kindle ed., Genesis Thought, 2018, pp. 230–71.

Barrett, Dorothea. Introduction. *Romola*, by George Eliot, edited by Barrett, Penguin, 2005, pp. vii–xxiv.

Barua, Ankur. "The Absolute of Advaita and the Spirit of Hegel: Situating Vedānta on the Horizons of British Idealisms." *Journal of Indian Council of Philosophical Research*, vol. 34, 2016, pp. 1–17.

Battersby, Christine. "'In the Shadow of His Language': May Sinclair's Portrait of the Artist as Daughter." *New Comparison: A Journal of Comparative and General Literary Studies*, vol. 33–34, 2002, pp. 102–20.

Baudelaire, Charles. *The Flowers of Evil*. Translated by James McGowan, Oxford UP, 1993.

Beane, Wendell C. "The Cosmological Structure of Mythical Time: Kālī-Śakti." *History of Religions*, vol. 13, no. 1, 1973, pp. 54–83.

Beaumont, Matthew. "Introduction: Reclaiming Realism." *A Concise Companion to Realism*, edited by Beaumont, Wiley-Blackwell, 2010, pp. 1–12.

Beiser, Frederick C. *German Idealism: The Struggle Against Subjectivism, 1781–1801*. Harvard UP, 2002.

———. *Hegel*. Routledge, 2005.

Bell, Michael. "The Metaphysics of Modernism." *The Cambridge Companion to Modernism*, edited by Michael Levenson, Cambridge UP, 2011, pp. 9–32.

Benjamin, Walter. "The Concept of Criticism in German Romanticism." *Walter Benjamin: Selected Writings, Volume 1: 1913–1926*, edited by Marcus Bullock and Michael W. Jennings, The Belknap Press of Harvard UP, 1996, pp. 116–200.

Bergonzi, Bernard. "Aldous Huxley and Aunt Mary." *Aldous Huxley: Between East and West*, edited by C. C. Barfoot, Rodopi, 2001, pp. 9–17.

Berkeley, Richard. *Coleridge and the Crisis of Reason*. Palgrave Macmillan, 2007.

Bevir, Mark. *The Making of British Socialism*. Princeton UP, 2011.

Bhattacharjee, Ritwick, and Saikat Ghosh. Introduction. *Horror Fiction in the Global South: Cultures, Narratives and Representations*, edited by Bhattacharjee and Ghosh, Bloomsbury, 2021, pp. 1–25.

Bhushan, Nalini, and Jay L. Garfield, editors. *Indian Philosophy in English: From Renaissance to Independence.* Oxford UP, 2011.

Bhushan, Nalini, and Jay L. Garfield. "Introduction: Whose Voice? Whose Tongue? Philosophy in English in Colonial India." *Indian Philosophy in English: From Renaissance to Independence*, edited by Bhushan and Garfield, Oxford UP, 2011, pp. xiii–xxvii.

Bleiler, Richard. "May Sinclair's Supernatural Fiction." *May Sinclair: Moving Towards the Modern*, edited by Andrew J. Kunka and Michele K. Troy, Routledge, 2006, pp. 123–38.

Bosanquet, Bernard. *Psychology of the Moral Self.* Macmillan and Co., 1897.

Boucher, David, and Andrew Vincent. *British Idealism: A Guide for the Perplexed.* Continuum, 2012.

Boyle, Nicholas. "General Introduction: The Eighteenth and Nineteenth Centuries." *The Impact of Idealism: The Legacy of Post Kantian German Thought*, vol. 1, edited by Karl Ameriks, Cambridge UP, 2013, pp. 1–40.

Bradley, F. H. *Appearance and Reality: A Metaphysical Essay.* 1893. Routledge, 2002.

———. *Ethical Studies.* 1876. Cambridge UP, 2012.

Brilmyer, S. Pearl. *The Science of Character: Human Objecthood and the Ends of Victorian Realism.* U of Chicago P, 2022.

Brown, Marshall. "The Logic of Realism: A Hegelian Approach." *PMLA*, vol. 96, no. 2, 1981, pp. 224–41.

Burnet, Thomas. *Archaeologiae Philosophicae: Or, the Ancient Doctrine Concerning the Originals of Things.* Translated by Thomas Foxton, E. Curll, 1729.

Burstein, Miriam Elizabeth. Introduction. *Robert Elsmere*, edited by Miriam Elizabeth Burstein, Victorian Secrets, 2018, pp. 5–12.

Butler, Samuel. *Erewhon.* 1872. Dover Publications, 2002.

———. *God the Known and God the Unknown.* A. C. Fifield, 1909.

———. *Luck, or Cunning as the Main Means of Organic Modification?* Jonathan Cape, 1922.

———. *The Note-Books of Samuel Butler.* Edited by Henry Festing Jones, A. C. Fifield, 1912.

———. *Unconscious Memory.* A. C. Fifield, 1920.

———. *The Way of All Flesh.* 1903. Dover Publications, 2004.

Candlish, Stewart, and Pierfrancesco Basile. "Francis Herbert Bradley." *The Stanford Encyclopedia of Philosophy*, edited by Edward N. Zalta, 2017, plato.stanford.edu/archives/spr2017/entries/bradley/.

Carlyle, Thomas. *Sartor Resartus.* Edited by Kerry McSweeney and Peter Sabor, Oxford UP, 1987.

Carroll, Noël. *The Philosophy of Horror, or Paradoxes of the Heart.* Routledge, 1990.

Cave, Terence. Introduction. *Daniel Deronda*, edited by Cave, Penguin, 2003, pp. ix–xxxv.

"Cellarius Genesis: Universe Guide." Genesis Thought, 2018.

"Cellarius: White Paper." Genesis Thought, 2018.

Chai, Leon. "Prospects for Idealism." *Modern Philology*, vol. 104, no. 1, 2006, pp. 96–104.
Coleridge, Samuel Taylor. *Biographia Literaria*. Edited by James Engell and W. Jackson Bate. 2 vols., vol. 7 of *The Collected Works of Samuel Taylor Coleridge*, Princeton UP, 1985.
———. *Collected Letters of Samuel Taylor Coleridge*. 6 vols., edited by E. L. Griggs, Clarendon Press, 1956–71.
———. *The Complete Poems*. Edited by William Keach, Penguin, 1997.
———. *The Notebooks of Samuel Taylor Coleridge*. 5 vols., edited by Kathleen Coburn, Princeton UP, 1957–90.
Collins, Wilkie. *The Moonstone*. Vintage, 2009.
Cook, Roy T. "Canonicity and Normativity in Massive, Serialized, Collaborative Fiction." *Journal of Aesthetics and Art Criticism*, vol. 71, no. 3, 2013, pp. 271–76.
Coole, Diana, and Samantha Frost. "Introducing the New Materialisms." *New Materialisms: Ontology, Agency, and Politics*, edited by Coole and Frost, Duke UP, 2010, pp. 1–43.
Culp, Andrew. *Dark Deleuze*. U of Minnesota P, 2016.
Danta, Chris. "Panpsychism and Speculative Evolutionary Aesthetics in Samuel Butler's 'The Book of the Machines.'" *Textual Practice*, 2019, pp. 1–20.
Deleuze, Gilles, and Félix Guattari. *A Thousand Plateaus: Capitalism and Schizophrenia*. Translated by Brian Massumi, U of Minnesota P, 1987.
den Otter, Sandra M. *British Idealism and Social Explanation: A Study in Late Victorian Thought*. Clarendon Press, 1996.
De Paolo, Charles. "Coleridge, Hegel, and the Philosophy of History." *The Wordsworth Circle*, vol. 26, no. 1, 1995, pp. 31–35.
Deutsch, Eliot. *Advaita Vedānta: A Philosophical Reconstruction*. U of Hawai'i P, 1969.
Dibble, Jerry A. *The Pythia's Drunken Song: Thomas Carlyle's* Sartor Resartus *and the Style Problem in German Idealist Philosophy*. Martinus Nijhoff, 1978.
di Giovanni, George. Introduction. *The Science of Logic*, by Georg Wilhelm Friedrich Hegel, translated and edited by di Giovanni, Cambridge UP, 2010, pp. xi–lxii.
Dimova-Cookson, Maria, and W. J. Mander, editors. *T. H. Green: Ethics, Metaphysics, and Political Philosophy*. Clarendon Press, 2006.
Disley, Liz. "General Introduction: The Twentieth and Twenty-First Centuries." *The Impact of Idealism: The Legacy of Post Kantian German Thought*, vol. 1, edited by Karl Ameriks, Cambridge UP, 2013, pp. 41–61.
Dixon, Joy. *Divine Feminine: Theosophy and Feminism in England*. Johns Hopkins UP, 2001.
Drew, John. *India and the Romantic Imagination*. Oxford UP, 1987.
Drewery, Claire. "Transgressing Boundaries; Transcending Bodies: Sublimation and the Abject Corpus in *Uncanny Stories* and *Tales Told by Simpson*." *May*

Sinclair: Re-Thinking Bodies and Minds, edited by Rebecca Bowler and Claire Drewery, Edinburgh UP, 2017, pp. 213–31.

Duncan, Ian. "George Eliot and the Science of the Human." *A Companion to George Eliot*, edited by Amanda Anderson and Harry E. Shaw, Wiley Blackwell, 2013, pp. 471–85.

Dunham, Jeremy, et al. *Idealism: The History of a Philosophy*. McGill-Queen's UP, 2011.

Eldridge, Richard. "Idealism in Nineteenth-Century British and American Literature." *Aesthetics and Literature*, vol. 3, 2013, pp. 121–44.

Eliot, George. *Daniel Deronda*. Edited by Terence Cave, Penguin, 2003.

———. *Essays of George Eliot*. Edited by Thomas Pinney, Routledge, 2016.

———. *The George Eliot Letters*. Vol. 6., edited by Gordon S. Haight, Oxford UP, 1956.

———. *George Eliot's* Daniel Deronda *Notebooks*. Edited by Jane Irwin, Cambridge UP, 1996.

———. *Impressions of Theophrastus Such*. William Blackwood and Sons, 1879.

———. *The Lifted Veil and* Brother Jacob. Oxford UP, 1999.

———. *Middlemarch*. Edited by Rosemary Ashton, Penguin, 1994.

———. *Romola*. Edited by Dorothea Barrett, Penguin, 2005.

———. *Selected Essays, Poems and Other Writings*. Edited by A. S. Byatt and Nicholas Warren, Penguin, 1990.

Ellermann, Greg. "Hegel, In and Out of the Woods: Nature, Reflection, Capital." *Essays in Romanticism*, vol. 23, no. 1, 2016, pp. 1–18.

———. "Late Coleridge and the Life of Idealism." *Studies in Romanticism*, vol. 54, no. 1, 2015, pp. 33–55.

Emerson, Ralph Waldo. *The Complete Essays and Other Writings of Ralph Waldo Emerson*. Edited by Brooks Atkinson, The Modern Library, 1940.

"Enter Cellarius, a Transmedia Universe 100 Years in the Future." *ConsenSys*, 1 May 2018, media.consensys.net/enter-cellarius-a-transmedia-universe-100-years-in-the-future-476876a27522.

Fawcett, Edward Douglas. *The Riddle of the Universe*. Edward Arnold, 1893.

———. "Some Observations Touching the Cosmic Imagining and 'Reason.'" *Mind*, vol. 27, no. 106, 1918, pp. 152–64.

Fedele, Cassandra. *Letters and Orations*. Edited and translated by Diana Robin, U of Chicago P, 2000.

Felski, Rita. *The Limits of Critique*. Kindle ed., U of Chicago P, 2015.

Fisher, Mark. *The Weird and the Eerie*. Repeater Books, 2016.

Fleishman, Avrom. *George Eliot's Intellectual Life*. Cambridge UP, 2010.

Frank, Adam J., and Elizabeth A. Wilson. *A Silvan Tomkins Handbook: Foundations for Affect Theory*. U of Minnesota P, 2020.

Frost, Samantha. "Fear and the Illusion of Autonomy." *New Materialisms: Ontology, Agency, and Politics*, edited by Diana Coole and Samantha Frost, Duke UP, 2010, pp. 158–77.

Gallagher, Catherine. "George Eliot: Immanent Victorian." *Representations*, vol. 90, no. 1, 2005, pp. 61–74.
Gang, Joshua. *Behaviorism, Consciousness, and the Literary Mind*. Johns Hopkins UP, 2022.
Gannon, Christiane. "Hinduism, Spiritual Community, and Narrative Form in *The Moonstone*." *Dickens Studies Annual*, vol. 46, 2015, pp. 297–320.
Gatens, Moira. "The Art and Philosophy of George Eliot." *Philosophy and Literature*, vol. 33, no. 1, 2009, pp. 73–90.
Geach, Peter. *Mental Acts: Their Content and Their Objects*. Routledge & Kegan Paul, 1957.
Gilbert, Pamela K. *Victorian Skin: Surface, Self, History*. Cornell UP, 2019.
Gillott, David. *Samuel Butler Against the Professionals: Rethinking Lamarckism, 1860–1900*. Routledge, 2015.
The Gospel of Sri Ramakrishna. Translated by Swami Nikhilananda, Ramakrishna-Vivekananda Center, 1942.
Greiner, Rae. *Sympathetic Realism in Nineteenth-Century British Fiction*. Johns Hopkins UP, 2012.
Grosz, Elizabeth. "Feminism, Materialism, and Freedom." *New Materialisms: Ontology, Agency, and Politics*, edited by Diana Coole and Samantha Frost, Duke UP, 2010, pp. 139–57.
———. *The Incorporeal: Ontology, Ethics, and the Limits of Materialism*. Columbia UP, 2017.
Guyer, Paul and Rolf-Peter Horstmann. "Idealism." *The Stanford Encyclopedia of Philosophy*, edited by Edward N. Zalta, 21 Mar. 2023, plato.stanford.edu/archives/spr2023/entries/idealism.
Haldar, Hiralal. *Neo-Hegelianism*. Heath Cranton Ltd., 1927.
Han, Lei. "The Idealistic Elements in Modern Semiotic Studies: With Particular Recourse to the *Umwelt* Theory." *Concentric: Literary and Cultural Studies*, vol. 47, no. 1, 2021, pp. 107–28.
Harries, Natalie Tal. "'The One Life Within Us and Abroad': Coleridge and Hinduism." *Coleridge, Romanticism, and the Orient: Cultural Negotiations*, edited by David Vallins et al., Bloomsbury, 2013, pp. 131–44.
Harrold, Charles Frederick. *Carlyle and German Thought: 1819–1834*. Yale UP, 1978.
Hedley, Douglas. *Coleridge, Philosophy and Religion: Aids to Reflection and the Mirror of the Spirit*. Cambridge UP, 2004.
Hegel, Georg Wilhelm Friedrich. *The Science of Logic*. Translated and edited by George di Giovanni, Cambridge UP, 2010.
Herling, Bradley L. *The German Gītā: Hermeneutics and Discipline in the German Reception of Indian Thought, 1778–1831*. Routledge, 2006.
Hetherington, Paul, and Cassandra Atherton. *Prose Poetry: An Introduction*. Princeton UP, 2020.

Hext, Kate. "Literary Form and Philosophical Thought in Nineteenth-Century Britain." *Literature Compass*, vol. 9, no. 11, 2012, pp. 695–707.
Hinton, Charles Howard. "An Accidental Meeting." *An Episode of Flatland*. Swan Sonnenschein & Co., 1907, forgottenfutures.co.uk/flat2/flat2-16.htm.
Hodgson, William Hope. *The House on the Borderland*. Dover Publications, 2008.
Hösle, Vittorio. "The Search for the Orient in German Idealism." *Zeitschrift der Deutschen Morgenländischen Gesellschaft*, vol. 163, no. 2, 2013, pp. 431–54.
Houlgate, Stephen. *The Opening of Hegel's Logic: From Being to Infinity*. Purdue UP, 2006.
Howell, Anthony. "The Prose Poem: What the Hell is it?" *Fortnightly Review*, 1 Apr. 2016, fortnightlyreview.co.uk/2016/04/prose-poetry/.
Humes, Cynthia Ann. "Wrestling with Kālī: South Asian and British Constructions of the Dark Goddess." *Encountering Kālī: In the Margins, at the Center, in the West*, edited by Rachel Fell McDermott and Jeffrey J. Kripal, U of California P, 2003, pp. 145–68.
Hurley, Kelly. "British Gothic Fiction, 1885–1930." *The Cambridge Companion to Gothic Fiction*, edited by Jerrold E. Hogle, Cambridge UP, 2002, pp. 189–207.
Huxley, Aldous. "The Doors of Perception." *Aldous Huxley: Complete Essays*, vol. 5, edited by Robert S. Baker and James Sexton, Ivan R. Dee, 2002, pp. 157–91.
———. "The Education of an Amphibian." *Aldous Huxley: Complete Essays*, vol. 5, edited by Robert S. Baker and James Sexton, Ivan R. Dee, 2002, pp. 191–209.
———. *Ends and Means: An Inquiry into the Nature of Ideals*. Routledge, 2017.
———. "The 'Inanimate' Is Alive." *The Divine Within: Selected Writings on Enlightenment*, edited by Jacqueline Hazard Bridgeman, HarperCollins, 2013, pp. 247–52.
———. *Island*. Vintage, 2005.
———. *The Perennial Philosophy*. HarperCollins, 2009.
———. *Time Must Have a Stop*. Vintage, 1953.
Iser, Wolfgang. "The Reading Process: A Phenomenological Approach." *New Literary History*, vol. 3, no. 2, 1972, pp. 279–99.
Jackson, Carl T. *Vedanta for the West: The Ramakrishna Movement in the United States*. Indiana UP, 1994.
James, Henry. "Middlemarch." *The Galaxy*, 1873, pp. 424–28.
Jameson, Fredric. *Postmodernism, or, The Cultural Logic of Late Capitalism*. Duke UP, 1991.
Jones, Charlotte. *Realism, Form, and Representation in the Edwardian Novel: Synthetic Realism*. Oxford UP, 2021.
Jordan, Alexander. "The Contribution of Thomas Carlyle to British Idealism, c. 1880–1930." *Scottish Historical Review*, vol. 98, no. 248, 2019, pp. 439–68.
Joshi, S. T. Introduction. *If the Dead Knew: The Weird Fiction of May Sinclair*, edited by Joshi, Hippocampus Press, 2020, pp. 7–16.

---. *Unutterable Horror: A History of Supernatural Fiction*. Vol. 2, Hippocampus Press, 2012.

---. *The Weird Tale*. Wildside Press, 2003.

Katzav, Joel. "The Disappearance of Modern Indian Philosophy from *Mind* and the *Philosophical Review*." *Digressions & Impressions*, 25 Jan. 2017, digressionsnimpressions.typepad.com/digressionsimpressions/2017/01/the-disappearance-of-modern-indian-philosophy-from-mind-and-the-philosophical-review.html.

Kendal, Gordon. "F. H. Bradley: An Unpublished Note on Christian Morality." *Religious Studies*, vol. 19, no. 2, 1983, pp. 175–83.

Kermode, Frank. *The Sense of an Ending: Studies in the Theory of Fiction*. Oxford UP, 2000.

King, Amy M. "George Eliot and Science." *The Cambridge Companion to George Eliot*, 2nd ed., edited by George Levine and Nancy Henry, Cambridge UP, 2019, pp. 175–94.

---. "Natural History and the Novel: Dilatoriness and Length and the Nineteenth-Century Novel of Everyday Life." *NOVEL: A Forum on Fiction*, vol. 42, no. 3, 2009, pp. 460–66.

Kinsley, David R. "Kālī." *Encountering Kālī: In the Margins, at the Center, in the West*, edited by Rachel Fell McDermott and Jeffrey J. Kripal, U of California P, 2003, pp. 23–38.

Kinyon, Kamila. "The Phenomenology of Robots: Confrontations with Death in Karel Čapek's *R. U. R.*" *Science Fiction Studies*, vol. 26, no. 3, 1999, pp. 379–400.

Kołakowski, Leszek. *Metaphysical Horror*. Edited by Agnieszka Kołakowska, U of Chicago P, 2001.

Kornbluh, Anna. *The Order of Forms: Realism, Formalism, and Social Space*. U of Chicago P, 2019.

Kramnick, Jonathan. *Paper Minds: Literature and the Ecology of Consciousness*. U of Chicago P, 2018.

Kripal, Jeffrey J. "Kālī's Tongue and Ramakrishna: 'Biting the Tongue' of the Tantric Tradition." *History of Religions*, vol. 34, no. 2, 1994, pp. 152–89.

Kripal, Jeffrey J., and Rachel Fell McDermott. "Introducing Kālī Studies." *Encountering Kālī: In the Margins, at the Center, in the West*, edited by McDermott and Kripal, U of California P, 2003, pp. 1–19.

Kucich, John. "Organicism." *Victorian Literature and Culture*, vol. 46, no. 3/4, 2018, pp. 791–95.

Lacoue-Labarthe, Philippe, and Jean-Luc Nancy. *The Literary Absolute: The Theory of Literature in German Romanticism*. Translated by Philip Barnard and Cheryl Lester, State U of New York P, 1988.

LaPorte, Charles. "Mathilde Blind, Constance Naden, and the Victorian Poetess." *Victorian Literature and Culture*, vol. 34, no. 2, 2006, pp. 427–41.

Leary, Timothy et al. *The Psychedelic Experience: A Manual Based on the* Tibetan Book of the Dead. Citadel Press, 1992.
Leone, Homo [Potaraju Narasimham]. "The Vedantic Absolute." *Mind*, vol. 21, no. 81, 1912, pp. 62–78.
Levine, Caroline. *Forms: Whole, Rhythm, Hierarchy, Network*. Princeton UP, 2015.
Levine, George. "George Eliot's Hypothesis of Reality." *Nineteenth-Century Fiction*, vol. 35, no. 1, 1980, pp. 1–28.
———. "Literary Realism Reconsidered: 'The World in Its Length and Breadth.'" *A Concise Companion to Realism*, edited by Matthew Beaumont, Wiley-Blackwell, 2010, pp. 13–32.
———. *The Realistic Imagination: English Fiction from* Frankenstein *to* Lady Chatterley. U of Chicago P, 1981.
———. "Victorian Studies." *Redrawing the Boundaries: The Transformation of English and American Literary Studies*, edited by Stephen Greenblatt and Giles Gunn, The Modern Language Association of America, 1992, pp. 130–53.
Lewes, George Henry. *The Principles of Success in Literature*. Edited by William Dallam Armes, University of California Students' Co-Operative Association, 1901.
———. "Realism in Art: Recent German Fiction." *Westminster Review*, vol. 70, 1858, pp. 488–518.
Lewis, Pericles. *Religious Experience and the Modernist Novel*. Cambridge UP, 2010.
Li, Hao. "Dialectical Envisioning: *Daniel Deronda* and British Ethical Idealism." *Literature Compass*, vol. 9, no. 11, 2012, pp. 774–85.
Lightman, Bernard. "'A Conspiracy of One': Butler, Natural Theology, and Victorian Popularization." *Samuel Butler, Victorian against the Grain: A Critical Overview*, edited by James G. Paradis, U of Toronto P, 2007, pp. 113–42.
Lovatt, Gabriel. "From Experiment to Epidemic: Embodiment in the Decadent Modernism of Arthur Machen's 'The Great God Pan' and 'The Inmost Light.'" *Mosaic: An Interdisciplinary Critical Journal*, vol. 49, no. 1, 2016, pp. 19–35.
Lovecraft, H. P. *At the Mountains of Madness*. Penguin, 2018.
———. "Supernatural Horror in Literature." 1927. *The H. P. Lovecraft Archive*, 2009, hplovecraft.com/writings/texts/essays/shil.aspx.
Luckhurst, Roger. "Gothic, Horror, and the Weird: Shifting Paradigms." *The Routledge Companion to Victorian Literature*, edited by Dennis Denisoff and Talia Schaffer, Routledge, 2020, pp. 83–94.
———. "Transitions: From Victorian Gothic to Modern Horror, 1880–1932." *Horror: A Literary History*, edited by Xavier Aldana Reyes, The British Library, 2016, pp. 103–29.
Machen, Arthur. "About My Books." *The Secret Ceremonies: Critical Essays on Arthur Machen*, edited by Mark Valentine and Timothy J. Jarvis, Hippocampus Press, 2019, pp. 41–60.

———. *Collected Fiction*. 3 vols., edited by S. T. Joshi, Hippocampus Press, 2019.

———. *Hieroglyphics*. Martin Secker, 1926.

Malabou, Catherine. *The Future of Hegel: Plasticity, Temporality and Dialectic*. Translated by Lisabeth During, Routledge, 2005.

———. *Ontology of the Accident: An Essay on Destructive Plasticity*. Translated by Carolyn Shread, Polity Press, 2012.

Mander, W. J. *British Idealism: A History*. Oxford UP, 2011.

———. "In Defence of the Eternal Consciousness." *T. H. Green: Ethics, Metaphysics, and Political Philosophy*, edited by Maria Dimova-Cookson and W. J. Mander, Clarendon Press, 2006, pp. 187–206.

———. Introduction. *Anglo-American Idealism, 1865–1927*, edited by Mander, Greenwood Press, 2000, pp. 1–19.

Mander, W. J., and Stamatoula Panagakou, editors. *British Idealism and the Concept of the Self*. Palgrave Macmillan, 2016.

Marshall, Catherine, and Stéphane Guy, editors. *The Victorian Legacy in Political Thought*. Peter Lang, 2014.

Matus, Jill L. "George Eliot and the Sciences of Mind: The Silence that Lies on the Other Side of Roar." *A Companion to George Eliot*, edited by Amanda Anderson and Harry E. Shaw, Wiley Blackwell, 2013, pp. 457–70.

Mazumder, Aparajita. "Coleridge, Vishnu, and the Infinite." *Comparative Literature Studies*, vol. 30, no. 1, 1993, pp. 32–52.

McFarland, Thomas. *Coleridge and the Pantheist Tradition*. Oxford UP, 1969.

McKeon, Michael. *The Origins of the English Novel, 1600–1740*. The Johns Hopkins UP, 2002.

McLuhan, Marshall. *Understanding Media: The Extensions of Man*. McGraw-Hill Book Company, 1964.

McSweeney, Kerry, and Peter Sabor. Introduction. *Sartor Resartus*, edited by McSweeney and Sabor, Oxford UP, 1987, pp. vii–xxxiii.

McTaggart, J. Ellis. "Time and the Hegelian Dialectic." *Mind*, vol. 3, no. 10, 1894, pp. 190–207.

Meillassoux, Quentin. *After Finitude: An Essay on the Necessity of Contingency*. Bloomsbury Academic, 2009.

Milbank, John, and Aaron Riches. "Foreword: Neoplatonic Theurgy and Christian Incarnation." *Theurgy and the Soul: The Neoplatonism of Iamblichus*, by Gregory Shaw, Angelico Press/Sophia Perennis, 2014, pp. v–xvii.

Mill, John Stuart, and Jeremy Bentham. *Utilitarianism and Other Essays*. Edited by Alan Ryan, Penguin, 1987.

Miller, D. A. "From *roman policier* to *roman-police*: Wilkie Collins's *The Moonstone*." *NOVEL: A Forum on Fiction*, vol. 13, no. 2, 1980, pp. 153–70.

Moi, Toril. *Henrik Ibsen and the Birth of Modernism: Art, Theater, Philosophy*. Oxford UP, 2006.

———. "Idealism." *The Oxford Handbook of Philosophy and Literature*, edited by Richard Eldridge, Oxford UP, pp. 271–97.

Morgan, Benjamin. *The Outward Mind: Materialist Aesthetics in Victorian Science and Literature*. U of Chicago P, 2017.
Morton, Timothy. *Humankind: Solidarity with Nonhuman People*. Verso, 2017.
———. *Hyperobjects: Philosophy and Ecology after the End of the World*. U of Minnesota P, 2013.
Muirhead, J. H. Foreword to *Thought and Reality: Hegelianism and Advaita*, by P. T. Raju, George Allen & Unwin Ltd., 1937, pp. 17–18.
Mukerji, A. C. "Absolute Consciousness." *Indian Philosophy in English: From Renaissance to Independence*, edited by Nalini Bhushan and Jay L. Garfield, Oxford UP, 2011, pp. 323–52.
———. "The Realist's Conception of Idealism." *Indian Philosophy in English: From Renaissance to Independence*, edited by Nalini Bhushan and Jay L. Garfield, Oxford UP, 2011, pp. 471–98.
Murphy, Patricia. *Reconceiving Nature: Ecofeminism in Late Victorian Women's Poetry*. U of Missouri P, 2019.
Naden, Constance. *Further Reliques of Constance Naden: Being Essays and Tracts for Our Times*. Edited by George M. McCrie, Bickers and Son, 1891.
———. *Induction and Deduction: A Historical & Critical Sketch of Successive Philosophical Conceptions Respecting the Relations Between Inductive and Deductive Thought and Other Essays*. Edited by Robert Lewins, Bickers and Son, 1890.
Nagel, Thomas. *Mind and Cosmos: Why the Materialist Neo-Darwinian Conception of Nature Is Almost Certainly False*. Oxford UP, 2012.
Nassar, Dalia. *The Romantic Absolute: Being and Knowing in Early German Romantic Philosophy, 1795–1804*. U of Chicago P, 2014.
Nazar, Hina. "The Continental Eliot." *A Companion to George Eliot*, edited by Amanda Anderson and Harry E. Shaw, Wiley Blackwell, 2013, pp. 413–27.
Neff, Rebeccah Kinnamon. "May Sinclair's *Uncanny Stories* as Metaphysical Quest." *English Literature in Transition, 1880–1920*, vol. 26, no. 3, 1983, pp. 187–91.
———. "'New Mysticism' in the Writings of May Sinclair and T. S. Eliot." *Twentieth-Century Literature*, vol. 26, no. 1, 1980, pp. 82–108.
Neiman, Susan. *Evil in Modern Thought: An Alternative History of Philosophy*. Princeton UP, 2015.
Newell, Jonathan. *A Century of Weird Fiction, 1832–1937: Disgust, Metaphysics and the Aesthetics of Cosmic Horror*. U of Wales P, 2020.
Ng, Karen. *Hegel's Concept of Life: Self-Consciousness, Freedom, Logic*. Oxford UP, 2020.
Nicholson, Peter. "Green's 'Eternal Consciousness.'" *T. H. Green: Ethics, Metaphysics, and Political Philosophy*, edited by Maria Dimova-Cookson and W. J. Mander, Clarendon Press, 2006, pp. 139–59.
Noel-Tod, Jeremy. "Introduction: The Expansion of the Prose Poem." *The Penguin Book of the Prose Poem: From Baudelaire to Anne Carson*, edited by Noel-Tod, Penguin, 2018, pp. xix–xliv.

Norrman, Ralf. *Samuel Butler and the Meaning of Chiasmus*. Palgrave Macmillan, 1986.

Nuzzo, Angelica. "The 'Absoluteness' of Hegel's Absolute Spirit." *Hegel's Philosophy of Spirit: A Critical Guide*, edited by Marina F. Bykova, Cambridge UP, 2019, pp. 207–24.

O'Bolger, T. D. "The Counsels of O'Riordan, The Rannmaker." *Poetry: A Magazine of Verse*, vol. 9, no. 3, 1916, p. 136.

Orlie, Melissa A. "Impersonal Matter." *New Materialisms: Ontology, Agency, and Politics*, edited by Diana Coole and Samantha Frost, Duke UP, 2010, pp. 116–36.

Oxford English Dictionary. Oxford UP, oed.com.

Pahl, Katrin. *Tropes of Transport: Hegel and Emotion*. Northwestern UP, 2012.

Parker, Reeve. *Coleridge's Meditative Art*. Cornell UP, 1975.

Parkin-Gounelas, Ruth. "Mind Matters: Butler and Late Nineteenth-Century Psychology." *Samuel Butler, Victorian against the Grain: A Critical Overview*, edited by James G. Paradis, U of Toronto P, 2007, pp. 195–220.

Pasi, Marco. "Arthur Machen's Panic Fears: Western Esotericism and the Irruption of Negative Epistemology." *The Secret Ceremonies: Critical Essays on Arthur Machen*, edited by Mark Valentine and Timothy J. Jarvis, Hippocampus Press, 2019, pp. 139–59.

Peterson, William S. *Victorian Heretic: Mrs Humphrey Ward's* Robert Elsmere. Leicester UP, 1976.

Pickrem, Faye. "Disembodying Desire: Ontological Fantasy, Libidinal Anxiety and the Erotics of Renunciation in May Sinclair." *May Sinclair: Re-Thinking Bodies and Minds*, edited by Rebecca Bowler and Claire Drewery, Edinburgh UP, 2017, pp. 119–38.

Pinch, Adela. "The Appeal of Panpsychism in Victorian Britain." *Romanticism and Victorianism on the Net*, vol. 65, 2014–15, pp. 1–24.

———. *Thinking about Other People in Nineteenth-Century British Writing*. Cambridge UP, 2010.

Pinkard, Terry. "Hegel's *Phenomenology* and *Logic*: An Overview." *The Cambridge Companion to German Idealism*, edited by Karl Ameriks, Cambridge UP, 2000, pp. 161–79.

Piper, H. W. *The Active Universe: Pantheism and the Concept of Imagination in the English Romantic Poets*. Athlone Press, 1962.

Plotz, John. "Science Fiction." *Victorian Literature and Culture*, vol. 46, no. 3/4, 2018, pp. 854–58.

Poe, Edgar Allan. *Eureka: A Prose Poem*. Geo. P. Putnam, 1848.

———. Review of *Twice-Told Tales*, by Nathaniel Hawthorne. *Graham's Magazine*, vol. 20, no. 5, 1842, pp. 298–300.

Pong, Foong-Ee, and Tzu-Wei Hung. "The Kyoto School's Influence on Taiwanese Philosophy under Japanese Rule (1895–1945)." *Tetsugaku*, vol. 3, 2019, pp. 70–88.

Prabhavananda. *The Spiritual Heritage of India*. Vedanta Press, 1979.
Pratt, Mary Louise. *Imperial Eyes: Travel Writing and Transculturation*. Routledge, 1992.
Prystash, Justin. "'The Grand Still Mirror of Eternity': Temporal Dualism and Subjectification in Carlyle and Dickens." *Victorian Literature and Culture*, vol. 38, no. 1, 2010, pp. 87–104.
———. "Leaning from the Human: Virginia Woolf, Olaf Stapledon, and the Challenge of Behaviorism." *Configurations*, vol. 28, no. 4, 2020, pp. 433–57.
———. "Times of the Timeless: May Sinclair, British Idealism, and the Stream of Consciousness." *Twentieth-Century Literature*, vol. 68, no. 2, 2022, pp. 179–98.
———. "Vexed Meditation: Romantic Idealism in Coleridge and Its Afterlife in Bataille and Irigaray." *Romantic Legacies: Transnational and Transdisciplinary Contexts*, edited by Shun-liang Chao and John Michael Corrigan, Routledge, 2019, pp. 158–74.
Putzell-Korab, Sara M. *The Evolving Consciousness: An Hegelian Reading of the Novels of George Eliot*. Institut fur Anglistik und Amerikanistik, Universitat Salzburg, 1982.
Quinney, Laura. "Romanticism, Gnosticism and Neoplatonism." *A Companion to Romantic Poetry*, edited by Charles Mahoney, Wiley-Blackwell, 2011, pp. 412–24.
Quinton, Anthony. "The Neglect of Victorian Philosophy." *Victorian Studies*, vol. 1, no. 3, 1958, pp. 245–54.
Raines, Melissa Anne. *George Eliot's Grammar of Being*. Anthem Press, 2013.
Rajan, Tilottama. Introduction. *Idealism without Absolutes: Philosophy and Romantic Culture*, edited by Tilottama Rajan and Arkady Plotnitsky, State U of New York P, 2004, pp. 1–14.
Raju, P. T. *Thought and Reality: Hegelianism and Advaita*. George Allen & Unwin Ltd., 1937.
Rathore, Aakash Singh, and Rimina Mohapatra. *Hegel's India: A Reinterpretation, with Texts*. Oxford UP, 2017.
Reid, Nicholas. "Coleridge and Schelling: The Missing Transcendental Deduction." *Studies in Romanticism*, vol. 33, no. 3, 1994, pp. 451–79.
Reiter, Geoffrey. "'The Abyss of All Being': 'The Great God Pan' and the Death of Metaphysics." *The Secret Ceremonies: Critical Essays on Arthur Machen*, edited by Mark Valentine and Timothy J. Jarvis, Hippocampus Press, 2019, pp. 221–38.
Reynolds, John Myrdhin, translator. *Self-Liberation: Through Seeing with Naked Awareness*. Snow Lion Publications, 2010.
Rickett, Arthur. "A Yellow Creeper." *Lost Chords: Some Emotions without Morals*, A. D. Innes & Co., 1895, pp. 17–23.
Rosenbaum, Ron. "Salinger, the Swamis, and the Secrets." *Slate*, 27 June 2013, slate.com/culture/2013/06/j-d-salinger-and-eastern-religion-are-there-any-lost-books-still-in-the-vault.html.

Roy, Ayon. "The Specter of Hegel in Coleridge's *Biographia Literaria*." *Journal of the History of Ideas*, vol. 68, no. 2, 2007, pp. 279–304.

Rylance, Rick. *Victorian Psychology and British Culture, 1850–1880*. Oxford UP, 2000.

Savarese, John. *Romanticism's Other Minds: Poetry, Cognition, and the Science of Sociability*. Ohio State UP, 2020.

Sawyer, Dana. *Aldous Huxley: A Biography*. Trillium Press, 2014.

Schor, Naomi. "Idealism in the Novel: Recanonizing Sand." *Yale French Studies*, vol. 75, 1988, pp. 56–73.

Sedgwick, Eve Kosofsky, editor. *Novel Gazing: Queer Readings in Fiction*. Duke UP, 1997.

Sencindiver, Susan Yi. "'It's Alive!' New Materialism and Literary Horror." *The Palgrave Handbook to Horror Literature*, edited by Kevin Corstorphine and Laura R. Kremmel, Palgrave Macmillan, 2018, pp. 483–97.

Shakespeare, William. *The Winter's Tale*. Edited by Stephen Orgel, Oxford UP, 1996.

Shaviro, Steven. *Discognition*. Repeater, 2015.

———. *The Universe of Things: On Speculative Realism*. U of Minnesota P, 2014.

Shaw, Gregory. *Theurgy and the Soul: The Neoplatonism of Iamblichus*. Angelico Press/Sophia Perennis, 2014.

Shuttleworth, Sally. *George Eliot and Nineteenth-Century Science: The Make-Believe of a Beginning*. Cambridge UP, 1984.

Simons, Thomas R. "Coleridge Beyond Kant and Hegel: Transcendent Aesthetics and the Dialectic Pentad." *Studies in Romanticism*, vol. 45, no. 3, 2006, pp. 465–81.

Sinclair, May. *A Defence of Idealism: Some Questions and Conclusions*. The Macmillan Company, 1917.

———. *If the Dead Knew: The Weird Fiction of May Sinclair*. Edited by S. T. Joshi, Hippocampus Press, 2020.

———. Workbook 14. May Sinclair Papers, U of Pennsylvania Library, Kislak Center for Special Collections, Rare Books and Manuscripts, Box 40, Folder 14.

———. Workbook 29. May Sinclair Papers, U of Pennsylvania Library, Kislak Center for Special Collections, Rare Books and Manuscripts, Box 40, Folder 29.

———. Workbook 34. May Sinclair Papers, U of Pennsylvania Library, Kislak Center for Special Collections, Rare Books and Manuscripts, Box 41, Folder 34.

Singh, Dhananjay. "*Bhayānaka* (Horror and the Horrific) in Indian Aesthetics." *The Palgrave Handbook to Horror Literature*, edited by Kevin Corstorphine and Laura R. Kremmel, Palgrave Macmillan, 2018, pp. 21–31.

Singhal, Samarth. "Genres from the Orient: Instability in Shweta Taneja's *Cult of Chaos*." *Horror Fiction in the Global South: Cultures, Narratives and Rep-

resentations, edited by Ritwick Bhattacharjee and Saikat Ghosh, Bloomsbury, 2021, pp. 80–89.

Skrbina, David. *Panpsychism in the West*. MIT Press, 2005.

Small, Helen. Introduction. *The Lifted Veil and* Brother Jacob, by George Eliot, edited by Small, Oxford UP, 1999, pp. ix–xxxviii.

Sorabji, Richard. *Animal Minds and Human Morals: The Origins of the Western Debate*. Cornell UP, 1993.

Stainthorp, Clare. *Constance Naden: Scientist, Philosopher, Poet*. Peter Lang, 2019.

Stevens, Wallace. *Collected Poems*. Faber & Faber, 2006.

Stewart, Garrett. *Death Sentences: Styles of Dying in British Fiction*. Harvard UP, 1984.

Stirling, James Hutchison. *The Secret of Hegel: Being the Hegelian System in Origin, Principle, Form and Matter*. Oliver & Boyd, 1898.

Subialka, Michael J. *Modernist Idealism: Ambivalent Legacies of German Philosophy in Italian Literature*. U of Toronto P, 2021.

Sullivan, Michael. "The Art of Liu Kuo-sung." *The Liu Kuo-sung Archives*, 1992, liukuosung.org/document-info1.php?lang=en&Year=&p=6.

Sutherland, John. *The Longman Companion to Victorian Fiction*. 2nd ed., Routledge, 2009.

Svoboda, Robert E. *Aghora I: At the Left Hand of God*. Rupa, 1986.

Sweet, William, editor. *Biographical Encyclopedia of British Idealism*. Continuum, 2010.

Taneja, Shweta. "Agni's Tattoo." *Whose Future Is It?: Cellarius Stories, Volume 1*, Kindle ed., Genesis Thought, 2018, pp. 213–28.

———. *Cult of Chaos: An Anantya Tantrist Mystery*. HarperCollins India, 2014.

———. "Tantric Twist: The Possibilities of the Occult in Fiction." *Open*, 14 June 2017, www.openthemagazine.com/lounge/books/tantric-twist/.

Taylor, Matthew A. *Universes without Us: Posthuman Cosmologies in American Literature*. U of Minnesota P, 2013.

Thacker, Eugene. *In The Dust of This Planet: Horror of Philosophy, Vol. 1*. Zero Books, 2011.

Thain, Marion. "'Scientific Wooing': Constance Naden's Marriage of Science and Poetry." *Victorian Poetry*, vol. 41, no. 1, 2003, pp. 151–69.

Thielke, Peter, and Yitzhak Y. Melamed. "Salomon Maimon." *The Stanford Encyclopedia of Philosophy*, edited by Edward N. Zalta, 2021, plato.stanford.edu/archives/sum2021/entries/maimon.

Thomas, Dylan. *Dylan Thomas: Poems Selected by Derek Mahon*. Edited by Derek Mahon, Faber and Faber, 2004.

The Tibetan Book of the Dead. 3rd ed., translated by Kazi Dawa-Samdup and edited by W. Y. Evans-Wentz, Oxford UP, 1957.

Treadwell, James. "Coleridge in *Sartor Resartus*." *The Wordsworth Circle*, vol. 29, no. 1, 1998, pp. 68–71.

Turner, Frank M. *The Greek Heritage in Victorian Britain*. Yale UP, 1981.
Urban, Hugh B. "'India's Darkest Heart': Kālī in the Colonial Imagination." *Encountering Kālī: In the Margins, at the Center, in the West*, edited by Rachel Fell McDermott and Jeffrey J. Kripal, U of California P, 2003, pp. 169–95.
Valentine, Mark. *Arthur Machen*. Seren, 1995.
Vallins, David. "Immanence and Transcendence in Coleridge's Orient." *Coleridge, Romanticism, and the Orient: Cultural Negotiations*, edited by Vallins et al., Bloomsbury, 2013, pp. 119–30.
———. Introduction. *Coleridge, Romanticism, and the Orient: Cultural Negotiations*, edited by Vallins et al., Bloomsbury, 2013, pp. 1–15.
———. "The Letter and the Spirit: Coleridge and the Metaphysics of Prose." *Modern Philology*, vol. 94, no. 1, 1996, pp. 39–59.
Versluis, Arthur. *American Transcendentalism and Asian Religions*. Oxford UP, 1993.
Vivekananda. *Jñāna Yoga*. In *Indian Philosophy in English: From Renaissance to Independence*, edited by Nalini Bhushan and Jay L. Garfield, Oxford UP, 2011, pp. 269–322.
The V21 Collective. "Manifesto of the V21 Collective." *V21: Victorian Studies for the 21st Century*, v21collective.org/manifesto-of-the-v21-collective-ten-theses/. Accessed 30 Oct. 2024.
Wallis, R. T. *Neoplatonism*. 2nd ed., Gerald Duckworth & Co., 1995.
Ward, Mary Augusta. "Preface to Westmoreland Edition." *Robert Elsmere*, edited by Miriam Elizabeth Burstein, Victorian Secrets, 2018, pp. 659–69.
———. *Robert Elsmere*. Edited by Miriam Elizabeth Burstein, Victorian Secrets, 2018.
Warren, Andrew. "Coleridge, Orient, Philosophy." *Coleridge, Romanticism, and the Orient: Cultural Negotiations*, edited by David Vallins et al., Bloomsbury, 2013, pp. 103–18.
Watt, Ian. *The Rise of the Novel: Studies in Defoe, Richardson and Fielding*. The Bodley Head, 2015.
Watts, Peter. *Blindsight*. Tor, 2006.
Wells, H. G. "Skepticism of the Instrument." *Mind*, vol. 13, no. 51, 1904, pp. 379–93.
White, Christopher G. *Other Worlds: Spirituality and the Search for Invisible Dimensions*. Harvard UP, 2018.
Whitman, Walt. "Carlyle from American Points of View." *Specimen Days & Collect*, Rees Welsh & Co., 1882, pp. 170–78.
Wilberding, James, and Christoph Horn, editors. *Neoplatonism and the Philosophy of Nature*. Oxford UP, 2012.
Wilkins, Charles, translator. *The Bhagvat-Geeta, or Dialogues of Kreeshna and Arjoon*. C. Nourse, 1785.
Willburn, Sarah. "Possessed Individualism in George Eliot's *Daniel Deronda*." *Victorian Literature and Culture*, vol. 34, 2006, pp. 271–89.
Williams, Raymond. *Keywords: A Vocabulary of Culture and Society*. New ed., Oxford UP, 2015.

Willis, Kirk. "The Introduction and Critical Reception of Hegelian Thought in Britain 1830-1900." *Victorian Studies*, vol. 32, no. 1, 1988, pp. 85-111.

Wilson, Horace Hayman. "Sketch of the Religious Sects of the Hindus." *Calcutta Review*, vol. 24, 1855, pp. 31-67.

Woodard, Ben. *The Patchwork Absolute: F. H. Bradley and the Divisions of Philosophy*. Leuphana University, Habilitation Qualification, 2020, *Academia.edu*, www.academia.edu/30942829/The_Patchwork_Absolute_F_H_Bradley_and_the_Divisions_of_Philosophy.

Woolf, Virginia. "Modern Fiction." *The Essays of Virginia Woolf*, vol. 4., edited by Andrew McNeille, The Hogarth Press, 1984, pp. 157-65.

Yates, Frances. *Giordano Bruno and the Hermetic Tradition*. Routledge, 2002.

Zantvoort, Bart. "Speculating on the Absolute: On Hegel and Meillassoux." *Speculations*, vol. 6, 2015, pp. 79-119.

Zemka, Sue. "*Erewhon* and the End of Utopian Humanism." *ELH*, vol. 69, no. 2, 2002, pp. 439-72.

Žižek, Slavoj. *Less than Nothing: Hegel and the Shadow of Dialectical Materialism*. Verso, 2012.

Index

Absolute idealism: and African philosophy, 124–25; and anthropocentrism, 2–4, 24, 26; and capitalism, 120, 200–01, 216; definition of, 5–7, 22–26; ethics of, 5–8, 94, 127–28, 211–17; as global phenomenon, 8–9, 170; history of, 7–10, 22–23, 26; and horror fiction, 132–37; and Indian philosophy, 23; and materialism, 15–16, 21–22, 24; and modernism, 171–72; and realism, 23–24, 57–59, 65; and science fiction, 113–15
Advaita Vedānta, 13, 116, 164, 170–72, 175–86
Alpert, Richard (Ram Dass), 173
Althusser, Louis, 96
analytic philosophy, 9, 134, 170
Asimov, Isaac, 118–19

Barnes, Steven, 123–26
Baudelaire, Charles, 148–49
Beatles, The, 196
Bergson, Henri, 194, 197, 203, 206
Bhagavad Gita, the, 30–31, 48, 175, 220n2
Bildungsroman, 5, 36, 42–43, 111, 169, 176, 184, 190, 201
Bosanquet, Bernard, 69–70, 116
Bradley, F. H., 3, 60, 94–108, 113–28 passim, 154, 195, 206, 211; *Appearance and Reality*, 101–07, 126–27; *Ethical Studies*, 95–98; as science fiction writer, 105–07; and the self, 102–04
British Idealism: and Advaita Vedānta, 174–76, 182; and Carlyle, 35; and Hegel, 43–44; history of, 8, 9, 22–23, 68, 93–94, 210, 217; and Lewes, 66; and literature, 12, 13, 107, 134, 167–71; politics of, 4, 104; and temporality, 187–88
Buddhism, 49, 89, 116, 135, 142, 168, 171, 188
Butler, Samuel, 6, 40, 95, 98–101, 107–13, 154, 191; *Erewhon*, 108–09, 115; and science fiction, 114–28 passim; *The Way of All Flesh*, 111–13

Ĉapek, Karel, 118–19
Carlyle, Thomas, 34–43; and Coleridge, 35–36; and philosophy, 34–36; *Sartor Resartus*, 35–43
Cellarius Universe, the, 119–28
Christianity, 59, 76, 111, 132, 155, 220n4; and Advaita Vedānta, 177, 180; and British Idealism, 8, 44–45, 94; and modernism, 167–68, 171

243

244 | Index

Coleridge, Samuel Taylor, 10, 11, 27–34, 147; *Biographia Literaria*, 29, 32–34; and hylozoism, 32–33; and pantheism, 27; poetics of, 29–30
Collins, Wilkie, 52–56; *The Moonstone*, 53–56

death, 133, 152, 154, 155, 158–65 passim, 171–74, 182, 186–188
defamiliarization, 41, 43, 163
Deleuze, Gilles, 111, 203
detective fiction, 53–56
Doors, The (band), 196
dualism, 24, 31, 39, 47, 62–63, 77, 125

ecological consciousness, 3, 8, 24–25, 65, 105, 113, 210–11
Eliot, George, 57–91, 222n10; and aesthetics, 73–74; *Daniel Deronda*, 86–91; and Kabbalah, 88–89; *The Lifted Veil*, 151–52, 161; *Middlemarch*, 82–86; and philosophy, 72–76; *Romola*, 76–82; and science, 71–72; "Shadows of the Coming Race," 115–16
Emerson, Ralph Waldo, 42
empiricism, 57–58, 65–68, 72
evolution, 99–100, 105, 108, 113–16, 154, 167

Fawcett, Edward Douglas, 116–18, 164
Foucault, Michel, 16, 55, 69

Great Expectations, 51
Green, T. H., 167–69
Grosz, Elizabeth, 206–07

Haldar, Hiralal, 168–69
Heard, Gerald, 170, 172, 196
Hegel, G. W. F., 3, 43–51, 59, 62, 66, 219n1; and the dialectic, 49; relation to Indian thought, 47–49, scholarly approaches to, 46–47; *Science of Logic*, 48–51
Herbert, Frank, 119
Hinduism, 27, 30, 62, 130–31, 164–65
Hinton, Charles Howard, 219n2
Hobbes, Thomas, 211–13
horror fiction, 133–36
Huxley, Aldous, 167–74, 186–99, 213–17; *Brave New World*, 114, 172; *The Doors of Perception*, 196–99; *Island*, 213–17; *The Perennial Philosophy*, 195–96; *Time Must Have a Stop*, 189–95
Huxley, T. H., 72, 172, 180, 189

India, 60, 170–71; colonial philosophy of, 176; horror literature of, 132
Iser, Wolfgang, 51
Isherwood, Christopher, 170, 172
Ishiguro, Kazuo, 114

Jameson, Fredric, 199–202

Kālī, 130–32, 143, 177, 179–80
Kant, Immanuel, 5, 7, 36, 44, 75, 94, 114, 161–62, 204

Leary, Timothy, 173, 196
Lewes, George Henry, 58, 63, 66–67, 72, 98
Lewins, Robert, 60–62
literary criticism: and idealism, 11–12, 15–16, 58, 65–69, 203–12, 216–18; as paranoid, 55, 201–202; and polemics, 13–16, 21, 207–09
Liu, Kuo-sung, 217
Lovecraft, H. P., 137, 163–64

Machen, Arthur, 139–51; *The Great God Pan*, 140–41, *Hieroglyphics*, 147–48; *The Hill of Dreams*,

142–44; *Ornaments in Jade*, 148–51; "The White People," 141–42, 145–47
Matrix, The, 119
McCarthy, Tom, 55
McTaggart, J. M. E., 46, 187–88
meditation, 28–33, 37, 48–49, 89–90, 179, 220n4
mereology, 24–25, 41–42, 70, 137
Metzner, Ralph, 173
Mill, John Stuart, 21, 23, 36, 44
Mind (journal), 108, 170, 187
modernism, 5, 10, 41, 171, 186–88
Morton, Timothy, 1–3, 113
Mukerji, A. C., 182–84
mysticism, 27, 136, 154–55

Naden, Constance, 59–65
Nagel, Thomas, 9, 224n1
Neoplatonism, 6, 26, 77, 88–89, 222n9
new materialism, 204–08
Nikhilananda, 179

objective idealism, 5, 24, 33, 203. *See also* objectivity
objectivity: in Collins, 53–56, 83, 143; in Hegel, 44–45, 47; of idealism, 24; in object-oriented ontology, 1–2; in realism, 210; and sympathy, 82, 84. *See also* objective idealism
object-oriented ontology, 2, 203–04
organicism, 25, 70, 95–99, 211–14
Orientalism, 23, 27, 47–48, 130–31, 182

panpsychism, 3, 98–100, 110, 117, 207–08
Plato, 6, 24, 47, 58, 67, 73, 77, 94
Poe, Edgar Allan, 134, 137
postmodernism, 9, 10, 16, 41, 68, 174, 195–204
Prabhavananda, 177–79

prose poetry, 148–49
psychedelics, 130, 173, 196–202, 214–16

Rabelais, François, 148
Ramakrishna, 176–80
realism: definition of, 57–59; idealism as, 6, 23–24, 26, 182–83; the literary genre of, 5, 12, 41–42, 64–71, 73, 82, 87, 91, 105, 210; postmodernism as, 200–01
retrospection, 49–51, 53, 54–56, 169, 183–84, 187, 199. *See also* subration
Romanticism: British, 11, 22–23, 25–26; German, 7–8, 52, 149

Salinger, J. D., 223n5
Śaṅkara (also Śaṁkara), 175, 178, 191, 194–95, 223n3
science fiction: and idealism, 5, 11, 100, 113–19; as realism, 41, 59, 65, 126, 136, 210; thought experiments as, 35, 102
sensation novels, 46
sexuality: of the Absolute, 131–33, 139–43; and death, 187, 192; importance of for idealism, 97, 153–54, 157–58, 163
Sinclair, May, 152–65, 188; *A Defence of Idealism*, 154–56; "The Finding of the Absolute," 160–63; "The Flaw in the Crystal," 156–59; and Hinduism, 164–65; "Where Their Fire Is Not Quenched," 159–60
solipsism, 5, 59–63, 71, 76–91 passim. *See also* subjective idealism, subjectivity
speculative realism, 45, 203–04
Sprigge, Timothy, 9, 224n1
Stapledon, Olaf, 117
Stirling, James Hutchison, 44–46
subjective idealism: and Advaita Vedānta, 178; Bradley's opposition

subjective idealism *(continued)* to, 97; as distinct from Absolute idealism, 3, 5, 61; in Eliot, 71, 76, 83; and literary history, 67–68, 201; and postmodernism, 174, 203; and realism, 23, 58–59. *See also* solipsism, subjectivity

subjectivity: Absolute idealism's conception of, 24, 44–47; in Carlyle, 38–39; in Coleridge, 27, 30; as ecological, 2–3, 6; in Eliot, 76–91 passim; Kant's and Fichte's emphasis on, 7; in Machen, 143; in Naden, 61; and new materialism, 205–06; and realism, 59; and science fiction, 118. *See also* solipsism; subjective idealism

subration, 175–76, 184–86. *See also* retrospection

Taiwan, 1–3, 217–18
Taneja, Shweta, 122–23, 129–31, 133

Tantrism, 129–31, 179
Tibetan Book of the Dead, The, 171–73, 188–89
Tomkin, Silvan, 224n3
totalitarianism, 137, 211–13
Traherne, Thomas, 148

Vaihinger, Hans, 52
Vedanta Societies, 172, 177–78
Vivekananda, 176–82

war, 190, 193–94, 211, 213, 215–16
Ward, Mary Augusta, 167–72
Watts, Peter, 116
weird fiction, 134–35, 163–64
Wells, H. G., 114, 171
Whitman, Walt, 44
Wilson, Horace Hayman, 130–31
Woolf, Virginia, 171

Žižek, Slavoj, 46–47, 51